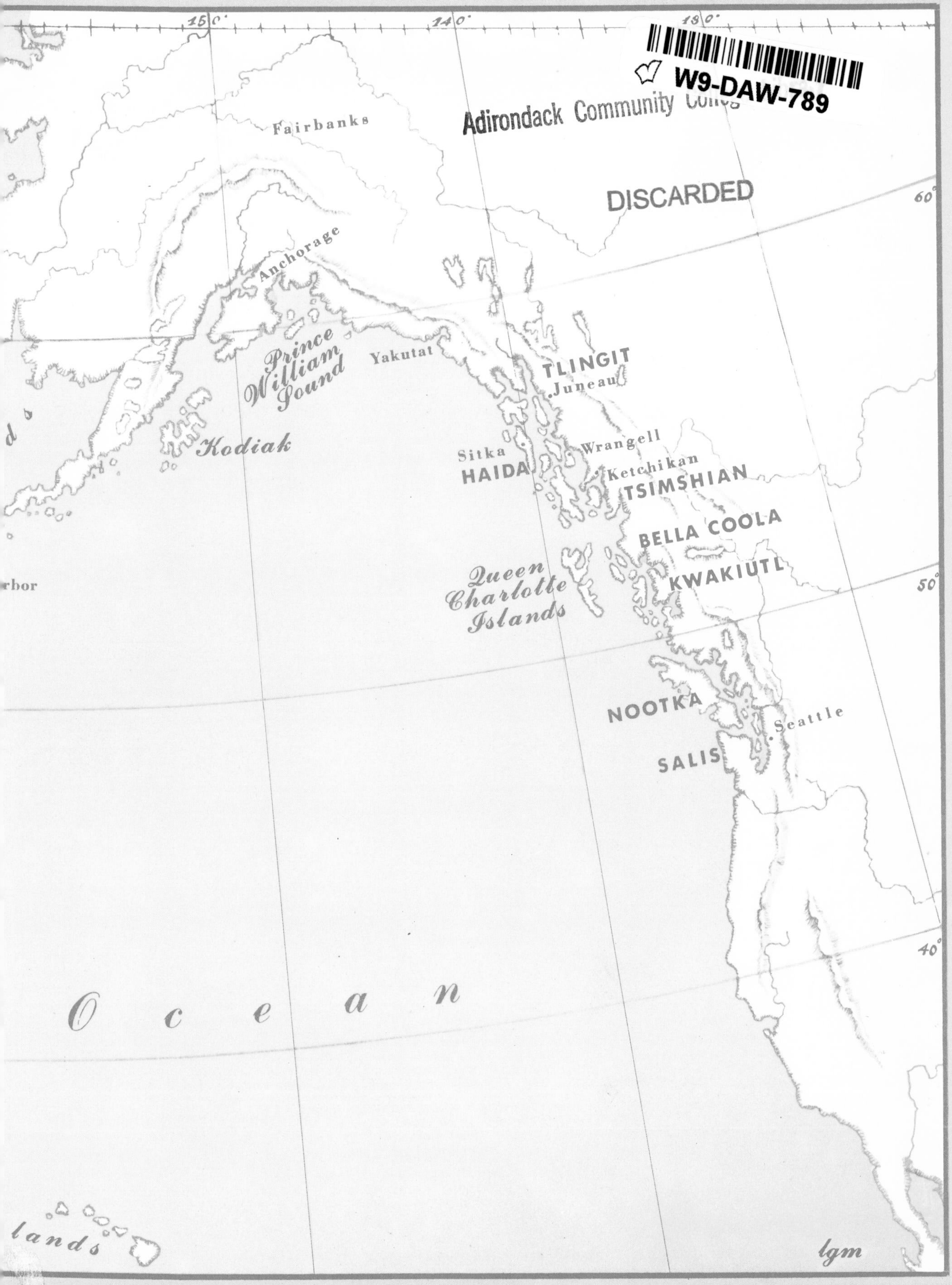

150°   140°   130°   60°

Fairbanks

Anchorage

Prince William Sound   Yakutat

TLINGIT
Juneau

Kodiak

Sitka
HAIDA

Wrangell

Ketchikan
TSIMSHIAN

BELLA COOLA

KWAKIUTL   50°

Queen Charlotte Islands

NOOTKA   Seattle

SALIS

40°

O c e a n

lands   lgm

LOST HERITAGE OF ALASKA

LOST HERITAGE

The Adventure and Art of

THE WORLD PUBLISHING COMPANY

OF ALASKA

the Alaskan Coastal Indians

NARRATIVE BY
POLLY MILLER

GRAPHICS AND AESTHETIC COMMENTARY BY
LEON GORDON MILLER

Cleveland and New York

7622

Published by The World Publishing Company
2231 West 110th Street, Cleveland, Ohio 44102

Published simultaneously in Canada by
Nelson, Foster & Scott Ltd.

First Printing 1967

Library of Congress Catalog Card Number: 67–15226

Printed in the United States of America

Typographical Design by Jeanette Young

To Brandt and Scott
for whom we value our heritage

Contents

Introduction

In *Lost Heritage of Alaska,* Polly and Leon Gordon Miller have vividly unfolded the story of the efflorescence and decline of the culture of the Indians of America's Northwest Coast. Theirs is a definitive account of a unique and intriguing chapter in the great American saga. Although, in one sense, an unfinished story, since the Tlingit and Haida of Alaska and British Columbia survive vigorously in a new phase of existence, it is nevertheless a completed epic in that the great cultural cycle that excited the curiosity, interest, and admiration of a succession of literate explorers and led to the dispersal of the indigenous handicraft treasures all over the world, has terminated.

The Millers' publication has an unusual timeliness in that both Alaska and British Columbia are in 1967 celebrating centennials. In Alaska it is the one hundredth anniversary of the purchase of Alaska by the United States from Russia. In British Columbia it is the participation in the continent-wide celebration of the consolidation in 1867 of the Hudson's Bay Company's far-flung outposts into the Dominion of Canada. These celebrations are inevitably occasions of reminiscence and retrospection, of estimation of past and contemporary performance, as well as projections of future prospects.

The Tlingits and Haidas are entitled to this comprehensive and understanding historiography of their great past—a past in which within "their homes they transformed structural houseposts into sculpture and room partitions into paintings"; a past in which "every tool and utensil which they used, was expertly carved, painted or both, to enhance the visual and tactile aspects in forms utilitarian and sculptural." The Millers have related all this admirably. Perhaps the greatest value of their voluminous compilation at this time lies in the information it conveys to a largely unknowing contemporary generation whose orientation is different and whose interest in a largely vanished heritage can at best be but uncertain and fleeting.

The authors have adopted the wise procedure of letting the original observers speak for themselves. Thus we see the Tlingits and Haidas, when their culture was in full flower, through the eyes and in the words of Captain Cook, perhaps— in the wide range of his discoveries—the greatest of all this planet's explorers, and of his successors, Vancouver, Portlock, Dixon, Meares, Billings, and, later, Belcher and Sir George Simpson, among the Britishers; of the Russians, Baranov, Khlebnikov, Rezanov, von Langsdorff, Lisiansky, and later, Veniaminov; of the Frenchmen, La Pérouse, Marchand, Camille de Roquefeuil; of the Americans, the "Boston men," Captain William Sturgis, Bernard Magee, Captain Richard Cleveland, John Bartlett, Captain Robert Gray, and his three officers, Robert Haswell, John Hoskins, and John Boit, who respectively kept the *Columbia's* log. They constitute a treasury of firsthand observers' recording.

These records are relatively sparse considering the extent and duration of the fur traffic. In the comparatively brief period, as the authors point out, between 1787 and 1809, at least sixty-four American ships traded off the Northwest Coast. On only a few vessels was there any serious attempt to describe the scene and the people. All the more creditable, then, is the wealth of material here assembled. It signalizes, incidentally, the achievement of one largely forgotten American explorer, Robert Gray, who discovered the Columbia River, which more famed explorers, such as Vancouver, had missed.

Except for the brutal subjection of the Aleuts by the early Russians, the promyshlenniki, or fur traders, and the Russians' bloody reprisals against them for rebelling against their enslavement, the nearly two centuries of contact between whites of several nationalities and the Northwest Coast natives, while by no means bloodless, were not periods of protracted strife. Certainly they were not as compared with the Indian Wars incidental to the conflict of whites and Indians in the westward march of the white man across what were to become the forty-eight states. There were outbursts of savage violence along the Northwest Coast, such as the massacre of the Russians in the destruction of Old Sitka, and others subsequently. These were usually precipitated by some incident, after which the superior arms of the trading outsiders prevailed and in which lives on both sides were lost. One of these local wars is vividly described by Judge F. W. Howay, whom the authors cite and who pieced together, from six contemporary journals, the story of Chief Coyah's battles, in the course of which several American and British ships' crews were massacred and the inevitable revenge taken on the Haidas. These savage episodes of an earlier period, the 1790's, never received the fame of Sitting Bull's much later slaughter of General Custer's troops at the Battle of the Little Bighorn, but they are graphically detailed in the Millers' narrative and are here collated perhaps for the first time for the general reading public.

But it is not to bodily conflict and killing that the deterioration of the Northwest Coast native cultures can be ascribed. The white man's imported diseases—smallpox, syphilis, and a variety of less lethal contagious fevers against which existed no immunity among the coastal primitives, took a far greater toll. Epidemics annihilated whole village populations. These, and the white man's introduction of fermented spirits, all produced a demoralization that destroyed "human cultural achievements not duplicated anywhere else. . . . one more bright tile in the complicated and wonderful mosaic of man's achievement on earth."

"America's Neglected Bargain" is the title of the sixth chapter in this book. The neglect was flagrant, unprecedented, and unparalleled in American history. It applied to Alaskans of all races. But the whites had the freedom, facility, and know-how to move out, to "go back where they came from" if they so desired, and many did—as the census figures reveal. But the Indians had no such choice. They were perforce obliged to adopt the white man's wage system, breaking—as the authors point out—"forever the tie with a life based on seasonal accord with the environment."

"Much praise has been showered on these industrious people for accomplishing the switch so efficiently," write the Millers, "but they did not make it eagerly."

The Indians' plaint was that the white man had taken their hunting and fishing grounds, which had provided their way of life. And a most abundant sustenance it furnished, with millions of salmon choking every stream on their way to the spawning grounds, a resource ever-renewing itself in limitless plenty. It provided the leisure that found expression in that "lost heritage" of great art. The white man—the commercial canners—came close to destroying that resource on which the aboriginal way of life was based.

The Indians' grievance took on crucial validity when the great salmon runs—America's greatest single fishery resource—during the 1940's and 1950's—were depleted almost to the vanishing point by the mismanagement of the Federal agency entrusted with their conservation, the Fish and Wildlife Service of the Department of the Interior. Indian claims could justifiably have addressed themselves to the destruction of their historic livelihood. Instead, their claim was based on the taking of their land (which was far less vital than the resources of the sea), virtually all of southeastern Alaska, withdrawn by the Federal government to create the Tongass National Forest. In 1967, one hundred years after the establishment of United States rule, the Tlingits and Haidas were still awaiting payment of such claim as the Federal courts had allowed.

In the period under the Stars and Stripes the authors likewise rely usefully on the verbatim testimony of the concerned observers. We thus read the pessimistic comments of Governors Alfred P. Swineford and John G. Brady; of government officials William Gouveneur Morris, William S. Dodge, I. C. Dennis, Vincent Colyer; of Captain L. A. Beardslee, the naval *de facto* ruler of Alaska from 1879 to 1884; of the missionaries, S. Hall Young, Sheldon Jackson, Armanda McFarland; of naturalist John Muir; and of one of the expert ethnologists in this field, Lieutenant George Thornton Emmons, of the U.S. Navy. Thus we are enabled, through the eyes of concerned and responsible witnesses, to see what happened.

They witnessed and participated in what the authors deplore: the "massive exodus of native art." In addition to the emissaries from museums in every land, "everyone who went to Alaska became a collector, the lowly tourist who quite unabashedly snatched up every object he could buy, the traders, missionaries, prospectors, school teachers, military personnel, naval officers, and even territorial officials. . . ." A whole chapter is devoted to the dispersal around the globe of the implements, masks, shaman's rattles, regalia, shields, carvings, hats, blankets, and garments of the Tlingit and Haida cultures.

It may be argued that at least most of these creations are preserved in museums, but the authors emphasize their belief that those treasures should be considered as art as well as mere ethnological manifestations.

The authors end on a somewhat more hopeful note. Despite their assertion that "the creative heritage is over," they see promise in the new attitude toward their heritage of the Alaska Native Brotherhood, constituted of Tlingits, Haidas, and Tsimpsians; in the Demonstration Workshop of the Indian Arts and Crafts Board at Sitka National Monument; in the twenty-year old programs located at Port Chilkoot (sponsored by Mimi and Ted Gregg and Carl Heinmiller) for training in wood carving, sculpture, block printing, textile design, lapidary work and in the revival of the Indian dances.

An enormous amount of research has gone into this readable and authoritative tracing of some two and a quarter centuries of maritime and ethnic history. It consolidates fragments into a harmonious whole and constitutes an invaluable addition to the growing body of Alaskana.

ERNEST GRUENING
United States Senator, Alaska

December 1966

ALASKA VISITED

The High Art of
Alaska's Coastal Indians

For well over two centuries the artistic accomplishment of the Indians of the Pacific Northwest Coast has astonished all who have experienced it. Russians, Englishmen, Frenchmen, Spaniards and Yankee merchant mariners visited Alaska and the adjacent coastal islands to explore and trade among these unusual people. All of the visitors who were sufficiently literate to record their experience registered also their intellectual and emotional responses to the all-pervading creative production of this unique coastal culture.

The writings, drawings and logs revealed an adventure and discovery of a new land of rich natural resources and a rich productive, creative native talent. As presented in this book, the observation of these native arts is placed in its historical context and perspective, recreating a vanished artistic glory as seen by these adventurous, courageous and observant men.

They described the art they saw as beautiful, curious, ugly, magnificent, repulsive, sophisticated, barbaric. But they never ignored it. Many of the early visitors recorded what they saw in logs, writings and drawings, and to these observers we are indebted for descriptions of a primitive culture in full flourish before its discovery and dislocation by white contact.

The journals of these adventurers depict a society closely oriented to nature, in which the Indians fished and hunted for life's basic needs, cured illness with shaman's rattles, small masks and magic, fought wars with ornate daggers, in carved wooden helmets and leather armor, and built ornamented fifty-man war canoes in which they paddled out to visit the white man's ships, wearing decorative masks and costumes. Within their homes they transformed structural houseposts into sculpture and room partitions into paintings. Every tool and utensil which they used was expertly carved, painted or both, to enhance its visual and tactile aspects in forms utilitarian and sculptural.

To understand the art and culture of Alaska's Tlingit and Haida requires more than the experience of seeing examples of their creative work. It requires an understanding of the motivation, the cultural order, the symbolism and the personal and community involvement in the creative process. For the art is part and parcel of the culture that its people created, distilled and projected through the medium of their most talented and creative artisans.

As a consequence the Indian artist was bound by the use of materials native to his region and by the traditional forms and symbolism of his culture. Yet within these stringent limitations, he created an endless variation of forms, stylistically similar, yet never exactly repeating an expression. In the thousands upon thousands of Tlingit carvings, no two bowls or spoons or boxes or totem poles are exactly alike.

This came about in part because they were made by numerous artists over a long history. But more important to its consequence as art is that no two pieces by the same artist were alike, yet different works by the same artist can be identified. It is this emergence of individual identity that transforms the purely ethnological specimen into a work of art. For the creation of a work of art is always a personal experience. Everything that an artist produces reflects his personal reaction to life's experience. This holds true even in the primitive society where art is integrated with the basic cultural expression and has a direct practical application to the objects of everyday use.

The white man discovered Alaska and the coast at a period when the culture of the Indian flourished. He watched it come to full flower, and in his way, plucked the seed to see the culture diminish. Today the art expressions of this culture are scattered over the world and only in recent years have become most desirable items for art collectors and museums of art.

Through the process of acculturation, the vigor of the native is being redirected. During this period of transition the emotional and personal stimuli to continue the traditional arts has died. The original motivation, cultural, communal and personal, has disappeared—the art heritage of the Alaskan Indian as an active process is lost.

The natives, their culture and their art are reflected in the personal experiences of men. The story brings one in contact with the artistic experience of the natives who produced a great art and culture, and the aesthetic experiences of the men who for over two centuries shared in the experience. *Lost Heritage of Alaska* reports, in their own words, what these men saw and felt, from Bering's voyage, sponsored by Peter the Great, through the achievement of Alaskan statehood in 1959 to the present day.

The date of birth of the native arts is conjecture. When white men first experienced this art it was already of age. From this moment of contact until today is a period of time of less than two hundred and fifty years in which we experienced the cycle of spring, summer, and winter of one of America's great cultures.

The cultural heritage is gone, but much of the art produced by it is with us to help us better understand the past and plan the future.

LEON GORDON MILLER

Cleveland, Ohio
1967

LOST HERITAGE OF ALASKA

Chapter I

VITUS BERING
DISCOVERS ALASKA

The first white men in recorded history to encounter the Tlingit Indians of Alaska were crew members of the Bering expedition in the year 1741.

Their impressions have never been learned, for the seventeen men who were sent to explore the fires on shore at latitude 57 degrees 15 minutes North, the site of modern Sitka, never returned. The men were sent ashore July 17th by Alexei Chirikov, commander of the *St. Paul,* sister ship to Vitus Bering's vessel, the *St. Peter.* This expedition, the second of Vitus Bering, marked the white man's first contact with the native population of the Pacific Northwest Coast of America, bringing them at last into the realm of recorded history. In its conception, the expedition itself was a massive and brilliant effort towards scientific discovery.

The disaster that befell Chirikov on this historic occasion is told by Lieutenant Sven Waxel, a Swedish seaman who served as first mate and pilot aboard the *St. Peter:*

"The coast was smooth and without islands or rocks and so it was not advisable to run in too close to it. The ship went to anchor a good distance from the shore and, being short of water, Chirikov decided to send a boat ashore. To command it he chose an officer called Avraam Demetiev, a very capable man, and gave

him a crew of ten of the best men he had. They were well equipped with guns and ammunition and also had a metal cannon with appurtenances. They were also given a signalling system and complete instructions how to behave and act in the event of the unexpected happening. Besides all this, they were supplied with provisions to last several days.

"The boat pulled away from the ship; they watched it disappear around a headland and some while later noticed various signal flashes corresponding exactly with the orders given, so that they had every reason for thinking that the party landed safely. However, two days passed and then a third day, and still the boat did not come back.

Vitus Bering

"Nevertheless, they could see the whole time that the signal fires continued to burn and so they began to think that perhaps the boat had been damaged on landing and that the party's return was being delayed by having to repair it.

"They then decided to send the little jolly-boat ashore with carpenters, calkers and all that they might need, so that the boat could be repaired if that should prove necessary. No sooner said than done. Six men were ordered into the jolly-boat, equipped with guns and ammunition and well supplied with everything else they might need. Their orders were to search out the boat and give all help that might be called for when they found it, after which both boats were to return to the ship immediately.

"Next morning two craft were seen coming out from the land, the one slightly larger than the other. Naturally it was assumed that these were the longboat and the jolly-boat, and very glad they were to see them. They began to get the ship ready to put to sea again, tightening the main ropes and stays and doing all the other necessary things, so that the entire crew was on deck, each busy at his work. But then, as the two craft drew near the ship, they discovered that the truth was the exact opposite of what they had

thought. These were American boats and they were filled with savages. They approached to within three cable lengths of the ship, then, seeing so many on deck, they turned back towards the land. Those on board the ship had now no boat left in which they could have put out after the Americans, and they had just to draw the melancholy conclusion that both the long boat and the jolly-boat were lost along with their entire crews."

The great adventure described by Waxel, the dauntless expedition which brought Alaska with its huge wealth and varied native peoples into the competitive thick of the white man's world, began with Czar Peter the Great of Russia. This enlightened, tempestuous despot, whose aim it was to transform a backward, insulated, and still oriental Russia into a nation of Western Europe, conceived of and ordered the expeditions that set Russia's hand on America.

Peter the Great had enlisted Vitus Bering into his newly created navy, calling upon him, as he called upon others from the courts of Europe, to help reshape Russian institutions and ideas. Bering was a Danish navigator who had spent twenty years in the Russian Navy, had served well, risen in rank, but resigned because further promotion had not been forthcoming. Then Peter called upon him again, this time to conduct an expedition from the Siberian shores of Kamchatka to discover whether Asia and America were connected.

In a modern day, the instructions handed to Bering in Peter's own handwriting, read like a page from *Alice in Wonderland:*

1. You are to construct at Kamchatka one or two boats with decks.

2. You are to proceed in these along the coast which extends to the North and which seems, in all probability (since we do not know where it ends) to be a part of America.

3. With this in view you are to try to find where it is joined to America and to reach some city in European possession and to inquire what it is called and to make a note of it and to secure exact information and to mark this on a map and then to return home.

Translated into harsh reality, this meant a six-thousand-mile trek across a Siberian wilderness of mountains, rivers, tundra and desert, as prelude to a voyage of how many thousand miles more into uncharted arctic seas, not to mention the awesome physical task of constructing and provisioning, in the Kamchatkan sub-arctic wilderness, ships capable of withstanding the stormy northern seas.

All this Bering accomplished and in 1725 embarked upon the first of his two historic voyages, establishing, as his ship passed through the strait that today bears his name, that Asia and America are di-

Peter the Great

vided by water, are indeed two separate masses of land.

Despite this accomplishment the voyage was a disappointment both to himself and to the Russian government. A new ruler sat on the throne, as Peter the Great had died shortly after having personally set down Bering's instructions. Bering petitioned Anne, Peter's niece, for permission to undertake a second voyage.

Once again, under what would seem like insuperable obstacles, and amid the additional confusion of a series of sub-explorations to Siberia and Japan authorized by the government, Bering set forth in 1733 on a second expedition, charged with no less a task than that of classifying the flora and fauna of Siberia, mapping the entire Arctic coast and thence voyaging eastward to explore America.

To his great credit, Bering overcame problems of hostile climate, bickering personnel, ship construction and provisioning, although eight long years were consumed in the prodigious effort. Finally, in 1741, his ships were ready, the *St. Peter* commanded by himself and his second in command, Lieutenant Sven Waxel, and the *St. Paul*, commanded by Alexei Chirikov.

"With God's help and a favorable wind we set sail from Avacha on 4th June, 1741. The *St. Paul* came out of the bay ahead of the *St. Peter*, on which I was, and there outside she waited for us to catch her up, and when we had done so we set course together in the direction decided by council." In these words Lieutenant Sven Waxel described the start of the voyage that was to begin the process of transforming native life in northwest America. Once started, the steady flow of explorers, followed by adventurers, traders, administrators, missionaries, anthropologists, settlers, and, finally, art lovers, never ceased. They came in waves, overlapping and mingling with each other like an oncoming tide, each depositing something of their own special stamp, each carrying away—along with their impressions—something indispensable to the continuance of native culture.

Of this chain reaction, Waxel, Bering, and Chirikov knew nothing. Of the ocean upon which they had embarked they knew even less, for the charts and maps on board had been drawn largely in the imaginations of impressionable cartographers.

"What we were to try to do," wrote Waxel, "was to determine the true distance along the parallel between North America and Asia. . . . All would have gone as we

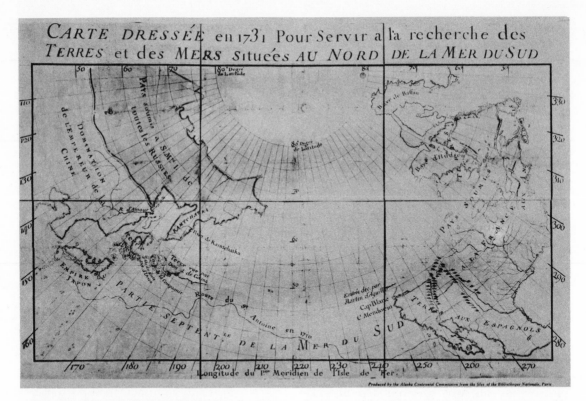

CARTE DRESSÉE en 1731 Pour Servir a la recherche des TERRES et des MERS Situées AU NORD DE LA MER DU SUD

wished, had we instead of SE. by E. sailed E. by N., for with that course we should have reached the American mainland in eight days. As it was, we were all led astray by the unreliable map of which I have already spoken."

Faulty maps were but one of the problems that beset the expedition. The *St. Peter* and *St. Paul* were separated during a storm, never again to meet. Antagonisms developed between the ship's officers. Georg Steller, the young German scientist attached to the *St. Peter*, was at bitter odds with Waxel, who for all practical purposes was in command of the ship. The crew itself was made up of criminals and malcontents who signed up for the expedition only under compulsion. Even worse was the condition of Bering, suffering from the accumulated hardships and the mountainous frustrations of the preceding years. He was both despondent and

ill and already had begun to show the tell-tale signs of the dreaded scurvy. As they thus made their way eastward, water ran low and tempers ran high and the month of June slid into July.

"On 16th July we were, according to an observation taken, on latitude 58 degrees 38 minutes north, and we calculated that we were 50 degrees east of Avacha. On this day we sighted land. This land consisted of huge, high, snow-covered mountains. [The range included lofty Mount St. Elias, which Bering named in honor of the day.] We attempted to sail closer in towards land, but as we had only light and shifting winds, it was not until 20th July that we drew near to it. At six o'clock in the evening of that day we let go our anchor in the neighborhood of an island of considerable size [Kayak Island], lying at no great distance from the mainland. A sounding showed 22 fathoms; the bottom was soft and clayey. At eight o'clock we sent the yawl ashore [under Steller's command] to look for water, and the longboat we sent in charge of Captain Sofron Khitrov on a reconnaissance round the curve of the islands.

"On the boat's return Khitrov reported that there was a good roadstead among some islands not far from where we were, where we would certainly be able to lie sheltered from almost every wind. However, Captain Commander Bering did not seem inclined to make a long stay here. Also, Khitrov had found on one of the islands a number of little houses, which the inhabitants presumably occupied when they came across from the mainland to fish. It appeared that the natives must have possessed axes and knives for these little houses were lined with smooth boards and decorated with small carvings. The inhabitants of these houses were not at home; either that or they must have been hiding on the island."

Waxel's second guess was correct. Some fifty years later the Russians sent a scientific expedition to the Northwest Coast of America under direction of Captain Joseph Billings. Billings' ship, too, anchored at Kayak Island and an old native came forward to relate that he "remembered that when he was a boy, a ship had been close to the bay on the west side of the island and had sent a boat ashore; but on its approaching land the natives all ran away. When the ship sailed, they returned to their huts and found in the subterraneous store room some glass beads, leaves [tobacco] and an iron kettle and something else."

For his part, the brilliant, embittered Steller, who was at first refused permission, was finally granted the opportunity to go on shore. There, in the space of ten hours, his keen naturalist's mind absorbed a rich lode of anthropological, biological and botanical data, the first ever to be recorded for the area. With Steller's writings,

The St. Peter *and* St. Paul—*from Steller's notebook*

the historic period of the Pacific Northwest Coast Indians really began. No wonder the shortness of time granted for those observations inspired his scathing comparison: "The time here spent in investigation bears an arithmetical ratio to the time used in fitting out: ten years the preparation for this great undertaking lasted, and ten hours were devoted to the work itself."

Bitterness, however, did not dull his powers of observation:

"As soon as I, with only the protection and assistance of my own cossack, had landed on the island and realized how scant and precious was the time at my disposal, I seized every opportunity to accomplish as much as possible with the greatest possible dispatch. I struck out in the direction of the mainland in the hopes of finding human beings and habitations. I had not gone more than a verst along the beach before I ran across signs of people and their doings. Under a tree I found an old piece of log hollowed out in the shape of a trough, in which, a couple of hours before, the savages, for lack of pots and vessels, had cooked their meat by means of red-hot stones, just as the Kamchadals did formerly. The bones, some of them with bits of meat and showing signs of having been roasted at the fire, were scattered about where the eaters had been sitting. I could see plainly that these bones belonged to no sea animal, but to a land animal, and I thought myself justified in regarding them as reindeer bones, though no such animal was observed on the island but was probably brought there from the mainland. There were also strewn about the remains of yukola, or pieces of dried fish, which, as in Kamchatka, has to serve the purpose of bread at all meals. There were also great numbers of very large scallops over eight inches across, also blue mussels similar to those found in Kamchatka and, no doubt, eaten raw as the custom is there. In various shells, as on dishes, I found sweet grass completely prepared in Kamchadal fashion, on which water seemed to have been poured in order to extract the sweetness. I discovered further (not far from the fireplace) beside the tree, on which there still were the live coals, a wooden apparatus for making

fire, of the same nature as those used in Kamchatka. The tinder, however, which the Kamchadals make from a species of grass, was here different, namely a species of fountain moss *(Alga fontinalis),* which was bleached white by the sun and of which I have kept a sample to be forwarded. From all this I think I may conclude that the inhabitants of this American coast are of the same origin as the Kamchadals, with whom they agree completely in such peculiar customs and utensils. . . .

"The chopped-down trees, as I came across them here and there, were miscut with many dull blows in such a way that in all likelihood the cutting of trees must be done by these savages, as in Kamchatka, with stone or bone axes similar to those used by the Germans of old and known today as 'thunderbolts.'

"After having made a brief examination of all this, I pushed on farther for about three versts, where I found a path leading into the very thick and dark forest which skirted the shore closely. I held a brief consultation with my cossack, who had a loaded gun, besides a knife and ax, as to what we should do in case we met one or more persons, and I commanded him to do nothing whatever without my orders. I myself was only armed with a Yakut palma [dagger] for the purpose of digging up rocks and plants. . . . After half an hour we came to a spot covered with cut grass. I pushed the grass aside at once and found underneath a cover consisting of rocks; and when this was also removed we came to some tree bark, which was laid on poles in an oblong rectangle three fathoms in length and two in width. All this covered a cellar two fathoms deep in which were the following objects: (1)

lukoshkas, or utensils made of bark, one and a half ells high, filled with smoked fish of a species of Kamchatkan salmon. . . . It was so cleanly and well prepared that I have never seen it as good in Kamchatka, and it also was much superior in taste to the Kamchatkan; (2) a quantity of *sladkaya trava* (or sweet grass), from which liquor is distilled; (3) different kinds of plants, whose outer skin had been removed like hemp, which I took for nettles, which grow here in profusion and perhaps are used, as in Kamchatka, for making fish nets; (4) the dried inner bark from the larch or spruce tree done up in rolls and dried; the same is used as food in time of famine, not only in Kamchatka but all through Siberia and even in Russia as far as Khlynov and elsewhere on the Vyatka; (5) large bales of thongs made of seaweed which, by making a test, we found to be of uncommon strength and firmness.

"Under these I found also some arrows in size greatly exceeding those in Kamchatka and approaching the arrows of the Tunguses and Tatars, scraped very smooth and painted black, so that one might well conjecture that the natives possessed iron instruments and knives.

"In spite of my fear of being attacked in the cellar I continued my search but, discovering nothing more, took away with me, as proof, two bundles of fish, the arrows, a wooden implement for making fire, tinder, a bundle of thongs of seaweed, bark, and grass and sent them by my cossack to the place where the water was being taken on, with instructions to bring them to the Captain Commander; at the same time I asked once more for two or three men to help me further in my investigations of nature. . . .

"In an hour or so I received the patriotic and courteous reply that I should betake myself on board quickly or they would leave me ashore without waiting for me. . . . I reflected that God gives to each one the place and the opportunity to do that which he is ordered to do. . . . However, since there was now no time left for moralizing, only enough to scrape together as much as possible before our fleeing the country, and as evening was already nearing, I sent my cossack out to shoot some rare birds that I had noticed, while I once more started off to the westward, returning at sunset with various observations and collections. . . . Here I was given once more the strict command that, unless I came on board this time, no more notice would be taken of me. I consequently betook myself with what I had collected to the ship and there, to my great astonishment, was treated to chocolate. . . .

"Although I did not need to trouble myself for the benefit of anybody except those who were capable of judging what I was doing, I nevertheless showed some of the objects and made known my ideas about various things, but only a single one of these was accepted. Namely, an iron kettle, a pound of tobacco, a Chinese pipe,

and a piece of Chinese silk were sent to the cellar, but in return the latter was plundered to such an extent that, if we should come again to these parts, the natives would certainly run away even faster or they would show themselves as hostile as they themselves had been treated, especially if it should occur to them to eat or drink the tobacco, the correct use of which probably could be as little known to them as the pipe itself. . . . A couple of knives or hatchets, the use of which was quite obvious, would have aroused the interest of these savages much more. But to this it was objected that such presents might be regarded as a sign of hostility, as if the intention were to declare war. How much more likely was it, particularly if they attempted to use the tobacco in the wrong way, for them to conclude that we had intended to poison them. . . .

"I had been on the ship scarcely an hour when Khitrov with his party of about fifteen men also returned in the great boat and made the following report: He had discovered among the islands lying close to the mainland a harbor where one could anchor without any danger. Although he had seen no human beings on

land, he had nevertheless come across a small dwelling built of wood, the walls of which were so smooth that it seemed as if they had been planed and in fact as if it had been done with cutting tools. Out of this building he brought with him various tangible tokens, for instance, a wooden vessel, such as is made in Russia of linden bark and used as a box; a stone which perhaps, for lack of something better, served as a whetstone, on which were seen streaks of copper, as if the savages, like the ancient Siberian tribes, possessed cutting tools of copper; further a hollow ball of hard-burned clay, about two inches in diameter, containing a pebble which I regarded as a toy for small children; and finally a paddle and the tail of a blackish gray fox."

To the anguish of both Steller and Waxel, Captain-Commander Bering appeared on deck the next morning and ordered that anchor be weighed. Waxel pleaded in vain to remain until the ship's water casks were filled. Steller's plea was that of a scientist whose fervent wish it was to explore the people of whom he had found abundant traces.

But his stormy protests were overruled. He railed in vain at the absurdity of coming so far a distance "only for the purpose of bringing American water to Asia."

However cautious it has been considered, Bering's decision was prompted by knowledge of several unpleasant facts. A third of his crew was sick with scurvy. They had but three months' provisions on board. They were in an unknown, unmapped sea, two thousand miles from their port of departure or, for that matter, any

known port. Contrary winds blew strong, and countless reefs lined the strange shore, which made navigation hazardous and grueling, even without the fogs and sleeting rain which constantly afflicted them. Waxel wrote:

"It was our intention to follow the land as it went, and it was by doing this that we first properly realized to what dreadful deception we had been exposed with that false map of which I have already spoken. We had been thinking that we would sail north to latitude 65 degrees, but instead we were forced to turn away as far as 52 degrees and then right down to 48 degrees, and things went ill with us on the way back. . . .

"Suddenly we would come out into large ocean waves and were scarcely able to manage the ship. I particularly remember one occasion. It was a dark night and we had not made a landfall for several days. About midnight we had a bad fright on finding ourselves in only 20 fathoms of water and not having any idea what sort of a bank or shallows it might be. We tried everything possible to escape from there, but in whatever direction we sailed we found only shallow water. . . . For a long time the depth remained the same, but fortunately we eventually came out into deep water."

The first death from scurvy to occur on the homeward voyage was that of a sailor named Shumagin. The need to obtain water became imperative. It was the end of August. The ship found anchorage at a group of islands off the southern tip of the Alaskan Peninsula. In the hope that the scurvy-stricken sailors might improve if taken ashore, some twenty were trans-

ferred. The name Shumagin, by which they are called today, was given the islands to commemorate the sailor's death. On the island brackish water was taken aboard, despite Steller's protests that its saltiness would increase disease among the crew.

By this time Bering was Captain-Commander mostly in name, reserving his authority for matters of policy. Exhausted by fifteen years of relentless efforts and deep in the grip of the depression which characterizes scurvy, Bering had taken to his bed, leaving Waxel in virtual command.

When the *St. Peter* put out to sea again, she was threatened by strong winds and a stormy sky. They anchored again. The date was September 5th. They heard "the screech of human voices and could see that a fire had been lit there. Shortly afterwards we saw two small kayaks made of sealskin coming out toward us, with one man in each. They stopped some 15 to 20 fathoms from the ship and, as we were unable to talk with them, made all sorts of signs and signals to us that we should go ashore to them. Come aboard to us they would not, but gradually they approached nearer and we threw various trifles down into the water to them, as presents."

This impasse of mutual suspicion and distrust between the white men and the natives was broken by a spontaneous transfer of personnel. Such exchanges of hostages to safeguard fair play became a set pattern during the next hundred years, and were used by the early Russian fur traders and the Aleuts whom they pressed into service.

"I could see," Waxel wrote, "that they

were afraid and mistrustful, and I wanted to show them that we were not afraid and also to convince them that their fears of us were unfounded. So I decided to send three men ashore, two Russians and an interpreter from the Chukchi peninsula. They pulled off their clothes and waded ashore (from the longboat that had been sent in from the ship) with the water right up under their arms. As soon as they had reached the shore, one of the Americans seated himself in his kayak and came out to me."

The boats and the dress of these Americans, as he called them, also caught Waxel's attention, both of which enabled these sea-going people to perform their crucial role in the often tragic and always violent century to follow.

"The two Russians and the interpreter had strolled about with the Americans quite a bit. They told us how they had seen nine kayaks, all made of sealskin. Only one person can sit in a kayak, which is sewn up tight both in front and behind. In the middle of the kayak is a raised part like a wooden bowl and in the center of this a hole large enough for a man to get the lower part of his body through and into the kayak. Round this hole is fastened a sealskin bag which in turn is fastened round the body with a long thong. Once [a man is] seated in the kayak and thus fastened in it, not a drop of water can find its way inside. The natives are accustomed to these craft from youth and are perfectly able to maintain their balance—the whole secret of sailing them—even in very rough weather. . . .

"We noticed no bows and arrows or other weapons of the kind such peoples are wont to have with them. Only one of them had a knife at his side. This knife was made in a fashion quite unknown to us. It was about eight inches long and in front broad and thick. These Americans' outer clothes or coats were made of whale guts cut up and sewn together again. Their trousers were of sealskin, while their caps were of sea-lion skin set around with various feathers, most of them, naturally, hawk's feathers. Their noses were plugged with tough grass of an unknown kind and when they took this out, it gave off a quantity of fluid which they licked up with their tongues. Their faces were red, but certain of them had painted theirs blue. Their individual features were like those of Europeans, in contrast to the Kalmuks who are all flat-nosed. They were long limbed and well formed. Their food seemed to consist of all kinds of sea animals and of the blubber, a piece of which they had wished to give me. They also eat herbs of all sorts, and wild roots. While I was watching, they pulled up some roots, shook off the sand and gobbled them up.

"On the following morning, 6th September, seven kayaks came out to us and lay off quite close to the ship. There was one man in each kayak, as I have already described. Two of them came right into the ship and took hold of our gangway. They made us a present of two of their caps and of a stick five feet long, to the thin end of which were fastened feathers of every conceivable kind. They also gave us a little human image carved out of bone, which we imagined must have been one of the idols they worshipped.

"They accepted presents from us as well and would have come aboard had not the wind got up and begun to blow hard, so that they had to betake themselves off in a hurry. As soon as they had got back on land, they all arranged themselves in a cluster and began screeching dreadfully. This they kept up for almost a quarter of an hour; yet I have no idea why they did so.

"It must be assumed that powder and guns were unknown to them, for they would hardly have come out to us again, and certainly not so close to the ship, if they had known that the two musket shots I had ordered to be fired the previous evening were connected with things which could kill them. . . .

"Shortly afterwards we got underway and as we sailed past the island the natives were on, they again stood all together in a clump and screeched as hard as they could. Whether this was to wish us a good voyage or an expression of their joy at seeing us departing, on that I shall not express an opinion."

For the balance of September, Waxel wrote, "We had to sail along without knowing what was what and that in an

unknown and undescribed ocean, like blind people who do not know whether they are going too quickly or too slowly. . . . Most of the time we were sailing with a headwind of almost storm strength, and we never saw land again until 25th September."

To describe the rest of the voyage is to describe misery so abject as defies belief. Most narratives simply summarize the bare facts of the *St. Peter's* shipwreck, Bering's death, and the eventual homecoming a year later of the sorry handful of crewmen. But, the survival of these forty-six bearded remnants of the *St. Peter* is a miracle transcended only in magnitude by the events that followed their deliverance. In this deliverance these men carried with them the coveted sea otter pelt that within fifty years would draw Europe and Russia together on America's Northwest Coast. The shipwreck of the *St. Peter* and the

winter spent by its survivors on Bering Island, not eight days' sail from the Kamchatkan port they so desperately sought, form a vital link in the chain which binds the Tlingit of Alaska to the fortunes of Russia and the western world.

Other explorers and adventurers of early days experienced similar trials. Some succumbed entirely and so left no record. Others survived but did not write of their experience. Some few, like Lieutenant Waxel and the scientist Georg Steller, had both the luck to survive and the wit and ability to put down their stories. By so doing, they emerge as the few out of thousands whose observations of the history they helped create are passed on for others. The final agonies of the *St. Peter* are an integral part of the history of Alaska. That someone else would have found it eventually, there is no doubt. But these men did. In their record one begins to realize the qualities of courage, fortitude and spirit that were required to write this first chapter.

"By now," Waxel wrote, "so many of our people were ill that I had, so to speak, no one to steer the ship. Our sails too, had worn so thin that I expected them to fly off at any moment. To bend on other sails was out of the question. I had not enough men for that. Indeed, when it came to a man's turn at the helm, he was dragged to it by two other of the invalids who were still able to walk a little, and set down at the wheel. There he had to sit and steer as well as he could, and when he could sit no more, he had to be replaced by another in no better case than he."

Throughout October violent winds, long, dark nights and days filled with snow,

hail and rain tormented the wretched crew. "Let no one imagine that our situation is here represented as too dangerous," wrote Steller, "let him rather believe that the most eloquent pen would have found itself too weak to describe our misery. Misery and death suddenly got the upper hand on our ship to such an extent that not only did the sick die off, but those who according to their own assertion were well, on being relieved at their posts, dropped dead from exhaustion. The small allowance of water, the lack of biscuits and brandy, the cold, dampness, nakedness, vermin, fright, and terror were not the least important causes."

On November 4 they sighted land and hope sprang up that it might be the desperately sought peninsula of Kamchatka.

"To Captain-Commander Bering, who had been tied to a bed of sickness for many weeks, I gave an account of our helpless condition in which we were more like a wreck than a ship," Waxel wrote. "The Captain-Commander ordered that all officers of whatever rank and the rest of the command should come down into his cabin to consult together on what measures might best serve to save us."

Illness, dwindling provisions, and the lateness of the season affected the decision. "We agreed, therefore, to make for the land and by that means seek to save our lives. Perhaps God would also help us to keep the ship."

The landing was no less a nightmare than had been the voyage. Twelve of the crew members had already died, and the rest were so weakened by scurvy that they could not maneuver the ship. They dropped anchor to avoid being carried onto a reef, "but it broke the cable at once and was as much help as though we had never dropped it.

"Here I must relate how in the midst of all our misfortunes we had an unexpected and undeserved stroke of good fortune," said Waxel. "It was just as we were making the sheet-anchor ready that the waves lifted us over the rocks and we found calm water. . . . We later realized that there was no other place anywhere round the entire island where a ship could have got in to shore, but only this one."

Yet even this small rejoicing was short lived. Some days later, after the crew had struggled ashore and lay resting in shallow pits dug in the sand—too weak to secure the ship for approaching winter—a savage storm broke and smashed the ship onto the shore, a wreck.

"Captain-Commander Bering died on 8th December," wrote Waxel. He had been carried ashore in a litter and placed like the others in a scooped hollow of sand. "I cannot forbear to tell of the wretched state of the Captain-Commander as he lay in his agony. The half of his body was already buried in the ground while he still lived, and even if it had been possible to pull him out again, it would have been against his wishes, for he said to us; 'The deeper in the ground I lie, the warmer I am; the part of my body that lies above ground suffers from the cold.' It had happened in this way: the Captain-Commander lay in a little hollow in the sand. The sand kept trickling down the sides and in the end had filled the hollow about half full. As the Captain-Commander was lying in the center of the hollow, it ended by the half of his body being covered by the falling sand."

Of this man of destiny, whose conduct of the expedition has been as much criticized as its results have been praised, Steller, who during the course of the voyage was one of the chief critics, praised his valor and fortitude in sticking with "so difficult an expedition, that had been made larger and more extensive" than a far younger man could have executed. "As it was," wrote Steller, "he perished almost from hunger, thirst, cold, hardship, and grief."

"Once we were all ashore," Waxel wrote, "the most important point to be considered was on what were we going to live during the winter." From the ship they had salvaged some water-soaked groats and an 800-pound sack of rye flour. The few men who could still move about began to explore and search for food. They soon learned the full horror of their situation. Their landfall was no part of the mainland, but an uncharted, sub-arctic island, inhabited by foxes.

"Everywhere on the shore," Steller wrote, "there was nothing but pitiful and terrifying sights. The dead before they

could be interred, were mutilated by the foxes, who even dared to attack the living and helpless sick, who lay about on the beach without cover, and sniffed at them like dogs." Yet out of prudence, he said, they did not want to exterminate even these hated animals, but only to frighten them.

In mid-November Steller and two others went hunting for the first time. They clubbed four sea otters and from the liver, kidneys, heart and meat, Steller wrote, "we made several palatable dishes. The precious skins of the sea otters we regarded already as a burden which had lost its value to us." These were thrown about until they spoiled, or were chewed to pieces by the foxes.

Although tough and sinewy, sea otter was their main source of subsistence, until by March this genial, sleekly pelted marine mammal had grown scarce. They became so wild from being hunted, said Waxel, that it was impossible to get near them. "When one saw a man 100 fathoms away, it would at once jump into the water; yet in the early days we had been able to ap-

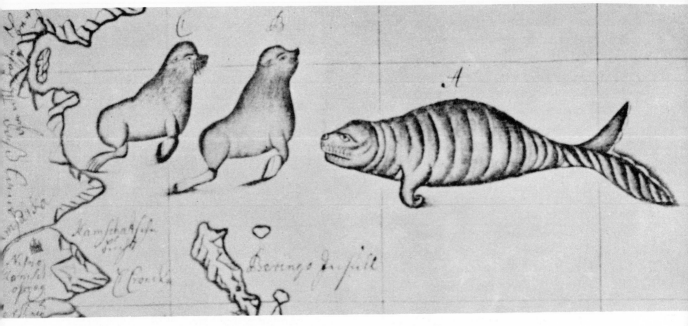

*Representation of a fur seal, a sea lion, and a sea cow on
the copy of Waxel's chart of the voyage of the* St. Peter

proach to within 5 or 10 fathoms of them without their being the least afraid."

Soon after the new year, 1742, the sea washed up a dead whale. "Its blubber was slightly rank," Waxel conceded, "but we were highly satisfied with that piece of good fortune and called the whale our provision store."

Nature's ceaseless natural rhythm for propagating the species, provided, with the annual migration of the fur seal, a replacement for the declining sea otter. Waxel who called them "sea bear" said, "They came ashore on the western side of the island in such numbers that the whole shore was, so to speak, covered with them." The scientist Steller rightfully concluded that "These and other Islands in the Channel must doubtless be the summer grounds of these animals where they bear their young. . . . countless herds followed and

within a few days covered the whole beach to such an extent that it was not possible to pass."

Just as Bering's survivors turned to the fur seal after exhausting their precious sea otter reserve, so a century later the avid fur seekers switched their attention to the fur seal, after their ruthless pursuit had all but extinguished the sea otter from the entire ocean.

"I had almost forgotton to mention," Waxel wrote, "that we also killed some young sea-lions, and these we regarded as the best eating of all."

Sustained by the miracle of arctic abundance, the castaways turned their thoughts to building from the wreck of the *St. Peter*—which providentially had been left half sunk in the protected waters near shore—a smaller vessel which could carry them to Kamchatka.

The closest thing they had to a ship-builder was a Siberian Cossack who had watched Bering's ships being constructed at Okhotsk. "He said that if I would give him the proportions of the new ship," said Waxel, "he would build it under my guidance and make her so solid that, with God's help, we should be able to put to sea in her without risk."

They salvaged all usable parts of the wreck and from such meager materials as they could scour up on the island, improvised what was wanting. Pitch to seal over the hull's caulking they obtained by melting from unused lengths of tarred rope, of which they had a quantity. "By the time our craft was almost ready we had also got our rigging, mast, sails, water containers and a store of provisions as good as it was possible to have in those miserable conditions," Waxel wrote.

"On 10th August, late in the afternoon, when there was full flood-tide, we let her run off. . . . When we had all come aboard and everything was ready, we weighed anchor on 13th August as evening was approaching.

"We named the vessel *St. Peter*, it being natural to call her after our old ship. She was rigged as a one masted hooker with mainyard and mainsail, flying topsail, foresail and jib: but we had no use for a spanker, for the mainyard and mainsail were so perfect that the main sheet reached right aft. . . . To put it shortly, the ship fulfilled all our expectations and I know too for certain that in 1752 she was still being used as a transport vessel between Okhotsk and Kamchatka.

"On 17th August we sighted the land north of Avacha. We then followed the

land southwards with various shifting winds, mostly southerly, and on 26th August arrived safely at Avacha Bay. On 27th August we reached Petropavlovsk.

"I am not able to describe the joy and heart-felt delight we one and all felt and exhibited on our deliverance. From the uttermost misery and distress we plunged into veritable superabundance, for there was a whole storehouse full of provisions, comfortable warm quarters and other amenities, none of which we had been able to have that last winter. All that made our joy and the sense of contrast so overwhelming that it just cannot be expressed in words."

The years that followed the miraculous return of the remnants of the *St. Peter's* crew were no less incredible than the expedition itself. Officially, the government of Russia took no action to follow up Bering's discoveries, proving as reluctant to publish an account of the new knowledge as it was to continue the quest for it. In

a sense this irony symbolized not only the misadventures of the expedition itself, but also the fifty turbulent, lawless years that followed. By her official default, Russia gave as a gift the thousand mile arc of the Aleutian Islands to a succession of hard, cruel and unprincipled fur-seekers who swarmed out over the waters in pursuit of the sea otter.

To the amazement of Bering's crew, the pelts of the sea otter, whose flesh and fur had sustained and warmed them, sold in China at fantastic prices. The men who heard the sea otter's call were the freebooting fur hunters, of Siberia, called *promyshlennik*i (pronounced "pro-meesh'len-eekee)", a term used to describe the hundreds of untamed adventurers, convicts, hard-driving, hard-living outcasts from society who had roamed Siberia in the search for furs. The news of prices brought in China by this newly discovered source of wealth was quickly communicated to them. By the tens, by the hundreds, these men pointed their crude crafts toward the islands of the north Pacific—the Near Islands, the Andreanof Islands, the Rat and the Fox—in frantic pursuit of the sea otter.

For the most part these rough adventurers kept no record of their actions beyond their collection from the natives of a tribute to the Czar, a tax in furs. They followed the custom earlier established in Siberia, when the chase of the Russian sable had led these same fur hunters across the continent, from the Urals to the Pacific. The tribute accrued to the Czar or Czarina, and such records as were kept of it were scanty at best and failed to mention the abuses committed by the men who collected it.

The first real knowledge of the epic story that was unfolding along the islands of Alaska came from the pen of William Coxe, Fellow of Kings College, Cambridge, and Chaplain to his Grace the Duke of Marlborough. The English scholar obtained permission from the Czarina, Catherine the Great, to study the sparse Russian archives. From his inquiry came an *Account of the Russian Discoveries between Asia and America,* a work that filled in the record between Bering and Cook, and one so popular that after publication in 1780, it ran through four editions. Although not always identified as the source, Coxe is the basis for all histories of this period.

"Since the conclusion of Bering's voyage, which was made at the expense of the crown, the prosecution of the New Discoveries began by him has been almost entirely carried on by individuals. These persons were principally merchants of Irkutsk, Yakutsk, and other natives of Siberia, who formed themselves into small trading companies, and fitted out vessels at their joint expense," explained Coxe.

"Most of the vessels which are equipped for these expeditions are two masted: they are commonly built without iron, and in general so badly constructed, that it is wonderful how they can weather so stormy a sea. They are called in Russian *Skitiki* or sewed vessels, because the planks are sewed together with thongs of leather.

"The risk of the trade is very great, as shipwrecks are common in the sea of Kamtchatka, which is full of rocks and very tempestuous. Besides, the crews are frequently surprised and killed by the islanders, and the vessels destroyed. In return the profits arising from these voyages are very considerable, and compensate the inconveniencies and dangers attending them. . . .

"Some notion of the general profits arising from this trade (when the voyage is successful), may be deduced from the sale of a rich cargo of furs, brought to Kamtchatka, on the 2d of June, 1772, from the new-discovered islands, in a vessel belonging to Ivan Popoff.

"The tenth part of the skins being delivered to the customs, the remainder was distributed in fifty-five shares. Each share consisted of twenty sea-otters, sixteen black and brown foxes, ten red foxes, three sea-otter tails; and such a portion was sold upon the spot from 800 to 1000 Roubles: so that according to this price the whole lading was worth about 50,000 Roubles.

"The principal furs and skins procured from the Peninsula of Kamtchatka and the New Discovered Islands are sea-otters, foxes, sables, ermines, wolves, bears, etc.— These furs are transported to Ochotsk by sea, and from thence carried to Kiachta upon the frontiers of Siberia; where the

greatest part of them are sold to the Chinese at a very considerable profit.

"Of all these furs the skins of the sea-otters are the richest and most valuable. These animals resort in great numbers to the Aleutian and Fox Islands: they are called by the Russians *Bobry Morski* or sea-beavers. . . .

"The fur of the finest sort is thick and long, of a dark colour, and a fine glossy hue. They are taken four ways; struck with darts as they are sleeping upon their backs in the sea, followed in boats and hunted down till they are tired, surprised in caverns, and taken in nets.

"Their skins fetch different prices according to their quality."

Coxe's story of this violent period omitted neither the wanton horrors inflicted upon the native population, nor the privation and hardships endured by the perpetrators of the violence.

As early as 1745 native blood was shed on the island of Agatoo when a Russian bullet pierced the hand of an Aleut islander. The same band of adventurers carried violence and bloodshed on to the island of Attu. Here they massacred fifteen male Aleuts in order to seize the native women.

No law, no order went with the tough promyshlenniki as they pushed eastward along the Aleutian Archipelago—only cruelty, drunkenness, the violation of women, the murder of men and the wholesale slaughter of the sea otter they so avidly sought.

Gradually a pattern of operations was established which Coxe described:

"The Russians have for some years past been accustomed to go to these islands in quest of furs, of which they have imposed a tax on the inhabitants. The manner of carrying on this trade is as follows. The Russian traders go in Autumn to Bering's and Copper island, and there winter; they then employ themselves in catching the sea-cat, and afterwards the Scivutcha, or sea-lion. The flesh of the latter is prepared for food, and it is very delicate. They carry the skins of these sea-animals to the Eastern islands. Next summer they go Eastward, to the Fox-islands; and again lay their ships up for the winter. They then endeavour to procure, either by persuasion or force, the children of the inhabitants, particularly of the Tookoos [Toyons or chiefs], as hostages. This being accomplished, they deliver to the inhabitants fox-traps, and also skins for their boats, for which they oblige them to bring furs and provisions during the winter. After obtaining from them a certain quantity of furs, by way of tax, for which they give them quittances; the Russians pay for the rest in beads, false pearls, goat's wool, copper kettles, hatchets, etc. In the spring they get back their traps, and deliver up their hostages."

If all did not go according to Russian pleasure—which, with the native women left behind, was at least partially satisfied —the hostages were, without a second thought, forfeit. Acts of needless cruelty fill the pages of Coxe's history. For real or trumped up offenses whole villages were burned and the inhabitants exterminated.

A man named Pushkarev is credited with being the first Russian to touch the mainland of the Alaskan Peninsula, at the place called by the natives Alaksu, from which comes the name Alaska. With this

fame goes the infamy of having kidnapped twenty-five girls. Coxe described how Pushkarev later sent some of them ashore on the pretext of picking berries. Two ran away, one was clubbed to death, some committed suicide by drowning themselves. Pushkarev solved the problem of witnesses by binding the balance who were on board ship and throwing them into the sea.

Another vignette is that of a Russian named Soloviev who was curious about the penerating powers of a musket ball. So frightful and bitter were Aleut memories of this man whose barbarism played a large part finally in crushing their spirit, that half a century later witnesses to the tragedy told Bishop Ivan Veniaminov that Soloviev tied a dozen Aleuts in a row. The bullet, they said, stopped at the ninth man.

Russian outrages stopped too—not all at once, not altogether, and certainly far past the ninth man. But gradually a renewed interest in the lands of Bering began to exhibit itself in the court at St. Petersburg. Catherine the Second, also called the Great, came to the throne. Catherine picked up the threads of the western empire begun by Peter. Official expeditions once more went out toward America and the tales of promyshlennik barbarism received an ear at court.

Of far greater practical consequence to Russian exploitation was a new name that appeared in the Aleutian fur trade, the name of a man credited with bringing a decisive change to the character of that exploitation. In 1777 Gregory Ivanovich Shelikov outfitted a ship for the fur trade. A scant seven years later he planted the first permanent Russian colony on American soil.

Unlike the fur-seekers before him, Shelikov had a vision. His gaze went beyond the Aleutians, on past the Alaskan Peninsula, all through the rich sea otter hunting grounds of coastal Alaska, down even to present-day Oregon and California. He envisioned the whole happy hunting ground as colonized by Russians for the purpose, as he told Czarina Catherine, of: (a) bringing the benefits of Christianity to the pagan natives and (b) enjoying exclusive rights of a fur trade protected by state charter.

Shelikov had read the handwriting that was already upon the waters. The once lush grounds for sea otter and fox, were rapidly receding before the Russian onslaught from Attu to Unalaska. By 1756,

only fifteen years after Bering's wreck on Bering Island, the once abundant animals were disappearing. Expeditions were yielding less furs on longer, more costly undertakings. Competition between rival trading companies was threatening extinction of the once abundant sea otter. Shelikov felt that consolidation into a single great fur monopoly was the only answer to preservation. Forming a partnership called the Shelikov-Golikov Company, Shelikov himself, along with his no less remarkable wife, Natalie, landed in 1784 on Kodiak Island opposite Prince William Sound. Here on the island's southeastern end they founded the first permanent Russian colony in America at Three Saints' Bay.

In the political frame of world affairs, Shelikov's entry into the Russian fur trade coincided with Spain's reawakened interest in exploration of her New World territories and with the final, brilliant explorations of England under Captain James Cook which closed the last gap in man's knowledge of the world.

As early as 1774 Spanish ships probed northward along the coast from San Blas, off the western coast of Mexico. In 1778 a Russian promyshlennik named Izmailov came face to face with the famed English navigator, Captain Cook. Out of their exchange on navigation and geography, came the news that spurred history. This was Cook's account of sea otters off the Alaskan mainland at Prince William's Sound. Cook's crew brought the same news back to England. But by the time the first English traders arrived to take advantage of it, the Russians were already entrenched.

Soon three major powers of Europe

poised over the spoils of sub-Arctic America, the merchant navigators of two of them bent on snatching a hapless sea animal, blessed or cursed with a high priced pelt. Today that animal is nearly extinct. The population of the Aleutian Islands declined from some 30,000 cheerful and vigorous people to a scant two thousands souls, few of whom can claim unmixed descent, and a not yet discovered, unique Indian culture populating the area of the American mainland known as the Pacific Northwest Coast, was cut nearly in half and the art which gained its fame ceased to exist, except in museums around the world.

The sardonic outcome of the struggle a century later is that none of the three powers won. Entering the race late, a new power burst through like a dark horse to take Alaska for its prize.

Before this happened, the interests of Russia, Spain, England and the newly emerged United States embroiled the far west coast of America in a century of diplomatic intrigue and commercial plunder that destroyed forever the last of America's colorful native cultures.

The man who made things start to hum was England's famous Captain Cook.

Chapter II

COMES THE
GREAT CAPTAIN COOK

For thirty years after Bering's discovery, Russia enjoyed exclusive sway over Alaska's wealth in furs. For this same time span the mild-mannered Aleuts of that land suffered the enslavement of forced labor by the tough, unprincipled promyshlenniki who used them to hunt down the coveted sea otter.

The Tlingit of Alaska and their neighbors along the coast down to Nootka had still some more time. Europe was not yet ready. Russia's expansion to the east did not bring her into collision with the states of western Europe whose trade and overseas empires kept them occupied elsewhere. To Spain, encroachment from the north on the western shore of her American empire was not yet threatening. England had yet to engage France in the Seven Years War which would strip the French of the rich fur-bearing regions of interior North America they had so brilliantly explored. Improvements in seamanship were still necessary before England would grasp and act on the idea that her long sought Northwest Passage might be found from the Pacific by sailing northeast.

Then, one day in March in the year 1778, Captain Cook sighted for England the "long looked for coast of New Albion. . . . The land appeared to be of a moderate height, diversified with hills and vallies, and, almost everywhere, covered with wood."

For the next twenty-two days Captain Cook's stout ships, the *Resolution* and *Discovery*, battled storms, contrary winds and thick weather.

"At length, at nine o'clock in the morning of the 29th, as we were standing to the North East, we again saw the land. Our latitude was 49° 29' North. The appearance of the country differed much from that of the parts which we had before seen; being full of high mountains, whose summits were covered with snow. But the valleys between them, and the grounds on the sea coast, high as well as low, were covered to a considerable breadth with high, straight trees, that

SANTA BARBARA in Lat.º 34°24' N.º and Long.º 240°15' E.º the PRESIDIO bearing N. 56° distant 2 Miles Var. 8 ½° Easterly.

formed a beautiful prospect, as of one vast forest. . . .

"We no sooner drew near the inlet than we found the coast to be inhabited; and at the place where we were first becalmed, three canoes came off to the ship. In one of these were two men, in another six, and in the third ten. Having come pretty near us, a person in one of the last two stood up, and made a long harangue, inviting us to land, as we guessed, by his gestures. At the same time, he kept strewing handfuls of feathers toward us: and some of his companions threw handfuls of a red dust or powder in the same manner. The person who played the orator, wore the skin of some animal, and held, in each hand, something which rattled as he kept shaking it. After tiring himself with his repeated exhortations, of which we did not understand a word, he was quiet; and then others took it, by turns, to say something, though they acted their part neither so long, nor with so much vehemence as the other. . . . After the tumultuous noise had ceased, they lay at a little distance from the ship, and conversed with each other in a very easy manner; nor did they seem to shew the least surprize or distrust. . . . The breeze which soon after sprung up, bringing us nearer to the shore, the canoes began to come off in greater numbers; and we had, at one time, thirty-

Captain James Cook

two of them near the ship, carrying from three to seven or eight persons each, both men and women. Several of these stood up in their canoes haranguing, and making gestures after the manner of our first visitors. One canoe was remarkable for a singular head, which had a bird's eye and bill, of an enormous size, painted on it; and a person who was in it, who seemed to be a Chief, was no less remarkable for his uncommon appearance; having many feathers hanging from his head, and being painted in an extraordinary manner. He held in his hand a carved bird of wood, as large as a pigeon, with which he rattled

The entrance of PORT St DIEGO in Lat.

as the person first-mentioned had done; and was no less vociferous in his harangue, which was attended with some expressive gestures.

"Though our visitors behaved very peaceably, and could not be suspected of any hostile intention, we could not prevail upon any of them to come on board. They shewed great readiness, however, to part with anything they had, and took from us whatever we offered them in exchange; but were more desirous of iron, than of any other of our articles of commerce; appearing to be perfectly acquainted with the use of that metal. Many of the canoes followed us to our anchoring-place; and a group of about ten or a dozen of them remained along-side the *Resolution* most of the night."

RESOLUTION.

As Cook entered these observations in his journal, so did contact begin between the white men of western civilization and the seven native tribes—more properly described as linguistic groupings —which together make up the Indians of the Pacific Northwest Coast. These seven major divisions occupy the coast from Yakutat Bay bounding the northern limits, to the Olympic Peninsula and adjacent mainland of the present-day State of Washington. Distinguished from each other by language into "nations" they yet form a characteristic native culture that differed markedly from that of the interior Indians and from the Aleut and Eskimo cultures farther north.

Captain James Cook has been called "the finisher" of the world's oceanic exploration. He sailed and mapped the last of the globe's diminishing unknown. With his discovery of America's Northwest Coast, Captain Cook completed a job begun nearly three hundred years earlier by Columbus.

Within a century and a half after Columbus, the seagoing powers of Europe had, through their natural pugnacity, superior technology and white man's diseases, decisively brought under their domination most of the populations of the globe. Only the highly civilized Orient and the Moslem world stood firm against Europe's onslaught.

At the moment when history called Captain Cook to greatness there remained unexplored only two portions of the vast and formidable Pacific Ocean. One was the giant expanse of the south, from Cape Horn on the southern tip of South America westward to the barely touched shores

of New Zealand and Australia. The other was the Northern Mystery, the Pacific coastline north of the California point touched briefly and named New Albion by the English explorer-buccaneer Sir Francis Drake, two hundred years earlier in 1578.

By the last quarter of the 18th century, new stirrings in Europe stimulated one final burst of maritime exploration. The power balance had shifted. England —no longer Spain—held command of the seas. England's defeat of France in the Seven Years' Wars brought her the French

holdings in Canada. The enterprising Dutch and Portuguese adjusted their mercantile sights to the political status of lesser powers.

But competition among the countries of Europe was far from dead. Elevated now to a status of political as well as commercial rivalry, the search for unclaimed lands and new markets was pressed vigorously and backed by the prestige and funds of the national states. In Cook's time the job of mapping the world was not quite finished. The need for new products and shorter trade routes was not yet over.

England under George III and Spain under the enlighted Bourbon, Carlos III, set the stage for what was destined to be the last act for each in their attempts to claim further territory in the New World. Ironically, their final gesture proved to be the prelude for the emergence of the new United States of America, which would shortly outdistance both Spain and England in trade along the Northwest Coast.

But at the time of Cook's third voyage, the American Colonists were absorbed in their fight for independence. They did not share England's urgent concern for a shorter trade route passing through the North American continent, a route that would aid England in the growing competition for the tea trade with the Orient. From the earliest explorations of Frobisher and later those of Henry Hudson, who was cast adrift by mutineers on the great northern bay he discovered, on down to the overland search by Alexander Mackenzie for a Northwest Passage to the Pacific, England never gave up hope. For

many years the British admiralty had offered a prize of twenty thousand pounds
to the discoverer of a passage from the
Atlantic to the Pacific. In 1775 the offer
was opened to members of the Royal Navy
and included discovery of a passage from
West to East.

Captain Cook had just returned from
his second expedition during which he
had completed mapping the essential
characteristics of the South Pacific. He
executed his task with such accuracy that
further exploration did not significantly
alter his findings. Celebrated, restless and
eager to continue doing that which he was
gifted to do, Cook asked for permission
to head an expedition to the American
Northwest Coast. Permission was enthu-
siastically granted, and once again Cook
equipped his vessels for a voyage of discovery in accordance with his own exact-
ing specifications, specifications that in following years would be accepted as standard for maritime expeditions.

Luck had undoubtedly played a part
in Cook's safe return from his two previous voyages. But far more important were
Cook's navigational genius and his scientific approach to the prevention of scurvy.
His contribution to seamanship in these
two areas broke the last chains binding the
art of navigation to the medieval world.
From Cook's day forward, navigation came
of age as a science, measurable and exact,
and health at sea was made possible even
on the longest of voyages.

Cook launched a two-fold attack on
scurvy, that dread disease of seamen that
softened the gums and loosened the teeth,
inflamed the joints, weakened the body,
depressed the mind and brought death over

the years to thousands of afflicted sailors. First, Cook imposed the strictest discipline to keep his ships and men clean, a revolutionary innovation in his day. Secondly, he introduced as a mandatory part of his crew's daily diet such innovations as sauerkraut and a steady variation of concoctions brewed from fresh fruit and vegetables.

Others before Cook possessed some understanding of the value to human health of these anti-scorbutics, but they were unable to apply their knowledge practically to diet at sea. Cook devised forms in which the crucial vitamin C, as we know it today, could be preserved on board ship far from port and made available to the crew, which for its part, did not necessarily appreciate their Captain's efforts on their behalf. A true man of science, Cook was constantly experimenting. And as all innovators find resistance to their new ideas, so too did Cook, who at one point in his journal related with some exasperation:

"Having procured a quantity of Sugar Cane and had upon trial made but a few

days before, found that a strong decoction of it made a very palatable beer, which was esteemed by every one on board, I ordered some more to be brewed, but when the Cask came to be broached not one of my Mutinous crew would even so much as taste it. Every innovation whatever though ever so much to their advantage is sure to meet with the highest disapprobation from Seamen. Soup and Sour Krout were at first both condemned by them as stuff not fit for human being[s] to eat. Few men have introduced into their Ship more novelties in the way of victuals and drink than I have done; indeed few men have had the same opportunity or been driven to the same necessity. It has however in a great measure been owing to such little innovations that I have always kept my people generally speaking free from that dreadful distemper the Scurvy."

In the end Cook's vision and dedication paid off. He returned from his second voyage in the Pacific having lost not one man from scurvy, and on his third voyage the observance of his strict measures by his officers after his own death in Hawaii confirmed his achievement. In 1795 the British Navy began issuing a daily ration of lime juice on all of Her Majesty's ships. To Cook goes the credit for this major breakthrough, credit early given by his contemporaries who strove thereafter to equip their own expeditions in accordance with Cook's standards. Official recognition was given as well by England's Royal Society which awarded to him its highest honor, the Copley Gold Medal.

The second major breakthrough in navigation accomplished by Cook was the perfection of a method to calculate longitude accurately. On his second voyage, in addition to conquering scurvy, Cook tested a marine chronometer that for the first time gave navigators a faithful measurement of longitude. Prior to his day, only latitude could be accurately determined, leaving the matter of east-west measurement to complex lunar calculations that were, at best, imprecise. Many accounts of early navigators mention discoveries—including most probably in the 1500's the Hawaiian Islands—that dissolved into fable for want of an accurate way to locate their position on maps.

Cook's inspired approach to hydrography—the study, description and mapping of water bodies, with especial reference to their navigational and commercial use—makes him the first modern navigator. When to this is added the banishment of scurvy, his accomplishment clearly marks the turning point in marine history.

The control of scurvy and the perfection of marine navigation may seem remote from the fortunes of the Tlingit of Alaska. In actual fact, both were requisite to the energetic pursuit of the maritime fur trade that came in Cook's wake and which brought about the permanent involvement of these peoples with white men's affairs.

Prior to Cook's time the long voyage from Boston or London, even had the riches in furs been known, was too hazardous to assure profits, the prime consideration of trade. Rumors had trickled through of the Russians' activities in America's frozen north, but these tough Russian adventurers suffered severely from scurvy and even Cook praised Bering, for having "delineated this Coast very well and fixed the latitude and longitude of the points better than could be expected from the methods he had to go by."

The newly won political freedom alone could not have sufficed to launch the young United States on an era of free trading with the Indians of the Pacific

Northwest. But the new factor of political independence, plus the changed state of marine science, combined to open this new market to the eager new merchants of Boston.

The great Captain Cook did more than discover for the western world the northern Pacific land arc stretching from Alaska to Vancouver Island. He brought to his discovery the two vital nautical advances that would sustain the discovery and bring this remote region, the home of a remarkable and unique Indian culture, into the mainstream of history.

The account of his discovery reached England and the western world in Volume Two of the now famous *A Voyage to the Pacific Ocean*.

Still to be mentioned is one more talent possessed by this remarkable sailor, his aptitude for anthropological observation. Born of humble parents and self-taught, Cook rose to fame and acclaim. So great, in fact, was his reputation that when France seized the opportunity of the American Revolution to declare war on England in 1778, the French Government issued an order exempting Captain Cook, then en route to the Northwest Coast, from attack. The order stated that Cook was free to sail without being molested. The British navigator, the French said, was the benefactor of every nation. Over and above his contributions to nautical science and modern medicine, Cook was the benefactor of modern anthropology as well. His curious and alert mind enabled him to observe what he saw, to sort the significant from the inconsequential, and to draw conclusions of insight and perception. In the months that he lay at anchor in Nootka

A VOYAGE TO THE PACIFIC OCEAN.

BOOK IV.

TRANSACTIONS AMONGST THE NATIVES OF NORTH AME-
RICA; DISCOVERIES ALONG THAT COAST AND THE EAST-
ERN EXTREMITY OF ASIA, NORTHWARD TO ICY CAPE;
AND RETURN SOUTHWARD TO THE SANDWICH ISLANDS.

CHAP. I.

*The Ships enter the Sound, and moor in a Harbour.—Inter-
course with the Natives.—Articles brought to barter.—
Thefts committed.—The Obfervatories erected, and Carpenters fet to work.—Jealoufy of the Inhabitants of the Sound
to prevent other Tribes having Intercourfe with the Ships.—
Stormy and rainy Weather.—Progrefs round the Sound.—
Behaviour of the Natives at their Villages.—Their Manner
of drying Fifh, &c.—Remarkable Vifit from Strangers, and
introductory Ceremonies.—A fecond Vifit to one of the Villages.—Leave to cut Grafs, purchafed.—The Ships fail.—
Prefents given and received at parting.*

THE fhips having happily found fo excellent fhelter
in an inlet, the coafts of which appeared to be inhabited by a race of people, whofe inoffenfive behaviour promifed a friendly intercourfe, the next morning, after coming to anchor, I loft no time in endeavouring
to find a commodious harbour where we might ftation our-
felves during our continuance in the Sound.

1778.
March.

1778.
March.

Monday 30.

Sound, he studied the Indians of the region as thoroughly and perceptively as any trained enthnologist, observing their daily lives, noting the unusal features of their culture as well as their similarities to other primitive peoples he had encountered during his many years in the Pacific. Unlike many of the merchant-navigators to follow, he was sensitive as well to the unusual quality of their native art.

The impressions which he recorded in his journal, and the artifacts he procured, many of which are treasured now by the British Museum, stand as the white man's introduction to the Northwest Coast Indians. His journal was the earliest written source material for the anthropologists who rediscovered these Indians a full century later.

Cook's conclusions still rate very high. His mind assimilated a wealth of facts and impressions. His deductions are astonishing in their accuracy. Even when confronted with practices he did not understand, his intuitive guesses, guided by his scientific bent, came close to the mark. When he encountered totem poles he ruled them out as being of religious significance, but rather, as we know today, he said they could be more closely described as "images of some of their ancestors whom they venerate as divinities."

Such insights as this, his power to see that which so many are blind to, and over and above all, his magnificent powers of verbal expression, place him high on the list of early anthropologists. If he is not the greatest, he is certainly among the most readable. And part of his readability comes from his own keen interest in the experiences which formed his life:

"A great many canoes, filled with the natives, were about the ships all day; and a trade commenced betwixt us and them, which was carried on with the strictest honesty on both sides. The articles which they offered to sale were skins of various animals, such as bears, wolves, foxes, deer, rackoons, polecats, martins; and, in particular, of the sea otters, which are found at the islands East of Kamtschatka. Besides the skins in their native shape, they also brought garments made of them, and another sort of clothing made of the bark of a tree, or some plant like hemp; weapons, such as bows, arrows, and spears; fishhooks, and instruments of various kinds; wooden vizors of many different monstrous figures; a sort of woolen stuff, or blanketing; bags filled with red ochre; pieces of carved work; beads and several other little ornaments of thin brass and iron, shaped like a horse-shoe, which they hang at their

nose and several chissels, or pieces of iron, fixed to handles. From their possessing which metals, we could infer that they had either been visited before by some civilized nation, or had connections with tribes on their continent, who had communication with them. But the most extraordinary of all the articles which they brought to the ships for sale, were human skulls, and hands not yet quite stripped of the flesh, which they made our people plainly understand they had eaten; and, indeed, some of them had evident marks that they had been upon the fire. We had but too much reason to suspect, from this circumstance, that the horrid practice of feeding on their enemies is as prevalent here, as we found it to be at New Zealand and other South Sea Islands. For the various articles which they brought, they took in exchange knives, chissels, pieces of iron and tin, nails, looking-glasses, buttons, or any kind of metal. Glass beads they were not fond of; and cloth of every sort they rejected.

"We employed the next day in hauling our ships into the cove, where they were moored head and stern, fastening our hawsers to the trees on shore. On heaving up the anchor of the Resolution, we found, notwithstanding the great depth of water in which it was let go, that there were rocks at the bottom. These had done some considerable damage to the cable; and the hawsers that were carried out, to warp the ship into the cove, also got foul of rocks; from which it appeared that the whole bottom was strewed with them. The ship being again very leaky in her upper works, I ordered the carpenters to go to work to caulk her, and to repair such other defects

Wolf mask, one of numerous artifacts brought back by Captain Cook from Nootka

as, on examination, we might discover.

"The fame of our arrival brought a great concourse of the natives to our ships in the course of this day. We counted above a hundred canoes at one time, which might be supposed to contain, at an average, five persons each; for few of them had less than three on board; great numbers had seven, eight, or nine; and one was manned with no less than seventeen. Amongst these visitors, many now favoured us with their company for the first time, which we could guess, from their approaching the ships with their orations and other ceremonies. If they had any distrust or fear of us at first, they now appeared to have laid it aside; for they came on board the ships, and mixed with our people with the greatest freedom. . . .

"The ships being securely moored, we began our other necessary business the

next day. The observatories were carried ashore, and placed upon an elevated rock, on one side of the cove, close to the *Resolution*. A party of men, with an officer, was sent to cut wood, and to clear a place for the conveniency of watering. Others were employed to brew spruce-beer, as pine-trees abounded here. The forge was also set up, to make the iron-work wanting for the repairs of the fore-mast. For, besides one of the bibs being defective, the larboard trestle-tree, and one of the cross-trees were sprung.

"A considerable number of the natives visited us daily; and every now and then we saw new faces. On their first coming, they generally went through a singular mode of introducing themselves. They would paddle, with all their strength, quite round both ships, a Chief, or rather principle person in the canoe, standing up with a spear, or some other weapon, in his hand, and speaking, or rather hollowing, all the time. Sometimes the orator of the canoe would have his face covered with a mask, representing either a human visage, or that of some animal; and, instead of a weapon, would hold a rattle in his hand, as before described. After making this circuit round the ships, they would come along-side, and begin to trade without further intercourse, . . . they were as light-fingered as any of our friends in the islands we had visited in the course of the voyage. And they were far more dangerous thieves; for, possessing sharp iron instruments, they could cut a hook from a tackle, or any other piece of iron from a rope, the instant that our backs were turned. A large hook, weighing between twenty and thirty

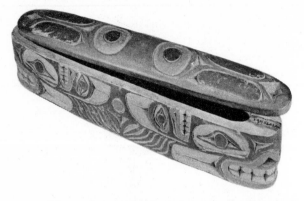

"After dinner, Eachtel shewed a small round box, which served him as a dressing case. It contained a comb, some necklaces and earrings, a mirror, some down to serve as powder, and several little bags, with black, white and a red dust, resembling black lead." Camille la Roquefeuil—Voyage Around the World, 1823

pounds, several smaller ones, and other articles of iron, were lost in this manner. And, as to our boats, they stripped them of every bit of iron that was worth carrying away, though we had always men left in them as a guard. They were dextrous enough in effecting their purposes; for one fellow would contrive ceremony. Very often, indeed, they would first give us a song, in which all in the canoe joined, with a very pleasing harmony."

March passed into April as Cook's crew worked to repair the *Resolution.*

"During these various operations, several of the natives, who were about the ships, looked on with an expressive silent surprize, which we did not expect, from their general indifference and inattention.

"On the 18th, a party of strangers, in six or eight canoes, came into the cove, where they remained, looking at us, for some time; and then retired, without com-

ing alongside either ship. . . . It was evident, upon this and several other occasions, that the inhabitants of the adjoining parts of the Sound engrossed us entirely to themselves; or if, at any time, they did not hinder strangers from trading with us, they contrived to manage the trade for them in such a manner, that the price of their commodities was always kept up, while the value of our was lessening every day. We also found, that many of the principal natives, who lived near us, carried on a trade with more distant tribes, in the articles they had procured from us. . . . Nothing would go down with our visitors but metal; and brass had, by this time, supplanted iron; being so eagerly sought after, that before we left this place, hardly a bit of it was left in the ships, except what belonged to our necessary instruments. Whole suits of clothes were stripped of every button; bureaus of their furniture; and copper kettles, tin cannisters, candlesticks, and the like, all went to wreck; so that our American friends here got a greater medly and variety of things from us, than any other nation whom we had visited in the course of the voyage. . . .

"During the time I was at this village, Mr. Webber, who had attended me thither, made drawings of everything that was curious, both within and without doors. I had also an opportunity of inspecting, more narrowly, the construction of the houses, household furniture, and utensils, and the striking peculiarities of the customs and modes of living of the inhabitants."

One can only marvel at the spread of these "particulars about the country, and its inhabitants" as came to Cook's knowledge during his short stay, between March 30th when his ships arrived and April 26th when he "cast off the Moorings and with our boats towed the ships out of the Cove" of the inlet he had honored with the name King George's Sound, adding that "its name, with the Natives is Nook ka."

He described the natives as generally under common stature, solidly built with high prominent cheeks, flattened foreheads and eyes that were small, black, and languishing rather than sparkling.

"They have either no beards at all, which was most commonly the case, or a small thin one upon the point of the chin; which does not arise from any natural defect of hair on that part, but from plucking it out more or less; for some of them, and particularly the old men, have not only considerable beards all over the chin, but whiskers, or mustachios; both on the upper lip, and running from thence toward the lower jaw obliquely downward. Their eye-brows are also scanty, and always narrow; but the hair of the head is in great abundance, very coarse and strong; and, without a single exception, black, straight, and lank, or hanging down over the shoulders. The neck is short; the arms and body have no particular mark of beauty or elegance in their formation, but are rather clumsy; and the limbs, in all, are very small in proportion to the other parts, and crooked, or ill-made, with large feet badly shaped, and projecting ankles. This last defect seems, in a great measure, to arise from their sitting so much on their hams or knees, both in their canoes and houses.

"Their colour we could never positively determine, as their bodies were incrusted with paint and dirt; though, in particular cases, when these were well rubbed off, the whitness of the skin appeared almost to equal that of Europeans; though rather of that pale effete cast which distinguishes those of our Southern nations. Their children, whose skins had never been stained with paint, also equalled ours in whiteness. . . .

"The women are nearly of the same size, colour, and form, with the men; from whom it is not easy to distinguish them, as they possess no natural delicacies sufficient to render their persons agreeable; and hardly any one was seen, even amongst those who were in the prime of

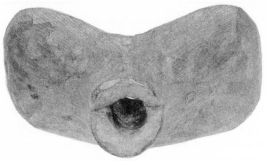

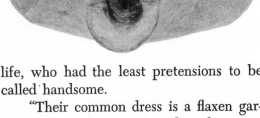

passes under the chin, to prevent its blowing off.

"Besides the above dress, which is common to both sexes, the men frequently throw over their other garments the skin of a bear, wolf, or sea-otter, with the hair outward, and tie it, as a cloak, near the upper part, wearing it sometimes before, and sometimes behind. . . .

life, who had the least pretensions to be called handsome.

"Their common dress is a flaxen garment, or mantle, ornamented on the upper edge by a narrow strip of fur, and, at the lower edge, by fringes or tassels. It passes under the left arm, and is tied over the right shoulder, by a string before, and one behind, near its middle; by which means both arms are left free; and it hangs evenly, covering the left side, but leaving the right open. . . . Their head is covered with a cap, of the figure of a truncated cone, or like a flower-pot, made of fine matting, having the top frequently ornamented with a round or pointed knob, or bunch of leathern tassels; and there is a string that

"Thus far of their ordinary dress and ornaments; but they have some that seem to be used only on extraordinary occasions; either when they exhibit themselves as strangers, in visits of ceremony, or when they go to war. Amongst the first may be considered the skins of animals, such as wolves or bears, tied on in the usual manner, but ornamented at the edges with broad borders of fur, or of the woollen stuff manufactured by them, ingeniously wrought with various figures. . . .

"The face, at the same time, is variously painted, having its upper and lower parts of different colours, the strokes appearing like fresh gashes; or it is besmeared with a kind of tallow, mixed with paint, which is afterward formed into a great variety of regular figures, and appears like carved work. Sometimes, again, the hair is separated into small parcels, which are tied at intervals of about two inches, to the end, with thread; and others tie it together, behind, after our manner, and stick branches of the *cupressus thyoides* in it.

"Thus dressed, they have a truly savage and incongruous appearance; but this is much heightened when they assume, what may be called, their monstrous decorations. These consist of an endless variety of carved wooden masks or vizors, applied on the face, or to the upper part of the head, or forehead. Some of these resemble faces, furnished with hair, beards, and eye-brows; others, the heads of birds, particularly of eagles and quebrantahuessos; and many, the heads of land and sea-animals, such as wolves, deer, and porpoises, and others.

"But, in general, these representations much exceed the natural size; and they are painted, and often strewed with pieces of the foliaceous mica, which makes them glitter, and serves to augment their enormous deformity. They even exceed this sometimes, and fix on the same part of the head large pieces of carved work, resembling the prow of a canoe, painted in the same manner, and projecting to a considerable distance. So fond are they of these disguises, that I have seen one of them put his head into a tin kettle he had

got from us, for want of another sort of mask. . . .

"The only dress amongst the people of Nootka, observed by us, that seems peculiarly adapted to war, is a thick leathern mantle doubled, which, from its size, appears to be the skin of an elk or buffalo, tanned. This they fasten on, in the common manner; and it is so contrived, that it may reach up, and cover the breast quite to the throat, falling, at the same

time, almost to the heels. It is, sometimes, ingeniously painted in different compartments; and is not only sufficiently strong to resist arrows; but, as they informed us by signs, even spears cannot pierce it; so that it may be considered as their coat of mail, or most complete defensive armour.

"Though these people cannot be viewed without a kind of horror, when equipped in such extravagant dresses, yet, when divested of them, and beheld in their common habit and actions, they have not the least appearance of ferocity in their countenances; and seem, on the contrary, as observed already, to be of a quiet, phlegmatic, and inactive disposition; destitute, in some measure, of that degree of animation and vivacity that would render

them agreeable as social beings. . . .

"The village at the entrance of the Sound stands on the side of a rising ground, which has a pretty steep ascent from the beach to the verge of the wood, in which space it is situated.

"The houses are disposed in three ranges, or rows, rising gradually behind each other; the largest being that in front. and the others less; besides a few straggling, or single ones, at each end. . . .

"Their furniture consists chiefly of a great number of chests and boxes of all sizes, which are generally piled upon each other, close to the sides or ends of the house; and contain their spare garments, skins, masks, and other things which they set a value upon. Some of these are double, or one covers the other as a lid; others have a lid fastened with thongs; and some of the very large ones have a square hole or scuttle, cut in the upper part; by which the things are put in and taken out. They are often painted black, studded with the teeth of different animals, or carved with a kind of freeze-work, the figures of birds or animals, as decoration. . . . .Their fishing implements, and other things also, lie or hang up in different parts of the house, but without the least order; so that the whole is a complete scene of confusion; and the only places that do not partake of this confusion are the sleeping-benches, that have nothing on them but the mats; which are also cleaner, or of a finer sort, than those they commonly have to sit on in their boats.

"The nastiness and stench of their houses are, however, at least equal to the confusion. For, as they dry their fish indoors, they also gut them there, which, with their bones and fragments thrown down at meals, and the addition of other sorts of filth, lie every where in heaps, and are, I believe, never carried away, till it becomes troublesome, from their size, to walk over them. In a word, their houses are as filthy as hog-sties; every thing in and about them stinking of fish, train-oil, and smoke.

"But amidst all the filth and confusion that are found in the houses, many of them are decorated with images. These are nothing more than the trunks of very large trees, four or five feet high, set up singly, or by pairs, at the upper end of the apartment, with the front carved into a human face; the arms and hands cut out from the sides, and variously painted; so that the whole is a truly monstrous figure. . . . Mr. Webber's view of the inside of a Nootka house, in which these images are represented, will convey a more perfect idea of them than any description. . . . It was natural, from these circumstances, for us to think that they were representatives of their gods, or symbols of some religious or superstitious objects: and yet we had proofs of the little real estimation they were in for with a small quantity of iron or brass, I could have purchased all the gods (if their images were such) in the place. . . .

"The chief employment of the men seems to be that of fishing, and killing land or sea animals, for the sustenance of their families; for we saw few of them doing any thing in the houses; whereas the women were occupied in manufacturing their flaxen or woollen garments, and in preparing the sardines for drying; which they also carry up from the beach in twig-baskets, after the men have brought them in their canoes. . . .

"Their manufactures, and mechanic arts, are far more extensive and ingenious, whether we regard the design, or the execution, than could have been expected from the natural disposition of the people, and the little progress that civilization has made amongst them in other respects. . . .

"To their taste or design in working figures upon their garments, corresponds their fondness for carving, in everything they make of wood. Nothing is without a kind of freeze-work, or the figure of some animal upon it; but the most general representation is that of the human face, which is often cut out upon birds, and the other monstrous figures mentioned before; and even upon their stone and their bone weapons. The general design of all these things is perfectly sufficient to convey a knowledge of the objects they are intended to represent; but the carving is not executed with the nicety that a dexterous artist would bestow even upon an indifferent design. The same, however, cannot be said of many of the human masks and heads; where they shew themselves to be ingenious sculptors. They not only preserve, with great exactness, the general character of their own faces, but finish the more minute parts, with a degree of accuracy in proportion, and neatness in execution. The strong propensity of this people to works of this sort, is remarkable, in a vast variety of particulars. Small whole human figures; representations of birds, fish, and land and sea animals; models of their house-hold utensils and of their canoes, were found amongst them in great abundance.

"The imitative arts being nearly allied, no wonder that, to their skill in working figures in their garments, and carving them in wood, they should add that of drawing them in colours. We have sometimes seen the whole process of their whale-fishery painted on the caps they wear. This, though rudely executed, serves, at least, to shew, that though there be no apearance of the knowledge of letters amongst them, they have some notion of a method of commemorating and representing actions, in a lasting way, independently of what may be recorded in their songs and traditions.

"Their language is, by no means, harsh or disagreeable, farther than proceeds from their using the k and h with more force, or pronouncing them with less softness than we do; and, upon the whole, it abounds rather with what we may call labial and dental, than with guttural sounds. The simple sounds which we have not heard them use, and which, consequently, may be reckoned rare, or wanting in their language, are those represented by the letters b, d, s, g, r, and v. But, on the other hand, they have one, which is very frequent, and not used by us. It is formed, in a particular manner, by clashing the tongue partly against the roof of the mouth, with considerable force; and may be compared to a very coarse or harsh method of lisping. It is difficult to represent this sound by any composition of our letters, unless, somehow, from iszthl." Tlingit pronunciation gives trouble even today. Many spellings have been used to convey the explosive force of KLING'-KET as the word *Tlingit* is pronounced.

"Were I to affix a name to the people of Nootka, as a distinct nation, I would call them *Wakashians;* from the word wakash, which was very frequently in their mouths. It seems to express applause, approbation, and friendship. For when they appeared to be satisfied, or well pleased with any thing they saw, or any incident that happened, they would, with one voice, call out *wakash! wakash!* I shall take my leave of them, with remarking, that, differing so essentially as they certainly do, in their persons, their customs, and language, from the inhabitants of the islands in the Pacific Ocean, we cannot suppose their respective progenitors to

have been united in the same tribe, or to have had any intimate connection, when they emigrated from their original settlements, into the place where we now find their descendants."

Cook left Nootka early in the spring in order to make full use of the navigable summer months for exploring the northern latitudes. He passed along the Queen Charlotte Islands and the scattered islands of the Alexander Archipelago to confront "the summit of an elevated mountain" which he concluded was Bering's Mount St. Elias, and so entered the landmark on his own charts.

Above the 60th parallel he found anchorage in protected waters of a great bay to which he gave the name of Prince William's Sound. Here, with the southernmost Eskimos of the north, Cook's men traded briefly, exchanging beads and pieces of iron with the natives for their cloaks made of the beautiful pelts of the sea otter.

On past Kenai and the Alaskan Peninsula, Cook probed a passage through the Aleutian chain to enter the Bering Sea. On to the north, he confirmed the discovery of Bering that a strait separated the continents of America and Asia. But, although he proceeded north by northeast around the contour of North America to a point past Icy Cape, almost to Barrow, Cook found no passageway through the great continent.

By the end of August, as the ships threaded their way through mountains of floating ice, Cook turned his expedition southward, paused briefly at Unalaska to hold the fateful meeting with the Russian promyshlennik, Gerasim Izmailov, and spread his sail to winter in the warmth and friendliness of the Sandwich Islands.

Cook, himself, never returned to England. He was killed by natives in the Hawaiian Islands that he had earlier discovered, en route northward and to which his expedition returned after proceeding north from Nootka Sound to explore the coast and confirm the Arctic Ocean discoveries of Vitus Bering. Of his death on the Hawaiian shore, observed in disbelief by members of his crew, Captain James King, who completed Cook's journal wrote:

"Thus fell our great and excellent Commander! After a life of so much distinction and successful enterprize, his death, as far as regards himself, cannot be reckoned premature; since he lived to finish the great work for which he seems to have been designed; and was rather removed from the enjoyment, than cut off from the acquisition, of glory. How sincerely his loss was felt and lamented, by those who had so long found their general security in his skill and conduct, and every consolation, under their hardships, in his tenderness and humanity, it is neither necessary nor possible for me to describe; much less shall I attempt to paint the horror with which we were struck, and the universal dejection and dismay which followed so dreadful and unexpected calamity."

But Captain Cook's story does not end with his death. His discoveries in the South Pacific led to the English-speaking occupation of Australia and New Zealand. More important to contemporary Americans, they set in motion events that led to ratification by Congress one hundred-eighty years later of Alaska and Hawaii, both discoveries of Cook's on his third voyage, as the forty-ninth and fiftieth states of the United States of America.

Cook himself realized the importance of these discoveries, recognizing the commercial value of the American northern coast and the tremendous strategic importance of the Hawaiian Islands. These, he noted "are extremely well situated for the ships sailing from New Spain to the Philippine Islands to touch and refresh at, being about midway between Acapulco and the Ladrone Islands."

His contemporaries grasped much more quickly the commercial potential of the Northwest Coast. Cook did not live to see the fur fever that seized his own crewmen in December of 1779 when they touched at Macao on the expedition's return home from the Arctic, along the east coast of Sibera to China. Captain King was dispatched from Macao to conduct negotiations for provisions with the Chinese merchants at Canton. King wrote, "As Canton was likely to be the most advantageous market for furs, I was desired by Captain Gore to carry with me about twenty sea otter skins." King met with a member of the Hong, a society of the principal Canton merchants, with whom he bargained the better part of the day. The merchant offered three-hundred dollars. "As I knew, from the price our skins had sold for in Kamtschatka, that he had not offered me one half their value," said King, "I therefore demanded one thousand." Finally, the merchant "proposed as his ultimatum, that we should divide the difference, which, being tired of the contest, I consented to, and received the eight hundred dollars."

Eight hundred dollars for twenty sea otter skins! Forty dollars per skin! King was impressed. He finished negotiations in Canton and made the return trip down channel to Macao, the only China port open at that time to foreign vessels. What he found added fuel to the fire:

"During our absence, a brisk trade had been carrying on with the Chinese, for the sea otter skins, which had, every day, been rising in their value. One of our seamen sold his stock, alone, for eight hundred dollars; and a few prime skins, which were clean, and had been well preserved, were sold for one hundred and twenty each. The whole amount of the value, in specie and goods, that was got for the furs, in both ships, I am confident, did not fall short of two thousand pounds sterling."

However astonished King may have been, Cook far earlier had seen the importance in the trade of the pelt of the sea otter. A year and a half before, while his ships lay at Nootka, Cook with characteristic thoroughness had examined the sea otter which "abounds here as it is fully described in different books taken from the accounts of the Russian adventurers in their expedition Eastward from Kamchatka.

"We, for some time, entertained doubts, whether the many skins which the natives brought, really belonged to this animal; as our only reason for being of that opinion, was founded on the size, colour, and fineness of the fur; till a short while before our departure, when a whole one, that had been just killed, was purchased from some strangers who came to barter; and of this Mr. Webber made a drawing. It was rather young, weighing only twenty-five pounds; of a shining or glossy black colour; but many of the hairs being tipt with white, gave it a greyish cast at first sight. The face, throat, and breast were of a yellowish white, or very light brown colour, which, in many of the skins, extended the whole length of the

belly. It had six cutting teeth in each jaw; two of those of the lower jaw being very minute, and placed without, at the base of the two middle ones.

"In these circumstances, it seems to disagree with those found by the Russians; and also in not having the outer toes of the hind feet skirted with a membrane. There seemed also a greater variety in the colour of the skins, than is mentioned by the describers of the Russian sea-otters. These changes of colour certainly take place at the different gradations of life. . . . The fur of these animals, as mentioned in the Russian accounts, is certainly softer and finer than that of any others we know of; and, therefore, the discovery of this part of the continent of North

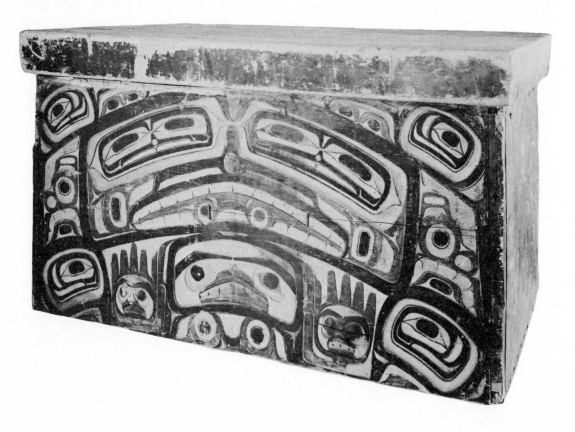

America, where so valuable an article of commerce may be met with, cannot be a matter of indifference."

To Captain King, who had just had the experience of selling his twenty skins for a sum of eight hundred Chinese dollars, or, when converted into the equivalent amount in English money, two thousand pounds sterling, the matter was far from one of indifference: "The rage with which our seamen were possessed to return to Cook's River, and, by another cargo of skins, to make their fortunes, at one time, was not far short of mutiny; and I must own, I could not help indulging myself in a project."

Visions of a thriving fur trade flashed into King's mind and as he wrote the ending to the journal of Cook's third voyage he could not forego outlining it:

"I proposed then, that the Company's China ships should carry an additional complement of men each, making in all one hundred. Two vessels, one of two hundred and the other of one hundred and fifty tons, might, I was told, with proper notice, be readily purchased at Canton; and, as victualling is not dearer there than in Europe, I calculate, that they might be completely fitted out for sea, with a year's pay and provision, for six thousand pounds, including the purchase. The expense of the necessary articles for barter is scarcely worth mentioning. I would, by all means, recommend that each ship should have five tons of unwrought iron, a forge, and an expert smith, with a journeyman and apprentice, who might be ready to forge such tools, as it should appear the Indians were most desirous of. For though six of the finest

skins purchased by us, were got for a dozen large green glass beads, yet it is well known, that the fancy of these people for articles of ornament, is exceedingly capricious; and that iron is the only sure commodity for their market. To this might be added a few gross of large-pointed case-knives, some bales of coarse woollen cloth (linen they would not accept of from us), and a barrel or two of copper and glass trinkets. . . .

"The vessels being now ready for sea . . . will shape their course for the Shumagins, and from thence to Cook's River, purchasing, as they proceed, as many skins as they are able, without losing too much time, since they ought to steer again to the Southward, and trace the coast with great accuracy from the latitude of 56° to 50°. . . . Having spent three months on the coast of America, they will set out on their return to China early in the month of October . . ."

That King's plan was put into operation, backed by private investors if not official English policy, provides one of the colorful episodes in the history of maritime trade. Of intensive duration for the next twenty-five years, ships from England, Spain, France and the United States followed the general outline of his instructions and set their courses for this far west coast that until so recently had been the Northern Mystery.

The story of this convergence is the story of the Tlingit and their coastal neigh-

"Icey Cape, Lat 70 29′ N., Long 197 20′ E . . . On the ice lay a prodigious number of Sea horses . . . They lay in herds of many hundreds upon the ice, huddling one over the other like swine, and roar or bray very loud, so that in the night or foggy weather they gave us notice of the ice long before we could see it. We never found the whole herd asleep, some were always upon the watch, these, on the approach of the boat, would wake those next to them and then the others, so that the whole herd would be awake presently. But they were seldom in a hurry to get away till after they had been once fired at, then they would tumble one over the other into the sea in the utmost confusion, and if we did not at the first discharge kill those we fired at outright we generally lost them tho' mortally wounded. They did not appear to us to be that dangerous animal some Authors have described, not even when attacked, they are rather more so to appearance than reality; Vast numbers of them would follow and come close up to the boats, but the flash of a Musket in the pan, or even pointing one at them would send them down in an instant. The female will defend the young one to the very last and at the expence of her life whether in the Water or on the ice; nor will the young quit the dam though she be dead so that if you kill one you are sure of the other. The Dam when in the Water holds the young one between her fore fins." Captain James Cook —Voyage to the Pacific Ocean, *1778*

"The Sea Otter—Altogether in life it is a beautiful and pleasing animal, cunning and amusing in its habits, and at the same time ingratiating and amorous. . . . They prefer to lie together in families, the male with its mate, the half-grown young and the very young sucklings. The male caresses the female by stroking her, using the fore feet as hands. . . . Their love for their young is so intense that for them they expose themselves to the most manifest danger of death. When their young are taken away from them, they cry bitterly like a small child. . . . In flight they take the suckling young in the mouth, but the grown-up ones they drive before them. If they have the luck to escape they begin, as soon as they are in the water, to mock their pursuers in such a manner that one cannot look on without particular pleasure. . . . If a sea otter is overtaken and nowhere sees any escape it blows and hisses like an angry cat. When struck it prepares itself for death by turning on the side, draws up the hind feet, and covers the eyes with the fore feet." From Georg Steller's Journal. *John Webber's illustration from the* Atlas of Captain Cook.

bors who, within the decade of their discovery by Cook, became an important part of a new global trade, a trade of paramount importance to the newly sovereign United States.

From the moment in March 1778, when three canoes "came off to the ship" and a person in one of them "stood up and made a long harangue," the Tlingit and their tribal brethren down the coast to Nootka ceased to be what they had been before. So fast, indeed, came the change that their vanished customs and beliefs have become the province of anthropologists, who themselves look back to such accounts as Captain Cook's and those of the adventurous traders who early followed him, to find out what these Indians were like at the time of their contact with the white man.

Chapter III

THE MERCHANT NAVIGATORS AND THE FUR FEVER

The England to which Captain Cook's ships returned in 1780 was embroiled on all sides in war. With the intervention of France, the American colonists had nearly won their freedom. Led by France the allied Bourbon powers of the continent were inflicting naval and commercial defeat on the mistress of the seas. In 1783 a beaten England signed treaties of peace with the newly born American republic that beneath its surface disorganization was inherently strong, and with an exultant France that concealed in her show of strength the seeds of approaching revolution.

Captain Cook's *A Voyage to the Pacific Ocean,* published that same year, brought to the western powers detailed knowledge of the far side of the new world. Cook's meticulous explorations, astute observations, and lucid account of his findings opened the waters of the northern Pacific to commerce. The sea otter provided the object on which to base the new trade.

England was in no shape to act officially on Captain James King's urgent recommendations for the immediate establishment of a fur trading factory. William Bolts, Esq., made an unfulfilled effort in 1781 to mount a maritime fur trading venture but his enterprise never got out to sea.

Then in April of 1785 a small brig of sixty tons, manned by a crew of twenty under command of Captain James Hanna, slipped out of a harbor, called the Typa, near Macao in China. By August it reached its destination of Nootka Sound, the King George's Sound of Captain Cook's discovery, and in trade with Captain Cook's same Indian friends procured the valuable pelts of five hundred-sixty sea otters. By February of the next year Captain Hanna was back in China where he sold the lot for $20,600.

Commercial temperatures soared and the fur fever was on. That same year, 1786, no less than five fur-seeking ventures were on the coast, three fitted out

Captain John Meares

by British merchants in England and the Orient, more or less in accordance with the specifications outlined by King in his concluding passages of Cook's journal. For the safety of the endeavor, King said, two ships should accompany each other. They should be properly provisioned and supplied with articles for barter.

These perilous ventures became known as merchant-navigator expeditions, as they called for the exploration of a treacherous coast in order to trade with its almost equally unknown people.

A group of English merchants who called themselves the King George's Sound Company, financed the most ambitious of the expeditions of this early date, dispatching it with a degree of ceremony that raised the enterprise to an almost official status. Commander of the expedition was Captain Nathanial Portlock, of the *King George*. Captain George Dixon commanded the *Queen Charlotte*. These two captains added greatly to scientific knowledge of the day, further delineated the coastal cartography of Cook, and affixed to the region's bays, sounds, straits, and islands, the names of important English personages. Prompt publication of Portlock's and Dixon's journals gave the world its first news of Alaska's Tlingit Indians and their coastal brethren since Cook's visit a decade earlier.

In the spring of the same year, 1786, one more English expedition sailed to America from Bengal, under command of Captain John Meares, an irrepressible opportunist whose audacity, unreliability and powers of eloquent expression altered the course of history. Lieutenant John Meares was mustered out of England's

Royal Navy in 1783 after the Treaty of Versailles brought peace back to Europe. As master of a merchant ship, he made his way to India where he helped organize "a set of Gentlemen, who stiled themselves the Bengal Fur Society and sailed from thence in March, 1786," wrote George Dixon, who not only described the scientific aspect of his discoveries, but also supplied eager English readers with their first account of the burgeoning maritime fur trade.

Captain Meares sailed out of Bengal, followed a few days later by the expedition's second ship under Captain Tipping, from Calcutta. Meares ship, *Nootka,* and Tipping's *Sea Otter*—in case there should be doubt of the expedition's objective—set sail via the northern route. Meares followed the Aleutian chain to Unalaska where despite continual fog, unruly currents and unmapped rocky shores, he found safe anchorage. With mixed feelings he learned that the entire region was claimed by Russia and was in the

hands of the promyshlenniki, the tough breed of Russian fur hunters who were reaping the rewards of Bering's discovery.

"The Russians of these isles," wrote Meares, "came from Ochotsk and Kamchatka in galleots of about fifty tons burthen, having from sixty to eighty men in each. They heave their vessels up in some convenient place, during their station here, which is for eight years; at the end of which time they are relieved by another party. They hunt the sea otters and other animals whom nature has cloathed in furs. The natives of the different districts are also employed in the same occupation, and are obliged to give the fruits of their toil, as a tribute to the Empress of Russia, to whom the trade exclusively belongs."

Meares turned the *Nootka* due east toward the mainland where he hoped to find trading grounds unclaimed by the Russians. Fog and storms kept him company on his run down the coast so that mid-September passed before he reached Prince William's Sound for an unkept rendezvous with Captain Tipping, who had vanished without trace.

Now Meares was faced with a crisis. He had overstayed the season for safe passage back to India. Yet if he directed his course to the Sandwich Islands, as the Hawaiian Islands were still called, he feared his men would jump ship, never to return to America's inhospitable coast. He elected to stay over, dropped anchor in Snug Cove, unrigged the ship, brewed spruce beer to ward off scurvy, and hoped for an early spring.

By January scurvy made its appearance. "Too often did I find myself called to assist in performing the dreadful office of dragging the dead bodies across the ice, to a shallow sepulchre which our own hands had hewn out for them on the shore. The sledge on which we fetched the wood was their hearse, and the chasms in the ice their grave." April passed and more men died, but with the return of warmer weather in May, the natives reappeared and brought them fresh fish and fowl daily.

On the 19th a boat, conducted by canoes, arrived in which was Captain George Dixon of the *Queen Charlotte*. A miracle, truly—from the opposite ends of the world, ships converged on the northern waters of the new continent to meet in this isolated spot. Dixon was welcomed, said Meares, "as a guardian angel with tears of joy."

Dixon and Portlock supplied Meares with sugar, flour, molasses and men to help fix up his ship, demanding in return that he quit the coast. Having stayed over at such great cost, Meares was furious, but in his weakened state had no alternative,

and on reaching China—where he managed to turn in 357 sea otter skins for $14,242—began at once to lay plans for his return to the American coast.

Meares's good Samaritans turned their attention to the object of their voyage. Determined to make the most of the season, they separated. Portlock stayed to the north. Dixon took the coastline down toward Nootka, where the two captains agreed to met for their joint passage back to the "Isle of Owhyee" [Hawaii], then China, and home to England.

Both men recorded in sober prose

what they saw. Portlock remained for some time in the vicinity of Prince William's Sound where he mapped and charted the tricky shores. In his trade dealings with the natives he ably observed their aptitude for the arts, but even so, his trader's mind stuck firmly to business.

"They have tolerable ideas of carving," Portlock wrote of the Sitka Tlingit in the area of Norfolk Sound. "Indeed almost every utensil they make use of has some kind of rude carving, representing one animal or another. . . . But as curiosities were not the articles we were in pursuit of, I gave strict charge to my people not to purchase any thing, being apprehensive that if I allowed a traffic of that nature, the natives would not have been induced to have brought us any skins for sale, as they are very useful, and necessary for their clothing, whilst the others are only the amusements of their leisure hours."

The Indian's fondness for ceremony pressed Portlock's patience. Describing a typical, lengthy prelude to the opening of trading operations, Portlock noted:

"After this long ceremony was over . . . I expected our trade to begin in good earnest; but in this I was again disappointed; for the singing again commenced, and by way of varying our amusement, the chief appeared in different characters during the time his people were singing;

and always changed his dress when he varied his character; in doing of which some of his companions held up a large mat, by way of scene, to prevent us from seeing what was going on behind the curtain. At one time he appeared in the character of a warrior, and seemed to have all the savage ferocity of the Indian conqueror about him. He shewed us the manner in which they attacked their enemies, their method of fighting, and their behaviour to the vanquished enemy. He next assumed the character of a woman, and

to make his imitation more complete, he wore a mask, which represented a woman's face with their usual ornaments; and indeed it so exactly resembled a woman's face, that I am pretty certain it was beyond the reach of Indian art, and must certainly have been left by the Spaniards in their last visit to this part of the coast."

In this guess, Portlock underestimated the talents of the coastal Indians among whom other female impersonation masks have been found and preserved. But he is not wrong as to their quality, which in subtlety of carving and color are ranked high in Tlingit artistic accomplishment.

Dixon displayed the spirit of a true adventurer. In the introduction to his *Voyage* he acknowledged that the "attention of every trader for skins on the American coast has been fixed on Cook's River, Nootka, and Prince William's Sound"; but, he insisted, "the Reader will find, on pursuing this Voyage, that a greater quantity of furs may reasonably be expected in many parts of the coast, than at the harbours just mentioned, and will not, I hope, accuse me of vanity in asserting, that a more spirited undertaking was never set on foot by individuals on true commercial principles."

Port Mulgrave [Yakutat] was Dixon's introduction to the Indians of the Pacific Northwest Coast. To the north of Yakutat live the Chugach, the most southerly of the Eskimo, affected in many of their customs, art, and habits of dress by trade with their southern neighbors. Along the islands of the Aleutian archipelago to the west lived the sea-faring Aleuts, already by Dixon's time enslaved by the advancing Russians.

*"Their hook is a large simple piece of wood, the shank at least half an inch in diameter; that part which turns up, and which forms an acute angle, is considerably smaller, and brought gradually to a point: a flat piece of wood, about six inches long, and near two inches wide, is neatly lashed to the shank, on the back of which is rudely carved the representation of an human face." Captain George Dixon—*A Voyage Around the World, *1789*

The region occupied by the Indians of the Pacific Northwest Coast, is—in contrast to these northern and westerly expanses—a small compact coastal strip stretching from Yakutat Bay at approximately 60 degrees North latitude to a southern boundary mid-way across present Washington State. Within these limits of approximately twelve hundred miles

are found seven linguistic groupings sometimes referred to for convenience as "nations."

The Tlingit of Alaska are the most northerly of these "nations," inhabiting the coastal region from Yakutat Bay southward, along the mainland and Alexander Archipelago to a latitude across Prince of Wales Island at approximately 55 degrees.

Next come the Haida, occupying the southern half of the Prince of Wales Islands within present-day Alaska, and the Queen Charlotte Islands, an off-coastal island group, stretching from approximately 56 degrees to 52 degrees North latitude, which are today part of Canada.

Opposite the Haida on the mainland are the Tsimshian, commanding the mouth of the important Skeena River which legend declares is the route taken by these peoples in their migration to the coast. This area, like the Queen Charlotte Islands, is part of the Canadian province of British Columbia.

Next to the south, between North latitude 52 degrees and 51 degrees, part on the mainland and sharing the northern end of Vancouver Island, are the Kwakiutl, also Canadian. The Bella Coola form a smaller geographic unit within Kwakiutl territory.

The Salish are the most southerly of the Indian groups from a point short of 51 degrees North latitude to the Olympic Peninsula in the State of Washington, approximately 48 degrees North latitude. Some authorities place the Salish as far south as the Columbia River in present day Oregon. If they did not live that far south, there is evidence that the Salish traded with the Chinook of the region.

There remains one more linguistic division, since neither the term "tribe" nor "nation" accurately describes the nature of these geographic groupings. These are the Nootka who occupy the west coast of Vancouver Island and the tip of the Olympic Peninsula. These are the Indians of Nootka Sound whose way of life so fascinated Captain Cook, and whose safe harbor became the rendezvous point for the early fur traders.

All of these divisions together form the Pacific Northwest Coast Indians. Similarities far outweigh differences in the many characteristics that are unique to their culture. They themselves raided, fought, traded and borrowed from each other in a constant flux that helped to diffuse both the expressions of their artistic impulse and the underlying ceremonial and social patterns that gave rise to them.

On his coastal adventure southward along the the bays and inlets of America's western shore, Dixon was one of the first to observe the distinguishing features that set "tribes" or "nations" apart from one another. "Indeed it was pretty evident at first sight," he wrote of the Indians at Port Mulgrave, "that these people were a different nation, from the construction of their canoes, which were altogether of wood, neatly finished, and in shape not very much unlike our whale boats.

"The number of inhabitants contained in the whole sound, as near as I could calculate, amounted to about seventy, including woman and children; they in general are about the middle size, their limbs straight and well shaped, but like the rest

of the inhabitants we have seen on the coast, are particularly fond of painting their faces with a variety of colours, so that it is no easy matter to discover their real complexion; however, we prevailed on one woman, by persuasion, and a trifling present, to wash her face and hands, and the alteration it made in her appearance absolutely surprised us; her countenance had all the cheerful glow of an English milk-maid. . . .

"However, their symmetry of features is entirely destroyed," Dixon continued, "by a custom extremely singular and that we had never met with before. An aperature is made in the thick part of the under lip, and increased by degrees in a line parallel with the mouth, and equally long: in this aperature, a piece of wood is constantly wore, and in eliptical form, about half an inch thick. . . . This curious piece of wood is wore only by the woman, and seems to be conferred as a mark of distinction, it not being wore by all indiscriminately, but only those who appear in a superior station to the rest."

This unappetizing adornment was worn by the women of rank among the Tlingit, Haida, and Tsimshian, and no trader who encountered the ugly and distorting object failed to enter his outraged protest against it. In shape the labret was an elliptical plug of wood or bone, of a size that increased as its wearer grew older, grooved around the edge like a pulley wheel so that it fit securely in the slit cut in the wearer's under lip. The custom lost favor as contact between Indian and white increased, but even after Alaska's purchase by the United States, old women could still be seen wearing the labret.

Having exhausted the Indians' supply of furs at Port Mulgrave, Dixon's voyage continued to "light and variable winds" southward, arriving in the month of June at Norfolk Sound (now Sitka). There, said Dixon, "we purchased about 200 excellent sea otter skins." The depletion of fur signalled the Captain to hoist anchor

and continue his run down the coast. July found his vessel off the northern shores of the Queen Charlotte Islands, so named by Dixon, and the scene of his most remarkable trading adventure. In a protected bay on tiny North Island, wrote Dixon:

"A scene now commenced, which absolutely beggars all description, and with which we were so overjoyed, that we could scarcely believe the evidence of our senses. There were ten canoes about the ship, which contained, as nearly as I could estimate, 120 people; many of these brought most beautiful beaver [sea otter] cloaks; others excellent skins, and in short, none came empty handed, and the rapidity with which they sold them, was a circumstance additionally pleasing; they fairly quarrelled with each other about which should sell his cloak first; and some actually threw their furs on board, if nobody was at hand to receive them; but we took particular care to let none go from the vessel unpaid. Toes [pieces of iron, drawn to a cutting edge] were almost the only article we bartered with on this occasion, and indeed they were taken so very eagerly, that there was not the least occasion to offer any thing else. In less than half

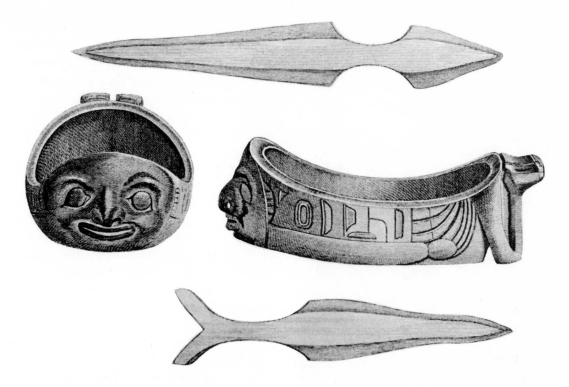

an hour we purchased near 300 beaver skins, of an excellent quality; a circumstance which greatly raised our spirits, and the more, as both the plenty of fine furs, and the avidity of the natives in parting with them, were convincing proofs, that no traffic whatever had recently been carried on near this place, and consequently we might expect a continuation of this plentiful commerce. That thou mayest form some idea of the cloaks we purchased here, I shall just observe, that they generally contain three good sea otter skins, one of which is cut in two pieces, afterwards they are neatly sewed together, so as to form a square, and are loosely tied about the shoulders with small leather strings fastened on each side."

The experience convinced Dixon he

had discovered the ideal technique for trade. "Thou mayest see that by the whole tenor of my last, that our coasting along these islands was the best and most expeditious method of trading we could possibly have hit on."

The voyage continued along the shores of the Queen Charlotte Islands in the strait that bears Dixon's name, pausing at likely bays and inlets to trade with the villagers who paddled out in their canoes. When "we had entirely stripped our numerous traders of every saleable article, on which they left us and paddled for the shore. . . . The number of sea otter skins purchased by us at the Queen Charlotte Islands," he wrote, "was no less than 1,821, many of them very fine."

The Indians are very fond of masks

or visors, and various kinds of caps," Dixon noted "all of which are painted with different devices, such as birds, beasts, fishes, and sometimes representations of the human face; they have likewise many of these devices carved in wood, and some of them far from being ill-executed. These curiosities seem to be greatly valued, and are carefully packed in neat square boxes, that they may the more conveniently be carried about.

"Whenever any large party came to trade, these treasures were first produced, and the principal persons dressed out in all their finery before the singing commenced. In addition to this, the Chief, who always conducts the vocal concert, puts on a large coat, made of the elk skin, tanned, round the lower part of which is one, or sometimes two rows of dried berries, or the beaks of birds, which make a rattling noise whenever he moves. In his hand he has a rattle . . . which is shook by the Chief with great glee, and in his opinion makes no small addition to the concert."

By August, just off the entrance to Nootka Sound strange sails appeared. "Our great joy to learn they were from London," said Dixon, "and fitted out by our own Owners." The ships were the *Prince of Wales* under Captain James Colnett, and *Princess Royal*, under Captain James Duncan. On board the *Prince of Wales* was one of the Etches brothers whose London firm had financed the ventures. The delighted travelers exchanged greetings and Dixon imparted to his colleagues news of his trading successes in the Queen Charlottes.

"At nine o'clock in the morning of the 9th, we parted company with our new brothers in trade, saluting them with three hearty cheers, and wishing them success at least equal to our own." Dixon set his course for the Hawaiian Islands where he met up with Portlock. They sold their joint cargoes of 2,552 sea otter skins for $54,-857 in China and sailed back to England.

While the English dominated the early years of the fur trade, other nations and particularly France, were keenly interested. On the eve of the French Revolution, France sent her noted navigator, Jean François de Galaup de La Pérouse on a round-the-world scientific exploring expedition, and instructed him to look into the fur trade. In June of 1786 La Pérouse sighted land just below Mount St. Elias where he entered the waters of Lituya Bay, a small inlet between Yakutat and Sitka, to gather wood, obtain water, and make needed ship repairs. La Pérouse named his landfall Port des Français.

"On the day of our arrival," La Pérouse wrote, "we were visited by the chief of the principal village. Before he came on board he seemed to address a prayer to the sun; he afterwards made us a long speech, which was terminated by some very agreeable songs."

La Pérouse did not pass a kindly judgment on the Tlingit, this most northerly of the coastal Indians. He was a navigator, not a sociologist and he looked at the Tlingit from a point of view that was typically French.

"I will however admit, if it be desired," he declared, "that it is impossible for a society to exist without some virtues; but I am obliged to confess, that I had not the penetration to perceive them; quarrelling continually among themselves, indifferent to their children, and absolute tyrants over their women, whom they incessantly condemn to the most painful labours; I have observed nothing among these people which will permit me to soften the colouring of this picture."

La Pérouse's own misfortune may have colored his views. He had sent two long boats to explore the mouth of the bay. Angry waves dashed them to pieces, killing twenty-one of his men. The accident cast a melancholy pall over his stay, but by prolonging it, enabled him to "procure infinitely more knowledge of the manners and customs of the Indians," which despite his obvious bias, shows that he

observed them closely. His description of them is as vivid as it is disapproving.

"I gave the name of village to three or four wooden sheds, of twenty-five feet in length, and fifteen in breadth, covered only to windward with the usual planks, or bark of trees; in the middle was a fire, over which were hung some flat fish and salmon drying in the smoke. . . .

"I think I may venture to assert, that this port is inhabited only in the favourable season, and that the Indians never pass a winter in it; I did not see a single cabin sheltered from the rain; and although there had never been collected together so many as three hundred Indians in the bay, we were visited by seven or eight hundred others.

"The canoes were continually entering and going out of the bay, and each of them brought and carried away their house and furniture, which consisted of a great many small boxes, in which were enclosed their most valuable effects: these boxes are placed at the entrance of their cabins, which possess a nastiness and stench, to which the den of no known animal in the world can properly be compared. They never remove themselves more

than two steps for the performance of any necessary occasion, in which they seek neither for shade nor privacy, as if they had not an instant to lose; and when this happens during a meal, they take their place again, from which they never were at a greater distance than five or six feet."

As Dixon had been, so was La Pérouse repelled by the labret.

"The young girls have only a needle in the lower lip, and the married women alone have the right of the bowl. We sometimes prevailed on them to pull off this ornament, to which they with difficulty agreed; they then testified the same embarrassment, and made the same gestures as a woman in Europe who discovers her bosom. The lower lip then fell upon the chin, and this second picture was not more enchanting than the first.

"These women, the most disgusting of any on the earth, covered with stinking skins, which are frequently untanned, failed not, however, to excite desires in some persons, in fact of no small consequence; they at first started many difficulties, giving assurances by their gestures that they ran the risk of their lives; but being overcome by presents, they had no objection to the sun being a witness, and absolutely refused to retire into the wood."

Outraged as were his deepest sensibilities, even this harshest of critics gave credit where credit was due. Their arts, he said, were more advanced than their morals.

"The Americans of Port des Français know how to forge iron, to fashion copper, to spin the hair of different animals, and, by the help of a needle, to fabricate with this yarn a tissue equal to our tapestry; they intermix in this tissue narrow strips of otter's skin, which gives their cloaks the semblance of the finest silk shag. In no part of the world can hats and baskets of reeds be plaited with more skill; they figure upon them very agreeable designs; they also engrave very tolerably figures of men and animals in wood and stone; they inlay boxes with mother of pearl, the form of which is very elegant; they make ornaments of serpentine, to which they give the polish of marble."

At the end of three months among the Tlingit, La Pérouse continued his circumnavigation of the globe. His ships arrived at Macao in January 1787, where he disposed of six-hundred sea otter skins for $10,000. Leaving the China coast his ships touched at New Holland in the South

"He was dressed in a much more superb style than any chief we had hitherto seen on this coast, and he supported a degree of state consequence . . . His external robe was a very fine large garment, that reached from his neck down to his heels, made of wool from the mountain sheep, neatly variegated with several colours, and edged, and otherwise decorated with little tufts, or frogs of woollen yarn, dyed of various colours . . . The whole exhibited a magnificent appearance, and indicated a taste for dress and ornament, that we had not supposed the natives of these regions to possess." Captain George Vancouver— A Voyage of Discovery, *1801*

found on the tiny island of Malicolo in the New Hebrides, far south in Pacific waters.

By destiny of a pleasanter sort, the natives' memory of La Pérouse has also been preserved. Stationed in Alaska around the turn of the century was a United States naval officer, Lieutenant George Thorton Emmons. An idea occurred to him which had occurred to no white man before and few since, and that was to reverse the usual patronizing practice of recording only the white man's impressions of the land's aborigines.

"In 1886, one hundred years after this event," Emmons said, "Cowee, the principal chief of the Auk quan of the Tlingit people, told me the story of the first meeting of his ancestors with the white man in Lituya Bay, where two boats of the strangers were upset and many of them were drowned. This narrative had been handed down by word of mouth for a century."

The loss of the long boats did not surprise the Tlingit: "The legend of Lituya, Emmons said, "tells of a monster of the deep who dwells in the ocean caverns near the entrance. He is known as Kah Lituya, 'the Man of Lituya.' He resents any approach to his domain, and all of those whom he destroys become his slaves, and take the form of bears, and from their watch towers on the lofty mountains of the Mt. Fairweather range they herald the approach of canoes, and with their master they grasp the surface water and shake it as if it were a sheet, causing the tidal waves to rise and engulf the unwary.

"It can be seen how this phenomenon appealed to the Tlingit, as of all deaths

Pacific. Then they were heard of no more.

By a stroke of divine fortune, La Pérouse had sent his journals and charts home overland, through Siberia and Russia, when his ships had stopped en route at Kamchatka. His journal reached France and was finally published in 1797, ten years after the events he recorded had occurred, far too late to affect the swift moving events in far west America, but no less important for the early descriptions of the Tlingit among whom he stayed while on the coast. The mystery of his disappearance ended a quarter of a century later, in 1826, when the wrecks of both the *Astrolabe* and *Boussole* were

The legend of Lituya tells of a monster of the deep who resents any approach to his domain. At the approach of a canoe, he and his slaves "grasp the surface water and shake it as if it were a sheet, causing the tidal waves to rise and engulf the unwary." George T. Emmons, "Meeting between La Pérouse and the Tlingit."

that by drowning was alone dreaded. The end might come in any other way and he met it unflinchingly, with perfect resignation. But his crude belief in a future life of comfort and warmth required that the body be cremated, while, if lost in the water, its spirit must ever remain in subjection to some evil power."

But when the two great ships had first sailed into the bay, Cowee told Emmons, "the people did not know what they were, but believed them to be great black birds with far reaching white wings, and, as their bird creator, Yehlh, often assumed the form of a raven, they thought that in this guise he had returned to earth, so in

their fright they fled to the forest and hid. Finding after a while that no harm came to them, they crept to the shore and, gathering leaves of the skunk cabbage, they rolled them into rude telescopes and looked through them, for to see Yehlh with the naked eye was to be turned to stone.

"As the sails came in and the sailers climbed the rigging and ran out on the yards, in their imagination they saw but the great birds folding their wings and flocks of small black messengers rising from their bodies and flying about. These latter they believed to be crows, and again in fear they sought the shelter of the woods.

"One family of warriors, bolder than the rest, put on their heavy coats of hide, the wooden collar and fighting head-dress, and, armed with the copper knife, spear, and bow, launched a war canoe. But scarcely had they cleared the beach when a cloud of smoke rose from the strange apparition followed by a voice of thunder, which so demoralized them that the canoe was overturned and the occupants scrambled to the shore as best they could.

"Now one nearly blind old warrior gathered the people together, and said that his life was far behind him and for the common good he would see if Yehlh would turn his children to stone, so he told his slaves to prepare his canoe, and, putting on a robe of the sea otter, he embarked and paddled seaward. But as he approached the ships the slaves lost heart and would turn back, and all deserted him save two, who finally placed him alongside. He climbed on board, but being hardly able to distinguish objects, the many black forms moving about still appeared as crows, and the cooked rice that they set before him to eat looked like worms, and he feared to touch it. He exchanged his coat of fur for a tin pan and with presents of food he returned to the shore. When he landed the people crowded about surprised to see him alive, and they touched him and smelled of him to see if it were really he, but they could not be persuaded to eat the strange food that he had brought to them.

"After much thought the old man was convinced that it was not Yehlh that he had gone to and that the black figures

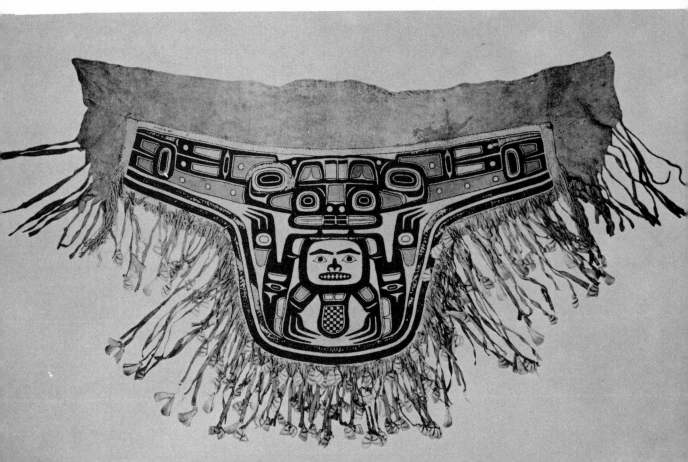

must be people, so the natives, profiting by his experience, visited the ships and exchanged their furs for many strange articles."

The man who so sensitively recorded this fragment from cultural memory became something of a legend himself during his sixty years on the North Pacific Coast. Emmons' participation in the Alaskan adventure belongs to a later period, after engines replaced sails and the Tlingit and Haida had exchanged their ways for the laws of westernized man.

The electronic world of the twentieth century is deeply in debt to the highly literate society of the eighteenth, which craved narratives of scientific exploration and adventure. Cook's *Voyage* set a fashionable journalistic precedent. Dixon's and Portlock's came next, and Europe suddenly found itself enjoying a rich vogue in narratives of adventure. Read for pleasure, they were also literary events and one critic even took Dixon to task for having his journal penned by a ghost, a practice evidently less common then.

Time has not validated this reviewer's complaint. For all who would learn of the early ways of the Pacific Coastal Indians, Dixon's narrative is a basic text, as is that of the Frenchman Etienne Marchand, who visited the North West coast a few years after La Pérouse and whose *Voyage Autour du Monde* was edited by the celebrated French historian Comte Charles Pierre de Claret Fleurieu from journals of Marchand's officers. Fleurieu used Marchand's story to expound his own theories on trade, anthropology, morality and the origin of the American Indian.

The "monstrous decorations" described

by Cook intrigued Marchand also. "Independently of their every day clothing," he said, "the men have another which may be called their holiday suit, or habit of ceremony." He prevailed upon a young native "to display part of his wardrobe which he kept carefully put by in a little box." Everywhere on the costume were grotesque figures—the head-dress carved and painted to represent "men, quadrupeds, and birds. . . . on each thigh, and knee, are placed pieces nearly similar, this difference, that that of the knee presents a grotesque head with a wooden nose, moveable and hooked, three or four inches in length.

"As soon as the actor had finished his toilet, the piece began: it neither was long nor over-charged with incidents; in it, the three unities were perfectly observed; he confined himself to agitating his body in every way, and to endeavouring, by a universal contortion of his limbs, to find motions that might multiply the

shocks of the sonorous gew-gaws with which his dress was loaded, in order to increase and diversify their sounds. At the same time, he made horrible grimaces, which Callot might have employed, with success, in his 'Temptation of St. Anthony': it cannot be said that he was the more ugly on that account; but he produced varieties in his ugliness."

To all who saw them, the Indians' ample-sized, wooden dwellings were works of wonder. The totem pole entrance Marchand described as an "opening made in the thickness of a large trunk of a tree which rises perpendicularly in the middle of one of the fronts of the habitation . . . it imitates the form of a gaping human mouth . . . and it is surmounted by a hooked nose, about two feet in length, proportioned, in point of size, to the monstrous face to which it belongs.

"Over the door, is seen the figure of a man carved, in the attitude of a child in the womb, and remarkable for the extreme smallness of the parts which characterize his sex; and above this figure, rises a gigantic statue of a man erect, which terminates the sculpture and the decoration of the portal; the head of this statue is dressed with a cap in the form of a sugar-loaf, the height of which is almost equal to that of the figure itself. On the parts of the surface which are not occupied by the capital subjects, are interspersed carved figures of frogs or toads, lizards, and other animals, and arms, legs, thighs, and other parts of the human body."

To Fleurieu back in France, the accomplished arts and architecture of these far away Indians raised the whole question of cultural origins. "These works of

sculpture cannot undoubtedly be compared, in any respect to the masterpieces
of which ancient Rome stripped Greece,
but can we avoid being astonished to find
them so numerous on an island which is
not perhaps more than six leagues in cir-
cumference, where population is not extensive, and among a nation of hunters
. . . men who choose not to be astonished
at any thing will say: The beaver also
builds his house: yes, but he does not
adorn it. . . ./ when we reflect on this
assemblage of useful arts and of those
which are merely agreeable, we are forced
to acknowledge that these arts have not
taken birth in the small island where they
are cultivated: they come from a greater
distance."

Perhaps time will prove Fleurieu right
in his assumptions. Theories range from
the one given by him, that the Pacific
Northwest Coast Indians were really Az-
tecs fleeing the Spaniards after Cortez, to
theories of pan-Pacific migrations. These
hold that the settling of the Americas could
have occurred, not only directly along the
land bridge once extant from Asia across
Bering Strait, but also via the ocean in
an extension of the oceanic migrations
that peopled the islands of the South Pacific. Only in this way, the argument runs,
can there be an explanation of the simi-
larity of many cultural and design elements common to the ancient cultures of
South and Middle America and the Pacific Northwest Coast.

Anthropologist Harry L. Shapiro of
the American Museum of Natural History
suggests that the peopling of the Pacific
Rim spread, through many millenniums,
outward from a dynamic center which he

places within the general geography of China. He does not rule out the possibility of extremely early trans-Pacific contacts which could have departed their ancient center to travel the Eastward Equatorial Current toward South America, or northward along the course of the Japanese Current which is held within the arc of the Pacific Rim by the Aleutian Islands to curl and pass southward along the Northwest Coast, past California to meet another current that flows on down the western shores of South America.

The concept, of a mutual southeastern Asian origin, explains more plausibly than other theoretical speculations (despite Captain Cook's question of a common root), the numerous similarities that exist in the language and arts of these widely separated peoples. It explains also the often remarkably oriental appearance of many of the coastal Indians' designs.

Fascinating as these speculations undoubtedly were to Europe's intellectuals of the late eighteenth century, a far more practical crisis had been shaping up along America's western shores. The Spanish claimed sovereignty over the entire Pacific West Coast. Russia occupied its northern portion, and the merchant-navigators were everywhere helping themselves to the sea otter bartered off by the Indians.

Resolution of the issue came with the flamboyant reappearance on the Coast of the audacious English ex-Navy lieutenant, Captain John Meares.

Upon his ignominious return to China from his ice-bound winter at Prince William Sound, Meares wasted no time in organizing a new venture for return to the American coast. Other captains were making fortunes selling furs to the wealthy Chinese mandarins. Within three months, by January of 1788, he managed the financial backing to purchase two ships, the *Felice* and the *Iphigenia,* arrange a partnership with Captain William Douglas and hire fifty Chinese artisans, his idea being to establish a factory at Nootka, build a small coasting vessel, and mark off for himself a permanent portion of the lucrative maritime trade in furs.

It was not in the nature of this unabashed gentleman, who brought England and Spain to the point of war, to sail simply across the Pacific expanse and engage inconspicuously in trade with the natives. On the *Felice*, Meares bore homeward a young Nootkan Indian, the brother of the region's famed chief, Maquinna, who in a not uncommon practice of the day had come away with an earlier trader. Meares saw in his transport home an opportunity to ingratiate himself with the people with whom he hoped to trade.

If Portlock and Dixon wrote sober prose for their readers at home, Captain John Meares supplied his countrymen with drama. One by one he introduced his vividly drawn cast of native characters. Where other traders dealt with natives in the plural, Meares saw them as individuals, each with his own personality and temperament. Through Meares's eyes the Indians among whom he stayed at Nootka become vital personages who step on stage as living men.

On this, his second voyage to the Northwest Coast, Meares anchored in Friendly Cove abreast of the village of Nootka on the 13th of May, 1788.

"Our earliest attention was invited to a multitude of the natives, assembled on the banks in front of the village, in order to take a view of the ship. Comekela, who for several days had been in a state of the most anxious impatience, now enjoyed the inexpressible delight of once more beholding his native land, to which he returned with the conscious pride of knowledge acquired by his voyage, and in the possession of those articles of utility or decoration, which would create the wonder, and increase the respect of his nation. His joy, however, received no inconsiderable interruption from the absence of his brother Maquinna, the chief of King George's Sound [Nootka Sound], and his relation Callicum, who stood next in rank to the sovereign. These chiefs were, at this time, on a visit of ceremony to Wicananish, a powerful prince of a tribe to the Southward. . . .

"At this time Comekela was dressed in

ately poured forth all its inhabitants to welcome him to his native home.

"Comekela had now arrayed himself in all his glory. His scarlet coat was decorated with such quantities of brass buttons and copper additions of one kind or other, as could not fail of procuring him the most profound respect from his countrymen, and render him an object of the first desire among the Nootka damsels. At least half a sheet of copper formed his breastplate; from his ears copper ornaments were suspended, and he contrived to hang from his hair, which was dressed en queue, so many handles of copper saucepans, that his head was kept back by the weight of them, in such a stiff and upright position, as very much to heighten the singularity of his appearance. For various articles of his present pride Comekela had been in a state of continual hostility with the cook, from whom he had contrived to purloin them; but their last and principal struggle was for an enormous spit, which the American had seized as a spear, to swell the circumstance of that magnificense with which he was on the moment of dazzling the eyes of his countrymen;—And situated as we were, this important article of culinary service could not be denied him. In such a state of accoutrement, and feeling as much delight as ever fed the pride of the most splendid thrones of Europe or the East, we set out with him for the shore, when a general shout and cry from the village assured him of the universal joy which was felt on his return.

"The whole body of inhabitants moved towards the beach, and with a most unpleasant howl, welcomed him on shore. At the head of them appeared his aunt, an

Maquinna and Callicum at Nootka
—Meares' Voyage

a scarlet regimental coat, decorated with brass buttons,—a military hat set off with a flaunting cockade, decent linens, and other appendages of European dress, which was far more than sufficient to excite the extreme admiration of his countrymen. . . .

"In a short time the ship was surrounded with a great number of canoes, which were filled with men, women and children; they brought also considerable supplies of fish, and we did not hesitate a moment to purchase an article so very acceptable to people just arrived from a long and toilsome voyage.

"In the evening the weather cleared up, and Comekela prepared to go on shore. The news of his intention was soon communicated to the village, which immedi-

old woman of about eighty years of age, and, from her apearance, might have been supposed to have lived in a continual state of filth and dirtiness from her birth to the moment in which we beheld such a disgusting object. She embraced her nephew with great affection, and shed the scalding rheum of her eyes on the cheek of Comekela.

"After the first ceremonies of welcome were over, and the first gaze of admiration satisfied, the whole company proceeded to the King's house, into which persons of rank were alone permitted to enter, and where a magnificent feast of whale blubber and oil was prepared. . . .

"Nootka is situated on a rising bank, which fronts the sea, and is backed and skirted with woods. In Friendly Cove the houses are large, and in the common fashion of the country. Each of these mansions accommodates several families, and is divided into partitions, in the manner of an English stable, in which all kinds of dirt, mixed with blubber, oil and fish, are discovered by more senses than one, to form a mass of undesirable filthiness.

"On the 14th, the weather was sufficiently fair to admit of our dispatching a party on shore to erect a tent for the wooders and waterers, as well as one for the sail-makers. For this purpose a spot was chosen at a small distance from the village, and contiguous to a rivulet. The rest of the crew were employed in unreefing the running rigging, unbending the

sails, and the other necessary duties of the ship.

"On the 16th, a number of war canoes entered the cove, with Maquinna and Callicum; they moved with great parade round the ship, singing at the same time a song of a pleasing though sonorous melody:—there were twelve of these canoes, each of which contained about eighteen men, the greater part of whom were cloathed in dresses of the most beautiful skins of the sea otter, which covered them from their necks to their ankles. Their hair was powdered with the white down of birds, and their faces bedaubed with red and black ochre, in the form of a shark's jaw, and a kind of spiral line, which rendered their appearance extremely savage. In most of these boats there were eight rowers on a side, and a single man sat in the bow. The chief occupied a place in the middle, and was also distinguished by an high cap, pointed at the crown, and ornamented at top with a small tuft of feathers.

"They paddled round our ship twice in this manner, uniformly rising up when they came to the stern, and calling out the word *wacush, wacush,* or friends. They then brought their canoes along-side, when Maquinna and Callicum came on board. The former appeared to be about thirty years, of a middle size, but extremely well made, and possessing a countenance that was formed to interest all who saw him. The latter seemed to be ten years older, of an athletic make, and a fine open arrangement of features, that united regard and confidence. The inferior people were proper and very personable men. A sealskin filled with oil was immediately handed on board, of which the chiefs took a small quantity, and then ordered it to be returned to the people in the canoes, who soon emptied the vessel of this luxurious liquor.

"A present, consisting of copper, iron, and other gratifying articles, was made to Maquinna and Callicum, who, on receiving it, took off their sea-otter garments, threw them, in the most graceful manner, at our feet, and remained in the unattired garb of nature on the deck."

Meares obtained permission to construct his ship. Maquinna not only gave him a plot of land for these operations, but appointed Callicum as a sort of guardian protector over the enterprise. Very soon the keel was laid and the vessel began to take shape. Meares left a work crew in charge and boarded the *Felice* to explore his surroundings.

"The district next to King George's Sound to the Southward," Meares found, "is that of Wicananish [At Çlayoquat Sound, called Port Cox by Meares]: though he is not considered as equal in rank to Maquinna, yet he is entirely free and independent, and by far the most potent chief of this quarter. In the same district reside the chiefs named Detootche and Hanna [the later had exchanged names with the trader, Captain Hanna], on two small islands, but who are entirely free and independent. These islands are situated a little to the Northward of Port Cox, and contain each of them about fifteen hundred people, and we did not understand that they had any other dependency.

"The general residence of Wicananish is in Port Cox, where he lives in a state of magnificence much superior to any of his neighbours, and both loved and

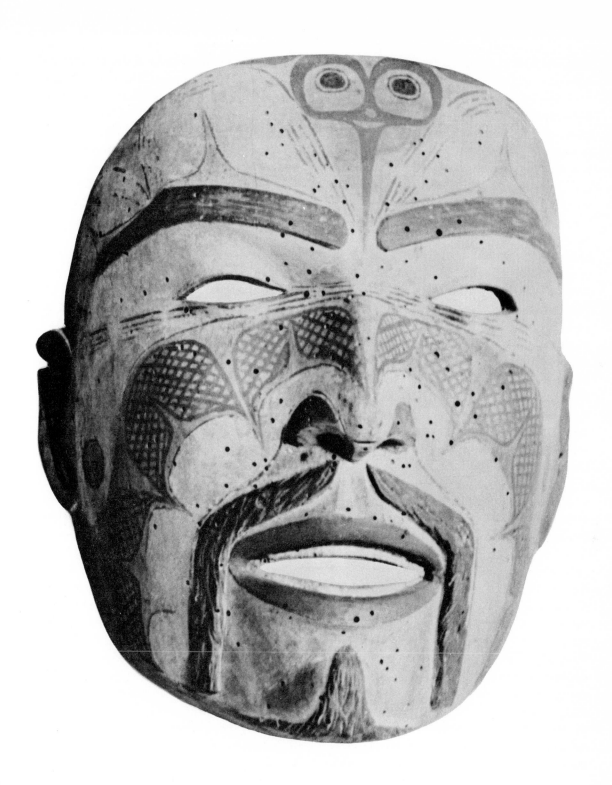

dreaded by the other chiefs. . . . In consequence of a message from the chief to invite us to a feast at his house, we landed about noon, when we were met by a large crowd of women and children, and conducted by the brother of Wicananish to the place of entertainment.

"On entering the house, we were absolutely astonished at the vast area it enclosed. It contained a large square, boarded up close on all sides to the height of twenty feet, with planks of an uncommon breadth and length. Three enormous trees, rudely carved and painted, formed the rafters, which were supported at the ends and in the middle by gigantic images, carved out of huge blocks of timber. [These same interior house posts are today on exhibit at the Field Museum of Natural History.] In the middle of this spacious room were several fires, and beside them large wooden vessels filled with fish soup. Large slices of whale's flesh lay in a state of preparation to be put in similar machines filled with water, into which the women, with a kind of tongs, conveyed hot stones from very fierce fires, in order to make it boil:—heaps of fish were strewed about, and in this central part of the place, which might very properly be called the kitchen, stood large sealskins filled with oil, from whence the guests were served with that delicious beverage. . . .

"The door by which we entered this extraordinary fabric, was the mouth of one of these huge images, which, large as it may be supposed, was not disproportioned to the other features of this monstrous visage. We ascended by a few steps on the outside, and after passing this extra-ordinary kind of portal, descended down the chin into the house, where we found new matter for astonishment in the number of men, women, and children, who composed the family of the chief; which consisted of at least eight hundred persons. . . .

"Before each person was placed a large slice of boiled whale, which, with small wooden dishes, filled with oil and fish soup, and a large muscleshell, by way of spoon, composed the economy of the table. . . .

"Wicananish, with an air of hospitality which would have graced a more cultivated society, met us half way from the entrance, and conducted us to a seat near his own, on which we placed ourselves, and indulged our curiosity during the remainder of the banquet, in viewing the perspective of this singular habitation.

"The feast being ended, we were desired to shew the presents which were intended for the chief:—a great variety of articles, brought for that purpose, were accordingly displayed, among which were several blankets and two copper tea-kettles. The eyes of the whole assembly were rivetted on these unusual objects, and a guardian was immediately assigned to the two tea-kettles, who, on account of their extraordinary value and beauty, was ordered to place them with great care in the royal coffers, which consisted of large chests rudely carved, and fancifully adorned with human teeth.

"About fifty men now advanced in the middle of the area, each of them holding up before us a sea otter of near six feet in length, and the most jetty blackness. As they remained in this posture, the chief made a speech, and giving his hand in token of friendship, informed us that these skins were the return he proposed to make for our present, and accordingly ordered them to be immediately sent to the ship."

Meares took his leave from Wicananish at Clayoquot to continue his trading explorations to the south. As he approached the entrance to the illusive Strait of Juan de Fuca he encountered the surly and hostile Chief Tatooche. He rounded Cape Flattery at the tip of the mountainous peninsula to which he affixed the name Olympic and coasted on toward the vicinity of the Columbia River, which he looked for but did not find.

Meares is not read for his contribution to cartography, much of which he invented or borrowed from the charts of others. He is read because he brings history to life, and more importantly, because his own unquenchable audacity created it.

The diplomatic impasse which he brought on at Nootka cast the entire American west coast in its present mold.

As September came on, Nootka was the scene of enormous activity. Meares returned and Captain Douglas joined him in the *Iphigenia* with a cargo of sea otter pelts gathered along the coast from Prince William Sound. Both the native and white occupants of the region were making final preparations for winter, Meares readying his ships for departure and the Indians moving their households to their winter village up river.

Into the thick of these preparations, a strange sail appeared unexpectedly in the waters of Nootka Sound. Meares sent his long boat, which he said, conveyed into the sound "a sloop, named the *Washington*, from Boston in New England."

Yankee Captain Robert Gray, who commanded the *Lady Washington*, was

the first of a new republic's merchant mariners to arrive on the continent's far northwestern coast. Neither he nor the English captain was aware of the symbolism in Meares's act of conveying Gray's ship into Nootka Sound at the moment of his own departure. Nor was Meares aware that his own ambitious plans would serve mainly to clear the way for Yankee traders, who would transform his dream of a thriving fur trade into a reality.

At the moment, each took the meeting at face value, and Gray watched with interest the launching of Meares's schooner, the *North West America,* then waiting to quit the stocks. Wrote Meares:

"As soon as the tide was its proper height, the English ensign was displayed on shore at the house, and on board the new vessel, which, at the proper moment, was named the *North West America,* as being the first bottom ever built and launched in this part of the globe.

"It was a moment of much expectation. . . . Maquinna, Callicum, and a large body of their people, who had received information of the launch, were come to behold it. . . . Our suspense was not of long duration; on the firing of a gun, the vessel started from the ways like a shot. . . ."

With this business successfully executed, Meares took his cargo of furs and set sail for China, elated at the prospect that lay ahead of a thriving fleet of coasting vessels based at the command point of Nootka. Douglas he left to close up the establishment for the winter and to then proceed with the *North West* to winter in the Hawaiian Islands, from which convenient mid-Pacific shelter he could return early the following spring for a head start on the trading season.

Robert Gray bid farewell to Meares and awaited his senior commander, John Kendrick, who arrived a few days later in the *Columbia Re-diviva,* in time to assist in preparations for Douglas's departure. Gray and Kendrick then settled down to a winter on the Pacific Northwest Coast. While in itself interesting because of the opportunity it offered to participate in a native winter, the presence of Gray and Kendrick on the coast over the winter of 1788–1789 was significant primarily because it gave them front-row seats to the diplomatic drama that opened the following spring.

The first performer to arrive was Captain Douglas, who in March returned from Hawaii. Gray was already trading at Clayoquot. Douglas had dispatched the *North West America* to the north. The *Iphigenia* and the *Columbia* lay at anchor in Nootka Sound.

To the surprise of Douglas and Kendrick, a Spanish ship, *Princesa,* commanded by Don Estevan Jose Martínez, entered the sound on May 6, 1789. The captains of the three ships enjoyed a period of cordial exchanges and reciprocal hospitality. On May 13 Martínez was joined by a second ship, the *San Carlo.* The following day Martínez invited Captain Douglas on board the *Princesa* and arrested him on grounds of "having been found anchored in the port of Nootka without having a passport, permission, or license from His Catholic Majesty for navigating or anchoring in seas or ports belonging to his dominion."

With this astonishing act, committed

in a small sheltered cove on Nootka Sound, began a decisive showdown between England and Spain known as the Nootka Controversy, an intense and acrimonious argument over ownership of a few rudely built structures on a small parcel of land claimed by both nations.

In retrospect, both events and issues appear less complex than they seemed to be at the time when distance and the sense of human and national outrage conspired to bring the two countries close to war. More important than the precipitating human events that set off the crisis, were the factors that led up to it.

Having failed to patrol the long stretch of northern coast over which she claimed sovereignty, Spain at last became alarmed over reports of encroachment. Her concern was particularly directed at the Russians and their advance along the Aleutians toward the Alaskan mainland and she sent Martínez to occupy Nootka as a sentinel to protect Spanish claims north of San Francisco.

Martínez may have exceeded his orders in arresting Douglas. He shortly thereafter released him with instructions to leave the coast. He then seized the *North West America* when the schooner sailed back into the sound, appropriating its 214 sea otter skins in the name of King Carlos III, in whose name also he had taken possession of Nootka.

Two more ships sailed into the tense waters. As fortune would have it, both were the property of Captain John Meares. Back in China Meares had profitably disposed of his cargo of skins just as Captains Colnett and Duncan arrived at the China port, bearing on board Mr. John

Etches. By April a new Captain, Thomas Hudson, was on his way to the coast in the *Princess Royal,* followed in May by Captain Colnett in the *Argonaut,* carrying, as the *Felice* had done, a frame for construction of a new ship. The joint Meares-Etches venture envisioned a thriving monopoly of the sea otter trade.

During the course of the summer at Nootka, Martínez seized both the *Argonaut* and the *Princess Royal,* confiscated their cargoes and made prisoners of their crews. He did not molest the Yankees, but to the contrary, sent his furs and some of the captured English seamen to China with Robert Gray, who exchanged ships with Kendrick, to take command of the *Columbia.* Colnett, Hudson and their ships Martínez sent to San Blas, New Spain's Pacific port. The crew of the schooner *North West America* went to China with Gray. Colnett went temporarily out of his mind. Meares in China learned of the affair from Douglas and from Gray. He went to England, protesting to the House of Commons that Spain had confiscated British property and violated British rights.

The controversy finally brought rivalry between England and Spain to a head. Each claimed the coast by virtue of discovery, a claim in which Spain had, per-

haps, a slight edge. England replied that discovery without occupancy, negated exclusive possession. In the end, growing British might prevailed over Spanish glory past its zenith, and on October 28, 1790, the Nootka Convention was signed by England and Spain, declaring Nootka an open port.

The treaty was a major diplomatic defeat for Spain. Inability to enforce her claim revealed her weakness. Following her withdrawal from Nootka, she made a half-hearted attempt to found a settlement on the Olympic Peninsula, then retired to San Francisco to await the furies of revolution that after 1822 switched California's allegiance to Mexico.

Two years passed before Spanish and English representatives arrived on the coast to execute the Convention and during this time the maritime trade spurted forward. By 1792 it reached a record peak of twenty-eight vessels under the flags of France, Portugal, England and the United States.

In this year the English representative Captain George Vancouver arrived to receive from the Spanish "the buildings and districts [Meares's work sheds] which were occupied by his majesty's subjects in the month of April 1789." Vancouver was charged as well with a second task of an even more formidable nature: to complete the mapping of the Northwest Coast.

Sent by Spain on the diplomatic mission was the admirable Juan Francisco de la Bodega y Quadra, who had already made two voyages of exploration along the coast, one before Cook and one after. Vancouver, himself, had sailed with Cook,

both on that great captain's second voyage to the Pacific and on his third, to the Northwest Coast.

These two seasoned gentlemen hit it off very well personally. Diplomatically, however, they came to loggerheads. Quadra offered to evacuate Nootka, but claimed that the British had not been dispossessed of lands or buildings and there was, therefore, nothing left to restore. The two men's inability to reach agreement sent the matter back to their respective courts where it dragged on two more years before final signatures were affixed.

Meanwhile, all was not work. In addition to numerous exchanges of cordiality, the occasion afforded a splendid glimpse into the ceremonial repertoire of the most powerful chief of the Nootka Indians, to whom the two Captains paid a diplomatic visit.

"We reached Tahsheis about two in the afternoon," wrote Vancouver. "Maquinna received us with great pleasure and approbation, and it was evident that his pride was not a little indulged by our shewing him this attention.

"After dinner, Maquinna entertained us with a representation of their warlike achievements. A dozen men first appeared, armed with muskets, and equipped with all their appendages, who took their post. . . . and were followed by eighteen very stout men, each bearing a spear or lance sixteen or eighteen feet in length. . . . These men made several movements in imitation of attack and defence, singing at the same time several war songs. . . . Their different evolutions being concluded, I was presented with two small sea-otter skins, and the warriors having laid

by their arms, performed a mask dance, which was ridiculously laughable, particularly on the part of Maquinna, who took a considerable share in the representation. We were not backward in contributing to the amusements of day, some songs were sung which the natives seemed much to admire, and being provided with drums and fifes, our sailors concluded the afternoon's diversion with reels and country dances.

"In the evening we took leave of Maquinna, who was scarcely able to express the satisfaction he had experienced in the honor we had done him, saying, that neither Wicananish, nor any other chief, had ever received such a mark of respect and attention from any visitors, and that he would in a few days return us the compliment; on which he was given to understand, he should be entertained in the European fashion."

On this note of keen anticipation, Maquinna, Wicananish and their people pass from stage center into the wings of the region's fast moving history. Further honor and respect from European visitors, Maquinna was not to know.

Awaiting instructions, Vancouver turned his full attention to completing the great work of his life. In three summers on the coast, he minutely mapped and charted the American coastline from California to Cook's Inlet, and on his return home in 1795 presented to the British Admiralty the stunning completion of the cartography begun by Bering and Cook.

Actual transfer of properties occurred the same year. Nootka was abandoned by both sides and no further white settlement ever occurred at this first rendezvous point on the Pacific Northwest Coast. Nootka's glory waned. Trading ships no longer made Nootka a prime port of call. A year later Maquinna took possession, transferring his village to the abandoned Spanish post.

Eclipse of this small port in an Indian wilderness brought to an end the period of international exploration, leaving behind no restraints to govern the actions of ambitious men. Yet even as an era ends, another issues from it. Robert Gray, an ambitious and resourceful Yankee, had arrived on the coast in time to see the curtain ring down on the brief, international North Pacific explosion. As he gathered his furs he watched the Spaniards act out their diplomatic requiem over a fading Pacific empire.

By the time Vancouver had completed his monumental survey of America's west coast, the Yankees had already taken possession and a new era of rampant free trade was in full progress, commensurate in its intensity with the quickened pace of change that back home was to transform an agrarian, colonial fledgling into an industrial giant. Having won by default

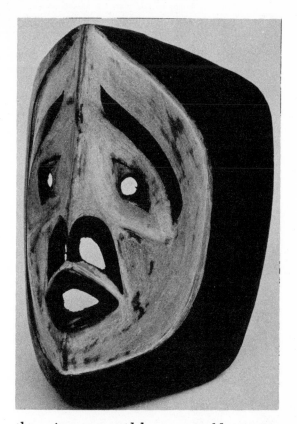

the prize contested by two world powers, the Yankee traders pursuing their commercial destinies around Cape Horn drew in the geographical boundaries of their republic's far western shores.

Chapter IV

CAPTAIN ROBERT GRAY
AND THE YANKEE TRADERS

In the newly independent United States of America the news of a wealth in furs came like the answer to a prayer. On its own at last, the young country found that having cut itself off from England, it had cut itself off from world trade as well. Predictably, England closed her ports to the rebel states' merchants, and the other nations were not tempted by the pioneer country's homespun products. The rich China trade was based on specie, of which the new republic had none.

In the shipbuilding center of Massachusetts, where war had wiped out the sailing fleets of the cod fishermen and the whalers, the yards lay idle for want of orders and capital. Its maritime commerce becalmed, Massachusetts, like the balance of the new nation, was in the grip of economic depression.

Grappling with this problem, six prominent citizens in Boston heeded the exhilarating words of Cook. Their attention was indeed engaged, as Dixon had suggested, at the prospect of "embarking in the new channel of commerce." Awakened to the possibilities of a maritime trade in furs, these enterprising merchants equipped two ships, the *Columbia-Redi-*

viva, for whom they chose John Kendrick as Captain, and a smaller companion vessel, the sloop *Lady Washington,* whose command they entrusted to an ex-naval officer, Robert Gray.

The plan was a long shot, brimming with hazards to match the rewards. The two vessels were to sail around Cape Horn and up the shores of two continents to America's far northwest coast, there to exchange cheap trade goods for the pelts of the sea otter. This coveted fur they would carry westward across the Pacific to China and trade for tea and other commodities in demand back home. The scheme envisioned a three-cornered trade, based not on gold or silver, but upon exchange—an ingenious answer to the struggling economy of a very young republic.

To open this lucrative trade Gray and Kendrick sailed with high hopes out of Boston harbor the last day of September 1787. In the spirit of a public enterprise they carried on board commemorative medals struck off in copper and silver for distribution among the natives. The ship was laden with trade goods calculated to appeal to the taste of the untutored Indians.

The ships touched at Cape Verde in the Atlantic and paused at the Falkland Islands off South America's eastern tip before making the treacherous run around gale-lashed Cape Horn the next April. Storms separated the *Columbia,* under Kendrick's cautious command, from the smaller ship, the *Lady Washington,* in which Gray made full speed northward. He fell in with the coast of New Albion at a point now called Tillamook Bay, carved into the coastline of Oregon, fought off hostile natives and continued northward.

Finally, on a day in mid-September, nearly a year since he had left Boston, Robert Gray entered the waters of Cook's storied Nootka Sound. Instead of the virgin wilderness he had expected, the *Felice* and the *Iphigenia* greeted his eyes and a third ship a-building sat on its ways almost ready for launching. The captain of the *Felice* dispatched his longboat to tow the *Lady Washington* in to anchor. That night the three captains wined and dined on ham and eggs, spiced with romantic inventions supplied by their gracious host, the irrepressible English adventurer, John Meares.

"All the time these Gentlemen were onboard they fully employed themselves fabricating and rehearsing vague and improvable tales relative to the coast of the vast danger attending its navigation of the Monsterous Savage disposition of its inhabitants adding it would be madness in us so weak as we were to stay a winter among them," wrote Gray's young Second Mate, Robert Haswell.

"Captain Meares protested both vessels ever since they had been on the coast had not collected fifty skins; on our smiling (for we had been differently informed) he said it was a fact upon his sacred word and honor, so intent was this Gentleman in deceiving us that he hesitated not to forfit his word and Honour to what we were convinced was a notorious falsity." Haswell's spelling might be curious, but his insight was sound. "The fact was they wished to frighten us off the Coast that they alone might menopolise the trade but the depth of there design could be easily fathemed."

Despite Meares's inventions, Gray and Kendrick, who arrived a week later in the *Columbia*, elected to remain over winter at Nootka Sound. They cheered the

launching of the little schooner, bade Meares God speed on his voyage back to China, and a month later helped tow the *Iphigenia* and *North West America* out of the harbor for their winter run to Hawaii.

"The natives no sooner saw the snow [a two-masted square-rigged vessel] *Iphigenia* clear of the Sound," wrote Haswell, "than they flocked to us in great numbers with fish oil and some venison and a very friendly intercourse soon commenced by which we were plentiously supplied with provisions and some skins. the natives are harmless and inofencive people, and well discribed by the Great Cap. Cook."

In this assumption Haswell was quite wrong, as Gray and the Yankee traders who followed would bitterly learn. But for these nautical pioneers on the far coast, their first winter passed peacefully, with no ugly incident beyond the theft of some small cannon and water casks, to color their impressions of the coastal inhabitants. The crews spent most of the time putting their ships back into condition for the trading season ahead.

"The natives visated us allmost every day with fish deer and oil and a fue skins. our chief amusements were fouling and hunting. in both we had tolerable sucess. the weather was generally rainey and very disagreeable. . . .

"Our constant converce with the Natives," wrote Haswell, "enabled us to gain a considerable knoledge of their Language Manours and customs [Which nowhere have been described in such utilitarian English as used by Captain Gray's youthful second mate]. The natives of the sound are below the middle size. they indid are prity Large about the sholders and those

parts of there body they keep in exercize are well proportioned thier principle employment being paddling their arms and bodies become more muscular while thier Legs are crooked and ill shaped indeed they not only in their canoes but in the Houses set on their hams that when they walk they never straten their knee but from constant habit keep it on a bend walking parot towed. . . ."

"Their weepens are bows arrows Separs Dagers and stone axes they now use firearms but their usual method of fighting is with the speer they generly surprise their enamey in the night and do the chief of the buseness before the rest awake with their stone axes these are of diferent forms some of them are made with a long wooden handle and at the top representing a mans head with hare on it and the stone placed in its mouth to represent an enormious tongue others are mearly a wedge with a handle cut round on the stone about 9 inches from the edge and above the handle is a human face with distorted features and are realy curious. their are but fue of the native that are good bowmen nor do they throw a speer

with dexterity it is a custom to adorn ther weepons with the teeth of their vanquished enemies."

The abundance of wild life impressed the Yankees even though their own city life in Boston was not yet so very far removed from the frontier wilderness.

"Here are Bears Wolves Moose fallow and rain deer Foxes racoons squrrels minks Land and sea otters Dogs Beavers Martins wild Cats and Mice," Haswell wrote.

"In the woods we find several sorts of woodpeckers, Robbins the Vergina red bird snow birds, yellow birds, long tailed thrush ground birds, tomtits, sparrows wrens, parterages, Quales, hawks, owls, Eagles of several sorts Ravens, Crows, swallous, Doves and pidgeons of water fowl are Geese, Ducks, Brants two sorts of shags several sorts of Shrill drake, two sorts of teel, large Loons several sorts of divers and Gulls, Murs, Marsh larks, kingfishers, and swans.

"Fish their air plenty of whales, but fue spermasity maney right Whales and an abundants of humpbacks, Porpoises Salmon of various spesies Breem flounders Cod and halibut Sculpins Frost fish Their are fish resembling the West india Red and white snapers black fish dog fish Herrins Serdenas and Seals The shell fish are oisters Scollops Clams Limpts coules mussles pearl sea egs and starfish."

From this rich roster of land and marine life, it is not difficult to see how the Pacific Northwest Coast Indians sustained both their physical and spiritual existence. From the land and the sea, although their food came primarily from the sea, the Indian drew on nature's abundance. From it also they created a vigorous mythology in which the birds and beasts slipped in and out of daily life in roles that were part human and part divine.

Of the coastal Indians the only whale hunters were the Nootka. Among the experiences of Gray's small crew on the *Lady Washington* was the excitement of

joining a whale hunt early the next year at Clayoquot, the village of Wicananish.

"About Noon," wrote Haswell, "I was surprized at hearing a very suden and Loud shout and seeing almost every Boddy running from the village to their canoes I was soon eased from my suspence by my Friend Hannah who told me Wickananish had struck a Whale and that the Villagers were going to his asistance I was curious to see them kill this large fish with such simple impliments and went in a canoe accompaneyed by Mr. Treet to be spectators

"On our arrival at the place of action I found the Whale with sixteen Bladders fastened to him with harpoons the whale was laying at this time unmolested waiting the return of the Chief who was in pursute of another but immediately on his return he gave the order for the atack his mandate was answered by a low but universal acclamation the next brother to the Chief Tatoochcosettle invited me into his canoe this I rediely complied with we were paddled up to the fish with great speed and he gave him a deadly pearce and the enormious creature instantly expired they fastened a number of Bois on the Fish and took it in tow to the Village

"I had many invitations to visate and partake with them but with this I did not comply on my Return on board I made particular inquieries relative to their custom in whaling. they told me the first Whale that was killed in a season it was their custom to make a sacrefise of one of their slaves the corps they lay besid a large piece of the Whales head adorned with eagle feathers after it has lay'd their a sertain time they put it in a Box as usual.

"They say it is particularly pleasing to their Deaty to adorn a Whale with Eagle fethers for they suppose thunder is caused in conflicts between that Bird and fish that an Egle of enormious size takes the Whale high in the air and when it falls causes the noice Thunder."

From Clayoquot Gray headed north to test the trading grounds of that scarcely explored stretch of coast. His small sloop, measuring only ninety feet, slipped in and out of the rocky coves and narrow passageways that more ample vessels could not negotiate. Yet even Gray's expert seamanship could not outwit the hidden dangers of navigation across the surface waters of a submerged mountain chain. Near Bucareli Bay the *Lady Washington* lodged on a submerged ledge. Careful maneuvering and cool heads extricated the ship from her predicament and she turned south toward the Queen Charlotte Islands. Here, by sheer chance, because the coasting trade was still in its infancy, Gray's small craft found Dixon's Cloak Bay, a village on Parry Passage which separates tiny North Island from Graham Island of the Queen Charlotte group.

"At 6 PM a vast number of Natives men Women and Children came off and brought with them several sea otter skins we understood of them that their was a large tribe not far off the weather was very thick hazey and we were but little distance from the land We soon saw their village from which they launched twenty or thurty very large canoes and came off in great perade padleing off swiftly and singing a very agreable air.

"of those people were purchaced to the amount of two hundred skins in a very

fue moments for one chizle each we bought all the skins they appeared to have by 10 in the evening when they returned to their Village for the night no doubt intending to bring off more in the morning but we did not stop but stood on to the southward the natives called their villag Custa it is situated in a sandy bay on the NW end of the Island their Chiefs name is Cuneah and appears to be a very good old Fellow his wife was off and had vast authority over every person alongside I was greved to leve them so soon, as it appered to me the best place for skins that we had seen."

Advertised first by Dixon and then by Gray, Cloak Bay—or Kioosta, as the deserted site is called today—became a favorite stop for the early traders, and its chief, Cunneah, despite various spellings, a familiar name in the coastal trade's growing native cast. Within a few days the skins that Haswell lamented leaving behind were collected by Captain Douglas who steered his *Iphigenia* north, instead of proceeding directly to China as Martínez had ordered him at Nootka.

Captain Kendrick was still at Nootka watching the Spanish Don Martínez tighten the tensions that crushed Meares's dreams of a commercial empire when Gray sailed back into the harbor with skins collected from the Straits of Juan de Fuca to Southern Alaska. Into Gray's capable hands passed the confiscated English furs and captured seamen, Kendrick's first mate, Joseph Ingraham, and the *Columbia*, which he received from Kendrick for the *Lady Washington*. By this switch Gray achieved the glory of being the first United States national to carry the Stars and Stripes around the world.

Gray set sail the end of July 1789, arrived at Canton in early December, exchanged his furs for tea, and eight months later, on a sunny afternoon in August, the town of Boston heard the boom of a thirteen-gun salute, heralding his return from a 41,000-mile circumnavigation of the globe. The citizens of Boston hurried to the wharf to watch as Gray, his crew and a dazzling young native from Owyhee, as Hawaii was then called, dressed in a flaming feather cloak of scarlet and gold, strode toward the mansion of the state's Governor John Hancock. Far more than a navigational feat, Gray's voyage had opened the China trade to the youthful United States.

Within five weeks the *Columbia* was on her way back to the Northwest Coast, again under the able Captain Robert Gray, who on this voyage would crown his commercial achievement with the discovery of the great river of the west, the Columbia, which he named after his ship.

Even prior to Cook its presence had been suspected. In 1775 Bruno Heceta was sent in the *Santiago* to explore the Spanish coast to latitude 65 degrees. He had noted a bay with strong currents and eddies at 46 degrees 9 minutes indicating a great river or strait. Later Meares had been deceived by the breakers extending across the mouth of the river and had named the bay Deception. "We can now with safety assert, that no such river as that of Saint Rock exists, as laid down in the Spanish chart," he declared. Vancouver, too, had passed it by, doubting the possibility of its existence.

Then on May 11th, 1792, as the *Columbia* bore due south, hugging the coast from Grays Harbor, his crew heard the thunderous roar of tide smashing

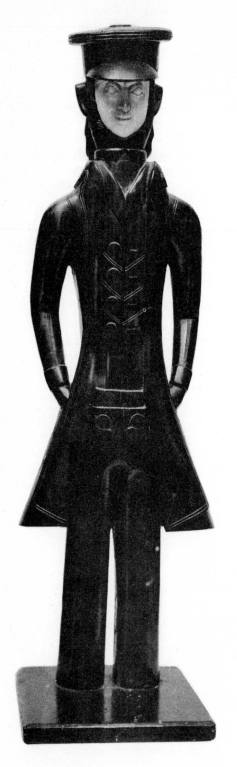

against the sand barrier at the river's entrance. With sails set they rode the crashing billows in over the bar. "At four A.M. saw the entrance of our desired port bearing east-southeast, distance six leagues," wrote Haswell, now Gray's first officer, "At eight A.M. being a little to windward of the entrance of the harbor, bore away, and ran in east southeast between the breakers. . . . When we were over the bar we found this to be a large river of fresh water, up which we steered."

This achievement alone would have elevated Gray to the nation's hall of heroes, for upon his discovery of the Columbia River the United States based its claim to the whole Oregon Territory, bringing the country's western borders to the sea. His maritime exploration led directly to the annexation of Oregon and Washington and, indirectly, to the purchase of Alaska in 1867, culminating finally in admission of all three to statehood. These were the ultimate fruits, but in the early years after the Revolution, when westward expansion over the land had not begun in earnest, the sea lanes of two oceans tied national fortune to the far coast of the Pacific.

The period of the Nor'westers, as these adventurous maritime merchants were called at home, built many private Boston fortunes in the process of bolstering the nation's economic health and establishing the country as a maritime power. The substitution of furs for specie enabled American merchants to compete successfully with other nations in the China trade, and though the risk was great, the profits from a successful venture made it a risk well worth taking.

One of the wealthiest and best known of these merchants, Captain William Sturgis, rose to national prominence as a Nor'west trader. He shipped at the age of seventeen on the *Eliza* and in five years rose to master of his own trading ships and remained in the Nor'west trade after his own sailing days were done. In his close scrutiny of the trade, he said, he had more than once seen a capital of $40,000 yield a return exceeding $150,000. In one instance an outfit not exceeding $50,000 had returned a gross profit of $284,000.

"While most of these who have rushed into this trade without knowledge, experience, or sufficient capital to carry it on, have been subjected to such serious losses, they were compelled to abandon it," Sturgis told an audience on one occasion, "to all who pursued it systematically and perseveringly, for a series of years, it proved highly lucrative."

The thirteen-gun salute fired by the *Columbia* as she arrived in Boston Harbor served as the start. Before the *Columbia* sailed on her second adventure, a youthful third-generation Boston merchant named Thomas Perkins hired away Gray's first mate, Joseph Ingraham, to serve as captain of his own newly acquired brigantine, *Hope*. The *Columbia* sailed soon after. By the year's end the *Hancock* had sailed under Samuel Crowell as master, and the Lamb brothers, Thomas and James, were building the *Margaret* which set sail the following winter under Captain James Magee.

The next year saw seven United States vessels in the North Pacific, all in pursuit of furs. Each year thereafter for the next

quarter century, the small well-built brigs —early forerunners of the famous clipper ships—rounded Cape Horn, the passage deemed by captains of the day as the most dangerous in the world.

Youth was a prime characteristic of these Yankee sailors. As Sturgis had gone to sea at seventeen, so had others. Robert Haswell was only seventeen when he first sailed on the *Columbia,* nineteen when he sailed again as Gray's first mate. Even younger was John Boit, son of a Boston merchant, who shipped as fifth mate on the *Columbia's* second voyage at the age of fifteen.

"Sir, you'll please to let my mamma know that I am well," wrote John Hoskins, clerk of the *Columbia* to its principal owner. "Mr. Boit also requests you'l let his parent know he is in health." Four years later, not yet twenty, Boit commanded his own vessel, an eighty-nine-ton sloop with a crew of twenty-two, ten carriage and eight swivel guns, and a cargo of trade goods for the Indians.

Boston custom house records swelled with listings of ships sent out by the growing mercantile firms who pinned their hopes on the sea otter thousands of miles distant. Within fifteen years of Gray's historic voyage no less than sixty vessels had been dispatched by Boston firms regularly engaged in the trade for the skins.

Young Perkins joined the Lamb brothers to send out the *Hazard* under Swift, master; *Ulysses* under one of the Lambs; *Alert,* Bowles master; *Globe,* Magee master; *Alert,* this time under Ebbetts master; *Caroline,* Captain Sturgis; *Pearl* under Ebbetts; the *Hazard* again, Swift master; and *Pearl* under Captain John Suter.

Equally committed to the new commerce was Dorr and Sons, which over the next dozen years sent the *Dispatch,* Captain Bowers; *Indian Packet,* Rogers master; *Sea Otter,* Captain Ebenezer Dorr, first American vessel to call at the Spanish port at Monterey; the *Jenny,* Bowers master; *Hancock,* Crocker master; *Rover,* Davidson master; *Dispatch,* again Dorr, and again the *Jenny* under Crocker.

In the beginning days of the trade, other port cities had made efforts to reap its rewards, but one by one New York, Philadelphia, even Salem, dropped out, leaving the seafaring men of Boston in full control. English ships fell off also, plagued by almost constant warfare in Europe during the frantic scant three decades during which the fur trade flourished, and the handicap of monopoly control by the South Sea and East India Companies under which only licensed ships could trade with the Orient.

"With the exception of the Russian

establishment on the northern part of the coast," Boston's Captain Sturgis explained in his account of the Northwest fur trade, "the whole trade was in our hands; and so remained until the close of the war with Great Britain, in 1815. . . . So many of the vessels engaged in this trade belonged here, the Indians had the impression that Boston was our whole country. Had any one spoken to them of American ships, or American people, he would not have been understood. We were only known as Boston ships, and Boston people."

As the new maritime fur trade affected the destiny of the United States, so did its impact change the fate of some ten thousand Indians who lived on the narrow band of coast stretched along the Alaskan panhandle to Cape Flattery. Even as they touched the coast, the traders began to alter forever the Indians' way of life.

Until Cook's voyage and the two brief encounters earlier with Spanish ships the world of the white man had not intruded upon them. Farther north the Russians were relentlessly hunting the hapless sea otter in a fashion that brought even more drastic relationships between white and native. But the Russians' grasp had not

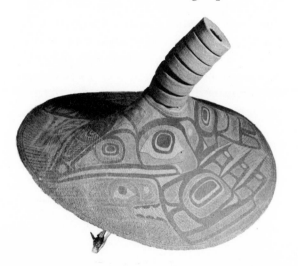

yet extended southward to the chief land-falls of the first English and Yankee traders, whose maritime adventures coincided exactly with the habitat of the seven linguistic groups forming the Pacific Northwest Coast Indians, from the Salish, Nootka and Kwakiutl around the Straits of Juan de Fuca and Vancouver Island, past the Tsimshian and Bella Coola of the mainland, Haida of the Queen Charlotte Islands and southern tip of Prince of Wales Island, and the Tlingit of Alaska from present Ketchikan up to Yakutat.

A glance at the map quickly shows the extent of this watery labyrinth, a reach of approximately eleven hundred miles, dotted with islands, indented by bays and inlets, connected by straits, passages and channels. It explains the inexorability of the fate that brought together seagoing merchants with maritime natives whose whole culture was adapted to this network of inland waterways.

While initially Dixon's iron "toes" and Gray's "chizels" were in eager demand, the Indians quickly began to covet the wondrous variety of civilized goods. A typical cargo, said Sturgis, might include "blankets, coarse cloths, great-coats, firearms and ammunition, rice, molasses, and biscuits, coarse cottons, cutlery, and hardware, a great variety of trinkets; in fact everything that one can imagine."

The canny Indians of the Northwest Coast and the traders from Boston had met their match in each other. The Indians' capricious taste spurred the Yankees to exercise their ingenuity and, when the standard objects of trade palled or ran out, to devise new and inviting ones to part the Indian from his furs.

Five years after Dixon's visit to Cunneah's Harbor at Cloak Bay, Captain Joseph Ingraham dropped the anchor of his little brigantine *Hope*. Two traders had already preceded him, Captain Douglas, Meares's old partner, now in the *Grace*, and Thomas Barnet, Englishman, in the *Gustavus*. Cunneah and his people had had their fill of iron chisels and they refused to trade.

Realizing that he had to capture their fancy with something new and bizarre, Ingraham directed his smith, an important member of a Nor'west trader's crew, to fabricate from the ship's supply of iron rods, a batch of showy, if heavy, iron collars, twisted and shaped to fit the neck and highly polished to catch the eye. His invention took the village by storm. Each collar brought three skins, and with them he cleared the village of its entire supply of three hundred skins. As he turned his ship north toward Alaskan waters, he set his crew to work sewing up garments of bright blue cloth, garnished with shiny buttons. In less than two months on the coast, he had exhausted his supply of trade goods, collected 1,400 sea otter skins and was ready to sail for China.

The *Gustavus* which had preceded Ingraham into Cunneah's Harbor had done as well. The experiences aboard the *Gustavus* are seen through the eyes of John Bartlett, common sailor, who shipped out on her from Canton when the vessel on which he had sailed from Boston was sold out from under its Yankee crew. "I and eight others," Bartlett wrote, "shipped on board the snow *Gustavus* bound for the Northwest Coast of America."

The *Gustavus* left China in November and "after a tedious passage of 70 days attended with gales and dirty weather" made the coast at the harbor of Wicananish. His village, Bartlett said, "contained about 200 houses or log huts of square form built about 20 yards from the water." Wicananish soon paid the *Gustavus* a visit. "He was a tall, raw boned fellow who came attended by thirty or forty canoes with fish and furs to sell."

The *Gustavus* was soon off, laying over just long enough to take on wood and to make repairs. Running along shore up Queen Charlotte Sound, the *Gustavus* paused at villages to trade with natives who paddled out to the ship. "At four o'clock a canoe came alongside with sixteen natives in her of whom we bought forty skins. Five prime skins could be bought here for a sheet of copper; one skin for about two feet of bar iron . . . on the morning of May 8th . . . saw a great number of whales—two or three hundred at a time . . . at 2 P.M. two canoes came off to us and soon there were a hundred canoes alongside. . . . We bought a hundred skins here. . . . We lay offshore all night and the next morning four canoes came off with their chief whose name was Comeeshier [Cumshewa, a powerful Haida chief whose village was mid-way along the East coast of the Queen Charlottes]. Bought seventy skins here bringing the whole number up to 775 now in the hold. The chief and his son remained on board all night. The next morning the tribe came off to the number of 250 men, women and children and we bought 210 skins."

The next stop brought one hundred and fifty skins from the village of "Skoitscut." This is one of the earliest references to Chief Skidgate who with his descendents achieved fame as virtuoso carvers of argillite, a malleable carbonaceous slate-like stone found only in the northern end of the Queen Charlottes, and worked into pipes, plates and model totem poles by the skilled carvers of Skidgate and Masset. "Got under way at 4 P.M. and stood offshore . . . bought one hundred and fifty skins here."

Trading along the coast in this manner the *Gustavus* reached the latitude of Mount St. Elias, which, because of the Russians' activity beyond it, tacitly marked the north extremes of the Yankee trading grounds. Here, noted Bartlett, "the men wore whiskers and the females ornamented themselves with fish bones. . . . On the 10th [June] four canoes came off with seventy natives. These were the stoutest men that we had seen on any part of the coast. They had no women with them and by their actions they seemed to have in mind an attempt on the vessel. At 11 o'clock they went away singing their war song and throwing their arms about them in a very savage manner. Bought nineteen skins of them which brought the total up to 1,218."

By mid-July the *Gustavus* had brought its cargo of sea otter skins up to a carefully counted total of 1,869 and, after laying

over several days to paint the ship and tar the rigging, "we left with pleasure the Northwest Coast of America, bound for the Island of O-why-hee."

By the second year following Gray's pioneer voyage the Pacific Coast Indians were treated to the spectacle of no less than twenty-eight vessels, cruising their inland waters. The flags of England, Spain, Portugal and France were still on the coast at this early period, and the Boston men began to arrive in force. Even in so large an expanse as the twelve-thousand-mile reach of trading waters, twenty-eight-ships all in search of a single prize could not fail but run into each other as each in turn made for the same known villages to trade. The spectacle was not lost on the natives who bargained shrewdly and with intelligent comprehension of the process,

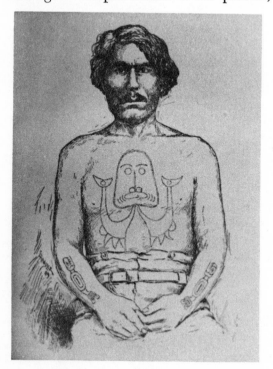

despite the naïveté of their taste.

In his ship's log, Bernard Magee, first mate of the *Jefferson,* wrote that on June 29th their ship, commanded by Captain Josiah Roberts, sailed out of Nootka Sound in company with the *Resolution,* his own schooner, constructed the previous winter in the Marquesas Islands, the *Amelia,* and the *Three Brothers,* and spoke the next day the English schooner *Prince William Henry.* Captain Kendrick, Magee said, they left behind at Friendly Cove, where the Spanish *San Carlos* also lay.

Shaking loose from the rival traders, the *Jefferson* came face to face with the effects of the mounting competition. In Coyah's Harbor at the far southern end of the Queen Charlottes, the natives had many sea otter skins, but would exchange them for nothing but dressed moose skins, called clemmons, which they used as war garments. At Cunneah's Harbor on the north end of the Islands, the Indians again had many skins, but had fixed the rate of barter at a coat and trousers, or an overcoat for a skin. The *Jefferson* obtained only sixty skins, wrote Magee, although they could easily have procured three hundred had they been able to meet the Indians' demand.

Turning north to the waters of Alaska, the *Jefferson* again encountered the *Resolution* and the *Amelia.* Skins were plentiful, said Magee, but again prices were exorbitant. The natives wanted thick copper and tanned moose hides, neither of which Captain Roberts possessed. In a month, he had collected only twenty-one skins, each of which cost a musket and two pounds of powder, or one and a half yards of cloth and two or three iron collars, for which native interest had shown a resurgence and which were being turned out frantically by the ship's armorer from the otherwise unsaleable supply of iron.

Captain Roberts was determined not to give up until every possibility was exhausted. Electing to winter on the coast, he sailed for Barkley Sound, a harbor on Vancouver Island south of Clayoquot. He set his smith to work turning out iron swords for the Indians on the Columbia River from whom moose skins, as well as sea otter, land otter, and beaver could be procured. He found the Columbia River people eager also for dentalium, a long slender shell found in abundance around Vancouver Island, and these he bought locally for exchange farther south. By the end of the winter Roberts had amassed a surprising trade goods supply of two hundred moose skins, one hundred and sixty fathoms of dentalium, sixty sheets of copper, four hundred iron swords, some iron collars, and a few small firearms, with which he set sail around mid-April to the north. Progressing along the eastern shore of the Queen Charlottes, he traded off his entire stock, so that when he reached Cunneah's Harbor where skins were abundant, he had swelled his supply of skins but had nothing left with which to barter.

Undaunted, he ransacked the ship for overlooked possibilities and then proceeded to dismantle the ship itself. Old sails, old clothes, old rope, the crews' trunks, and even the ship's crockery passed over the rail in barter. Bernard Magee, the first mate, recorded these transactions:

"Purchased from them 9 skins being mostly for the middle stay sail made into women's garments—being the last of the

light sails that we could possably spair —Having disposed in the same manner of 3 top-gallant steering sails, one top mast and two lower Ditto. In short every thing that could be spaired on board were purchass'd up by the natives with the greatest Evidity—seems in want of Every thing they got thire Eye on Excepting Iron which was in little or no Demand which we Could no more than purchase fish with & then wos obidged to work it up into different trinkets to thire fancy.

"I have no dount if we had a sufficiency of trade—Cloth thick copper &c— that there might be percured at this place between 1000 & 1500 Skins—of the best quality—as we have already procured upwards of 400 Skins—& that only with the drags—of all our trade—which we had no right to suppose according to the prices given the last season—to Command more then 150 Skins we have disposed of articles in this port this year that would not even Draw there atention the last season —&c at a very advantageous rate—and no End to the quantity of Skins brought on board and alongside Every Day for sale —of which we purchase dayly a few with some article or other."

His trade goods exhausted and his ship stripped nearly bare, Captain Roberts troubles were compounded by the arrival of Captain Hugh Moore's bark, *Phoenix* of Bengal, and two weeks later Captain Adamson's *Jenny* of Bristol, anchored in Cloak Bay. He yielded to the inevitable, hoisted anchor and set his course for China, leaving the coast to his replacements to whom the natives had already transferred their trade. Cleaned, aired and carefully repacked were 13,000 seal skins obtained at St. Ambrose Island at the very start of his voyage and 1,400 sea otters accumulated along America's west coast, from the Columbia River to Norfolk Sound.

Captain Sturgis did almost as well in a single afternoon. As he told the story, he had observed that the Indians were as eager for ermine as were the traders for sea otter. One year on his return from the coast he ordered 5,000 ermine skins from the Leipzig Fair at thirty cents each. The following season he sold the "clicks" to the eager Haida at the rate of three ermine per one sea otter. As sea otter was selling at the time in Canton for $50 each, his yield was $28,000 on an outlay of $840. And he succeeded, he said, in disposing of the balance of the ermine at the same advantageous rate, before other traders copied him and inundated the native market.

Multiply these experiences—of Captain Sturgis, of the *Hope,* the *Jefferson,* the *Gustavus*—by the dozens upon dozens of ships that visited the coast each year but left no record, and the cataclysmic impact of civilization's long reach begins to emerge. Within three brief decades, its intrusion had greatly altered native cultural patterns, and destroyed entirely nature's balance.

For most of the voyages, only sailing dates, ship, master and essential data are listed in custom house archives. The young captains and youthful crews were mostly untutored men who wrote their stories in seamanship rather than literature. Yet, year after year the Yankees visited the coast, anchoring in the protected harbors of the villages, called after the names of their

chiefs—Cunneah, Coyah, Skidgate—trading, competing, cajoling, conniving, in-
timidating and conducting themselves
generally like demons possessed, all for
the sake of the sea otter pelt. The ships
holds were bottomless pits, never filled to
capacity, the demand always exceeding
the supply.

Obligingly the Indians refashioned
their own practices to try to meet the
demand and keep a good thing going, ini-
tiating for the purpose a new and more
efficient technique which nearly exterminated the sea otter. Prior to the traders'
coming, the Indians had hunted the animals for their own use, esteeming the lux-
uriant pelt for its utility as much as for its
beauty. Their need for it was none-the-less
limited and other articles in their system
of values had greater worth. The hunt itself was as important as the prize, and the
hunter was highly regarded for his bravery.

Compared to taking the whale,
Meares wrote, "the taking of the sea otter
is attended with far greater hazard as
well as trouble. For this purpose two very
small canoes are prepared, in each of
which are two expert hunters. The instruments they employ on this occasion are
bows and arrows, and a small harpoon.
. . . notched and barbed and attached to
the shaft by several fathoms of line of sufficient strength to drag the otter to the
boat. Thus equipped, the hunters proceed
among the rocks in search of their prey.

"Sometimes they surprise him sleeping on his back, on the surface of the
water; and, if they can get near the animal without awaking him, which requires
infinite precaution, he is easily harpooned
and dragged to the boat, when a fierce

battle very often ensues between the otter and the hunters, who are frequently wounded by the claws and teeth of the animal.

"The more common mode, however, of taking him is by pursuit, which is sometimes continued for several hours. As he cannot remain under water but for a very short time, the skill in this chase consists in directing the canoes in the same line that the otter takes when under the water, at which time he swims with a degree of celerity that greatly exceeds that of his pursuers. They therefore separate, in order to have the better chance of wounding him with their arrows at the moment he rises; though it often happens that this wary and cunning animal escapes from the danger which surrounds him.

"It has been observed, in the account already given of the otter, that when they are overtaken with their young ones, the parental affection supersedes all sense of danger; and both the male and female defend their offspring with the most furious courage, tearing out the arrows and harpoons fixed in them with their teeth, and oftentimes even attacking the canoes. On these occasions, however, they and their litter never fail of yielding to the power of the hunter.

"The difficulty of taking the otter might indeed occasion some degree of surprise at the number of the skins which the natives appear to have in use, and for the purpose of trade. But the circumstance may be easily accounted for, by the constant exercise of this advantageous occupation; scarce a day passes, but numbers are eagerly employed in the pursuit of it."

Satisfactory as this method had proven for their own personal consumption and the first surprise burst of trading activity in the days of Meares, Portlock and Dixon, it no longer sufficed. The insatiable appetites of the swelling trade fleets demanded ever more pelts and the Indians obligingly stepped up their hunting tactics to provide them.

Instead of paddling out in pairs, the hunters went out in expeditions of twenty, thirty, or more canoes, spreading across the waters in a wide arc to encircle the sea otters in a floating trap. Each time the otter surfaced to breathe, he was met with a volley of arrows. The chase continued until the inevitable arrow pierced a vital spot, the otter was dragged lifeless into a canoe, and the hunting crew swept onward in pursuit of the next victim.

Some idea of the scope and effective-

ness of the mass hunting technique is given in an entry in Magee's log during the peak years of the trade. As the *Jefferson* waited at Cloak Bay, Cunneah, three other important family chiefs and their people paddled in from their winter village on Dall Island with their canoes full of sea otter skins, estimated by Magee to be in the vicinity of eight hundred.

William Tufts, who sailed as supercargo, or owner's business agent, on the *Guatimozin* in 1800, compiled one of the few lists of trading ships engaged regularly in the trade. He gives the following tabulation of sea otter skins shipped from the Northwest Coast to Canton:

1799	11,000
1800	9,500
1801	14,000
1802	14,000

This four-year total of 48,500 skins gives no figures on the number sold on the China market during the preceding fifteen years of frenetic trade, nor the thousands being taken annually by the Russians.

During the first lush days of the fur trade, when the sea otters were plentiful and the traders, mostly young in years, looked at everything in amazement, the Indians greeted the visitors with more cordiality than they were later to show, after increased numbers and debased trading tactics raised both prices and tempers. As the trade wore on, logs, diaries, and the news exchanged on board ship and at Canton became filled with descriptions of native treachery and violence. But in the few accounts that have been preserved, many early entries also described the ways of these unusual Indians.

Cunneah's village at Cloak Bay re-

ceived more than its share of visitors. In quick succession during the summer of 1791 had come Barnet in the *Gustavus*, Douglas in the *Grace*, the *Gustavus* again, and Ingraham in the *Hope*, to name but some. Crew members from each of the ships had the opportunity to investigate the village at close range. Ingraham described two totem poles "40 feet high and curiously carved with representations of men, frogs and birds."

Said John Bartlett of the *Gustavus*, "We went ashore where one of their winter houses stood. The entrance was cut out of a large tree and carved all the way up and down. The door was made like a man's head and the passage into the house was between his teeth and was built before they knew the use of iron." He was so impressed that in his unskilled sailor's hand, he made a drawing of the house and its odd doorway which is believed to be the earliest known representation of a totem pole.

The first description of a potlatch was recorded at Cunneah's village. Magee, in his log for the *Jefferson*, does not call the event a potlatch, but all of the elements of this important custom are present, including the raising of a pole, which was frequently a means of commemorating a special event. The event, in this instance, was the ceremony attendant upon the practice of facial perforation.

In the midst of their furious trading, during which even the Captain's old clothes became currency, wrote Magee, Chief Cunneah asked Captain Roberts to help place a figure "cut and carved with a great deal of art," atop a recently erected totem pole. The next day Cunneah invited the Captain and members of the crew to attend a special celebration.

"The house was thronged with guests and spectators," Magee wrote, "the scene was then opened by the ceremony of introducing the wives of Enow and Cunneah and the candidates for incision or boring, each coming in separately and backwards from behind the scenes—being saluted by a regular vocal music of all present and which had no unpleasant effect. In the same manner the gifts were brought in and displayed to the view of all present and thrown together in a heap being a profuse collection of Clamons, racoons and other cutsarks, comstages both iron and copper and a variety of ornaments. This being done the spectators were dismissed and the guests placed in order round the house. The incision was then performed on the lips and noses of two grown and two small girls, which ended, the distribution was then begun of the above articles, the Captain receiving five otter skins the other articles were distributed among the different chiefs according to their distinction, after which the Captain took his leave and returned onboard."

Next to the totem pole the potlatch is the most widely known cultural invention of the Pacific Northwest Coast Indians. The totem pole was the visual symbol of an Indian chief's identity, rank and accomplishments; the potlatch was the festive social event given to commemorate the milestones of life.

The term potlatch comes from the Chinook jargon introduced by traders along the west coast. Its primary function revolved around the rights, obligations and priveleges of chieftainship. A living chief

The first known drawing of a totem pole—John Bartlett's Journal, *1792*

could introduce to invited guests his heir presumptive. A new chief gave a potlatch to mourn the death of the old and to establish his own claim to the inheritance. A potlatch could also commemorate a fearless deed or the construction by a lesser or greater chief of a new house, the elaborateness of the party usually being commensurate with the status of the chief.

Competitive potlatches, of which much has been written, were confined mostly to the Kwakiutl at Fort Rupert and Tsimshian at Fort Simpson after the mid-1800's. Here the potlatch reached elaborate proportions in the prestige-seeking competition between chiefs to outshine each other by the conspicuous giving of gifts or the public destruction of blankets, coppers, even their canoes. Since white men were by this time on the coast in considerable numbers, they observed these excesses and exaggerated their scope and importance.

A potlatch, none-the-less, whether elaborate or of simpler dimensions, was looked forward to by the Indians—sometimes for years ahead—and very frequently a totem pole, commissioned months, or even years in advance, might be erected as part of the festivities.

Students of Northwest Coast Indian culture have spent many hours debating the antiquity of both pole and potlatch. But until some new find illuminates the past, present inquiry must content itself with the knowledge that when Ingraham, Gray, Bartlett, and others burst in upon their lives, both institutions were in full sway.

Another practice that mystified the early traders was Indian medicine. Robert Gray and his crew members were treated, if that is the word, to a sick-room scene in which they watched the Indian doctor, or shaman, perform his duties.

When Gray came back to the coast on his second visit, he brought on board the *Columbia* framing timbers from Boston to make a small sloop. Construction required a suitable harbor, and since the Spanish had taken over Nootka, Gray selected the district of Wicananish for his enterprise and set up a small shipyard in Clayoquot Sound.

Young Boit, Gray's fifth mate, aged fifteen, wrote in his diary that as the ship "sail'd into which we call'd Adventure Cove and moor'd Ship for winter, vast many of the Natives along side, and appear'd to be highly pleas'd with the idea of our tarrying among them through the Cold Season." During the months to follow, the men from Boston lived in close contact with the Indians and by good fortune, their experiences were recorded by three different members of Gray's crew, John Boit, Robert Haswell and John Hoskins.

"The Natives made us frequent visits," wrote Boit, "and brought a good supply of fish and some Sea Otter Skins, and by keeping a small boat down sound with 4 of our seaman we procured a constant supply of Wild Geese, Ducks and Teal. . . . October 13. The frame of the Sloop was up Complete . . . this is what I call dispatch. Wickananish, high Cheif, came on board, with sevrall of the Royall family. he inform'd that his winter village was a great way off, which occasion'd his visiting us so seldom."

In December, Boit wrote, "Capt. Gray went to an Indian Village for to look at a Chief, said to be very sick. on his arrivall he was rec'd very cordially and conducted to the sick mans house, which was full of people. In one Corner lay the Sick Cheif, Yethlan, youngest brother of Wickananish and arround him eight strong men which kept pressing his stomach with their hands, and making a most hideous Bow-wowing, in the poor fellows ears.

"Upon the Captain's approach, he suppos'd the Cheif to be nearly dead, and order'd this band of Doctors to desist, having made him some gruel to take. The cheif soon came too a little, and order'd two Sea Otter Skins as a present. After giving a Wine toast he order'd him to be left to sleep."

Hoskins' version is more descriptive: "At the earnest solicitation of a number of the Chiefs I on the 22d accompanied Captain Gray to the village of Opitsitah [Clayoquot] to see Yeklan the youngest brother of Wickananish   we were received at the beach by a Chief with about forty young men who conducted us to the house of the sickman chanting an agreeable though solemn air as we went and making our arrival known to every one in the avenue   we were greeted by a number of the populace who had assembled on the occasion   on entering the house we were received by Wickananish who presented us to his father and mother   they received us with the most cordial affection and said or seemed to say save the life of my son and restore him to health who until now we had not seen having been obscur'd by six stout men who are a set of priests and doctors that do every thing by magic   some of these were pressing on his belly and breast other sucking his throat making at times a most hideous noise which is answered by the voices of a great multitude that had thronged the house now and then those men would pretend to scoop something up (as though it was water) with their two hands and then blow it away   thus those men would continue to press and feel about the young man's body till they pretendedly would get hold of the evil spirit that was the cause of all his malady then seize on him as before mentioned and blow him away.

"The sickman was laid on a board covered with mats stripped perfectly naked   he appeared to be much emaciated those men had workt him into a high feaver and he had a pain in his bowels and limbs as we had judged the young man wanted nourishment so it was we had therefore brought him down some fowl soup and our servant made him some panado, boiled some rice etca. etca. we then left him though not until both he and his father made us promise a daily visit we were frequently asked by him his father and several of the other chiefs if we thought he would die   they were answered in the negative provided those men were not allowed to press him any more which was promised should be the case.

"The cause of this young man's illness is an excess of grief at the loss of his only child which died a few months since this he took so much to heart as scarce to be persuaded by his friends to receive sustenance sufficient to keep him alive add to this about three weeks since he visited us at the ship on his return he caught a bad cold and he will ere long in all human probability fall a sacrifice to his immoderate grief   such is the affection of people whom we deem savages to their children."

Whether from soup or the shaman's incantations, the young man improved. "I made the excursion to this same Village not long after," wrote Boit. "found the sick Cheif much better, and releived from his pressing and noisy friends."

By staying over the winter, Gray's people shared with the Indians their social

season. The Pacific Northwest Coast Indians adapted their habits to four divisions in the year, using three seasons in which nature displays her lush abundance for the gathering and preparation of supplies to last over the lean months of winter. With the coming of spring they loaded their possessions into their canoes and left the winter village to take up residence at inherited fishing sites, there to catch the salmon and halibut which they prepared and dried. During the summer they gathered salmon berries, huckleberries and other wild fruits and vegetables, some to be eaten and the rest to be preserved and carried back to the winter village at the summer's end.

During these mid-winter months, the coastal Indians filled the short days and long nights with social conviviality that called into play all their various arts. They told stories, sang and danced, costumed themselves in bizarre and fanciful masks and garments for spectacles designed to portray the various characters from their mythology.

Around the first of January Wicananish invited Gray's men to an entertainment he was giving for all the warriors of his villages. "We had not been there long," wrote Hoskins, "before a number of women came in and ranged themselves on each side of the room three deep and about twenty yards in length   then the chief ordered them to entertain us with a song which was performed by upwards of two hundred men and women   the music was rude but agreeable it being both vocal and instrumental the vocal part being performed by the women and the instrumental by the men   their instru-

ments are various   one was an empty chest slung to a beam very handsomely painted and adorned with eagle feathers   a man with a stick bound round with caeder bark struck on this which served for a drum several others with long poles striking against the boards on the roofs of the house others again with various hollow instruments in shape men, birds or any other figure their fancey suggests   these had a few pebble stones in them which they struck against their hands and had a very good effect."

Toward spring the Yankee visitors were invited to a final round of merriment. "The purport of these harangus were to the following effect," wrote Hoskins, "that whereas the eldest son of Wickananish to whom he had given his name and taken upon himself that of Hiyoua had become old enough to head his whaling canoe (a lad about 12 years old)." To properly celebrate the important event, Wicananish told his visitors, ancient custom required that many days be spent in "mirth and festivity."

"About ten o'clock," Hoskins wrote, "they began their dancing and musick. . . . To describe their various dresses would fill a volume scarce any two being alike the principal part had their bodies painted of a dead red their faces variously some of a shining black others red, others white again other black and white or black red and white variegated according to fancy etca. their heads as various as their faces   in general they were incrustated with grease and paint strewed with down and dressed out with small branches of the cypress and the long feathers of the eagles tails stuck up on top of their heads

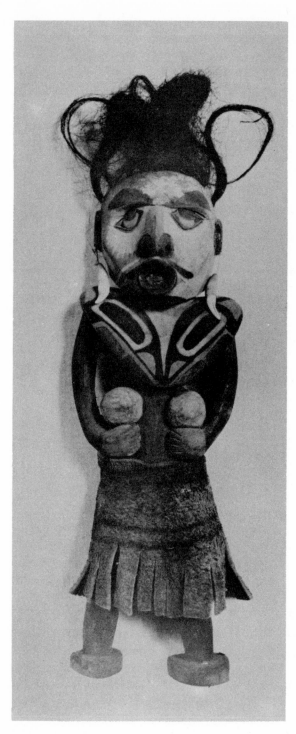

they wore a garment which was tied round their waist and hung as low as their knees a flaxen stuff tied in a bow just below the knees which hung to the ground and another bow of the same sort tied round the thick of the arm. . . . taking the whole together they formed the most savage grotesque appearance I ever beheld."

But deep beneath the show of cordiality, things were not what they seemed. Only a stroke of luck, the over-protestations of innocence on the part of Ottoo, a native boy whom they'd brought with them to the coast from the Sandwich Islands, saved Gray's crew from bloody annihilation.

"This day sevrall cheifs came on board, one of which we found was busily employ'd talking with our Sandwich Island lad," Boit wrote. "Their conversation was soon put a stop too, and the Lad examin'd, but he denyd that the Cheif ask'd him any improper questions. These Natives, always behaving so freindly, occasion'd us to place too much confidence in them, and what a pity it is, that we wou'd not leave this port with that opinion of them which we had held; But alas! We find them to be still a savage tribe, and only waiting an opportunity for to Massacre the whole of us in cold blood."

Ottoo confessed finally that Wicananish wanted him to help "take the Ship and Massacree all the Crew." Much alarmed, Gray's men worked around the clock to ready the vessel, which had been hauled on shore for graving. Wrote Boit, "I beleive never was more work don in so short a time. But *Men determin'd can do most any thing* . . . By midnight one side of the Ship was finish'd, when we heard a most hideous hooping of Indians, and ev'ry shout they seem'd to come nearer, every man immediately took his arms, and stood ready both on board ship and at the Log house, they kept hooping about one hour, when they ceas'd and 'tis probable retreated, lamenting their hard luck that the Cruell plan was so completely frustrated."

Wicananish's motive mystified them all. They were not aware, as others who came later would learn, that humiliation of one's person was the most grievous injury that anyone could inflict upon an Indian of the Pacific Northwest Coast. Even though they themselves did not associate the attack as revenge, the three chroniclers on Gray's ship had put the Yankees' high-handed behavior into the record.

Arriving from Boston the previous June, Gray had anchored at Clayoquot. "Ottoo, our Sandwich island boy," wrote Haswell, "found means to leave the ship and to go among the natives. Captain Gray therefore determined to take the first Chief that came along."

The unfortunate chief was Tootiscoosettle who, as Wicananish's eldest brother, was also a chief of high prestige. Gray enticed him on board and took him prisoner, threatening to carry him to sea unless he delivered the Sandwich Islander. "The chief was much frightened and asked if we meant to kill him, acknowledged he knew where Ottoo was, and immediately dispatched his servant in a canoe to the village; which was soon seen returning, with several others; hollowing as they came, with Ottoo.

"It was now necessary, as an example to deter others, who should be guilty of the like in future, that Ottoo should be punished; this as he was a Sandwich is-

lander Captain Gray willingly would have dispensed with. The Chief was ordered to be present at this punishment; and gave to understand that the man who carried Ottoo away, if he was found, would be punished the same; and if in future, any of the people ran away to his village, and he did not immediately send them back; the first Chief that was caught should also be punished; the Chief was now liberated, when he, and all the others in their canoes, left us; nor did we see any canoes stirring, or any come nigh the ship."

Innocent of the workings of the Indian mind, Gray had thought of the incident involving Ottoo and the chief as being of no consequence and after the summer's trading had returned to stay the winter at Clayoquot. Angered, and, by the seeming treachery of the attack, Gray used his technical superiority to teach the savages a lesson.

"I am sorry to be under the nessescity of remarking," wrote Boit, "that this day I was sent with three boats, all well man'd and arm'd, to destroy the Village of Opitsatah [Clayoquot] it was a Command I was no ways tenancious off, and am greived to think Capt. Gray shou'd let his passions go so far. This Village was about half a mile in Diameter, and Contained upwards off 200 Houses, generally well built for Indians ev'ry door that you enter'd was in resemblance to an human and Beasts head, the passage being through the mouth, besides which there was much more rude carved work about the dwellings some of which was by no means innelegant. This fine Village, the Work of Ages, was in a short time totally destroy'd."

The attack on Gray signalled a changing temper along the coast in which awe gave way to distrust and suspicion. Ingraham reported that at Cumshewa Inlet the threat of attack forced him to answer with "a discharge from his swivel and several muskets." A few years later this same tribe, led by Cumshewa, seized the sloop *Resolution* and "killed in an instant" its eleven man crew.

Except for *A Narrative of the Adventures and Sufferings of John R. Jewitt, only Survivor of the Crew of the Ship Boston During a Captivity of Three Years Among the Savages of Nootka Sound,* a volume avidly read in the States after its publication in 1815, firsthand accounts of these sudden brutal and terrifying attacks do not exist. The stories came through in bits and fragments, passing from ship to ship, until some trader, more literate than the rest, entered the account in his log.

Young John Boit, now in command of his own ship, *Union,* heard in Hawaii of Chief Coyah's massacre of the *Eleanor's* captain and crew. A sailor named Young "inform'd me old Capt. Metcalfe in a brig from the Isle of France had been cut of at Coyar's, in ye Queen Charlotte Isles by ye Natives of that place and ev'ry soul murder'd except one man who got up in ye Main top and was taken alive." The prisoner was rescued by a later trader and taken to Hawaii from where Young got the story that he passed on to Boit. The *Eleanor* was Coyah's second victim in 1794, the earlier ship being an unidentified British vessel.

As trade continued vessels were increasingly set upon, by the Chilkats at the head of Lynn Canal in Alaskan waters, on down the coast to the domain of Maquinna who took the *Boston* and made

Jewitt his captive. Few accounts of the atrocities include mention of the cause. The harsh justice of the traders, who punished petty theft and seeming threat with arrogant acts and the fire of guns, was rarely linked with the retaliation.

"The numerous tragical occurrences on the Coast show the personal hazards incurred by those engaged in the trade," said Boston's dean of the maritime traders, Captain Sturgis. But those who ascribe it to the treachery and ferocity of the Indians, he said, do not know the facts. "I, with better opportunities for investigating and ascertaining the truth, find the cause in the lawless and brutal violence of white men; and it would be easy to show that these fatal disasters might have been averted by a different treatment of the natives, and by prudence and proper precaution on the part of their civilized visitors."

Only one story has come down from the beginning. It has been put together bit by bit from the few surviving logs and journals. The story is that of Coyah's village on Houston Steward Channel at the southern tip of the Queen Charlotte Islands in territory now identified ethnologically as that of the Kunghit Haida Indians of Anthony Island. Coyah is first mentioned in Haswell's log of 1789 as a "chief who bartered for all his subjects." Coyah's village was much visited by the traders who found the yield in furs good, and trade conducted in an agreeable manner.

The first hint of trouble was noted by Gray on his return to the Coast in July of 1791. "When we first cast anchor in the Sound," wrote Hoskins, "we were visited by about twenty natives, men, women, and children in two canoes, most of whom recollected Captain Gray; both men and women came on board the ship without the least reserve.

"On Coyah the chief's being asked for, we were informed by several of the natives . . . that Captain Kendrick was here sometime ago in a vessel with one mast; that he took Coyah, tied a rope around his neck, whipt him, painted his face, cut off his hair, took away from him a great many skins, and then turned him ashore; Coyah was now no longer a Chief, but an 'Ahliko,' or one of the lower class."

By August the *Columbia* caught up with Kendrick back at Clayoquot Sound. Here John Boit filled in details the natives had neglected to mention. "Captain Kendrick inform'd us that he had had a skirmish with the Natives at Barrell's sound [In Queen Charlotte Isles] and was oblig'd to kill upwards of 50 of them before they wou'd desist from the attack. It appear'd to me from what I cou'd collect that the Indians was the aggressors."

Hoskins revealed the provocation. After Kendrick had sent Gray off to China and lasting fame, the previous year, he took the *Lady Washington* up to the Queen Charlottes where he anchored at Coyah's village to trade. "Having been there a short time the natives found means to steal his linnen etc & that had that day been washed," explained Hoskins. "this with some other things they had at times robbed him of induced him to take the two Chiefs Coyah and Schulkinanse he dismounted one of his cannon and put one leg of each into the carriage where the arms of the cannon rest and fastened down the clamps threatening at the same time if they did not restore the stolen goods to kill them nearly all the goods were soon returned. what was not he made them pay for in skins. . . . well knowing if he let those chiefs go they would sell him no more skins he therefore made them fetch him all their skins and paid them the same price he had done for those before purchased when they had no more the two Chiefs were set at liberty."

Kendrick, also, obviously knew nothing of the coastal Indian's code of vengeance, for when he returned the following spring, the friendliness of the natives

deceived him. "The day of the attack there was an extraordinary number of visitors several Chiefs being aboard," wrote Hoskins, "the arm chests were on the quarter deck with the keys in them the chiefs got on these chests and took the keys out when Coyah tauntingly said to Captain Kendrick pointing to his legs at the same time now put me into your gun carriage the vessel was immediately thronged with natives. . . . Captain Kendrick tarried on deck endeavoring to pacify the natives and bring them to some terms at the same time edging toward the companion way to secure his retreat to the cabbin a fellow all the time holding a huge marling spike he had stolen fixed into a stick over his head ready to strike the deadly blow whenever orders should be given the other natives with their daggers grasped and only waiting for the word to be given to begin a most savage massacre.

"Just as Captain Kendrick had reached the companion way Coyah jumpt down and he immediately jumpt on top of him Coyah then made a pass at him with his dagger but it luckily only went through his jacket and scratched his belly. The officers by this time had their arms in readiness . . . the natives on seeing this made a precipitate retreat . . . a constant fire was kept up as long as they could reach the natives with cannon or small arms after which they chased them in their armed boats making the most dreadful havock by killing all they came across."

Having repulsed the attack and left, Kendrick may have thought the incident closed. But in reality it was only just begun. The ensuing eclipse of the Anthony

tions of wealth. This humiliating violation of Koyah's person must have been shattering to his prestige in the tribe. . . . Kendrick had hurt Koyah more than he knew."

A reconstruction of events shows that Coyah's humiliation led him to avenge his injury by his attacks not only on Kendrick but also on the English brig and the *Eleanor*, for the coastal Indians held each white man accountable for the acts of every other. In an effort to restore his damaged prestige Coyah also declared war on his rival, Chief Skidgate. Even Cumshewa's seizure of the *Jefferson* was a bid to enhance his own prestige by emulating the warlike Coyah.

Then, in 1795 the *Union*, under Captain John Boit, anchored at Coyah's village. In the hostilities that followed, wrote Boit, "I killed their first chief, Scorch Eye, in the second mate's arms, while they were struggling together. The rest of the chiefs on board were knocked down and wounded, and we killed from the nettings and in the canoes alongside about 40 more when they retreated, at which time I could have killed 100 more with my grape shot, but I let humanity prevail and ceased firing."

Thus did the series of events that started with Kendrick's pique over his laundry, swell to make Coyah feared as the most savage chief on the coast, culminating finally in his death at the hand of a young master who was ignorant of the attack's provocation. From this moment Coyah's village began a descent into oblivion. No chief of power or prestige emerged to erase the stain from Coyah's title, and gradually his tribe declined so that a Hudson's Bay Company census in

Island Haida has been traced down to present times by two members of a salvage expedition of the Provincial Museum of British Columbia, Wilson Duff and Michael Kew. "What Kendrick regarded as a simple lesson," they wrote, "must to Koyah have been a monstrous and shattering indignity. No Coast Indian could endure even the slightest insult without taking steps immediately to restore his damaged prestige. To be taken captive, even by a white man, was like being made a slave, and that stigma could be removed only by the greatest feats of revenge or distribu-

1841 placed the village population at three hundred. Some years later the Eagle lineage of Chief Ninstints rose to ascendancy over the Raven lineage of Coyah.

Known today as Ninstints, the site is now abandoned, its past eminence marked by a "straggling line of bleached and weathered totem poles on the coast" and the remains of "posts and beams of the old houses lying in moss covered heaps on the ground, half hidden by the invading forest growth."

Other causes contributed to the destruction of the population. Smallpox took a disastrous toll, as it did among all tribes of the Pacific Northwest Coast during the epidemic of 1862, but many of them recovered their vigor. In 1884 an exploration of the village for the Canadian government found only thirty inhabitants, twenty-five carved poles and twenty burial columns. Some time later, their former enemies came down from Skidgate and helped them to pack their small belongings into canoes for a voyage north to Skidgate Mission. The number of persons who can today trace their ancestry to the village on Anthony Island is very few. This is illustrated by the fact that in 1957 the Provincial Museum Salvage Expedition was unable to locate anyone retaining sufficient identity with the village on Anthony Island to claim payment for the totem poles that it removed for preservation.

This today, then, is Ninstints. Duff and Kew wrote in their report, "A few fragments of memory, a few bright glimpses in the writings of the past, some old and weathered totem poles in a storage shed, and the mouldering remnants of once magnificent carved posts and

houses on the site of the old village—these are all that survive of the tribe and village of Chiefs Koyah and Ninstints. What was destroyed here was not just a few hundred individual human lives. Human beings must die anyway. It was something even more complex and even more human—a vigorous and functioning society, the product of just as long an evolution as our own, well suited to its environment and vital enough to participate in human cultural achievements not duplicated anywhere else. What was destroyed was one more bright tile in the complicated and wonderful mosaic of man's achievement on earth. Mankind is the loser. We are the losers."

This eloquent elegy might well be extended to mourn the passing of the entire coastal culture, for although its demise was not so sudden or dramatic, it was certainly as complete. For the Indian of the Pacific Northwest Coast there was no return to a prior state. Western man, in the garb of a merchant sailor from Boston, had tied his destiny to change.

For the Yankee sailing men from Boston the maritime trade off America's west coast ended nearly as abruptly as it had begun. After some years of decline, said Captain Sturgis, "the difficulties and uncertainty in procuring furs became so serious, that in 1829 the business north of California was abandoned." The success of four furious fur trading decades had extinguished the object on which the trade was based, a marine creature whose beauty of coat was its undoing.

Politically, too, the curtain had run down on Yankee free enterprise. While the Nor'west traders rounded Cape Horn each new season to hit the coast and make the fast run to China, another elemental force, in the form of a single, remarkable personality, had dug in at Sitka. From his vantage point in the Alexander Archipelago of Alaska, a short, balding human dynamo named Alexander Baranov had seized the American mainland for Russia. Even as the Yankee traders came and went, the focal point of Alaskan history switched to a sumptuously decorated frame structure that sat on a small rise overlooking Sitka Harbor. Here, from Baranov's Castle, the lord of Alaska ruled over his vast north Pacific empire.

Chapter V

BARANOV-RUSSIAN
RULE IN AMERICA

Few empires have begun less hopefully than the phenomenon known as Russian America. The man whom Gregory Shelikov chose to run his colony at Kodiak stepped ashore in July 1791, from an Aleut styled kayak he had fashioned from skins of the sea lion. He was suffering from pneumonia. The man was Alexander Baranov, an independent merchant whose caravan had been wiped out by wild Chukchee tribesmen in Siberia. Flying the flag of Russia high over his fortress at Sitka, Baranov alone, during his twenty-seven years tenure as manager of the Russian American Company, created the momenttum that kept the Slavs in America for nearly fifty more years after his death. Baranov *was* Russian America.

His task was awesome and the cards were stacked against him. The thriving colony Shelikov had described, consisted of "about 50 Russians . . . five houses after the Russian fashion" containing a court, commissary, store house and counting house, two eighty-ton galliots and a building for hostages. Shelikov himself had left the grumbling colony to petition the Czarina Catherine to grant his Shelikov-Golikov Company a royal fur trading monopoly. Foreign nations, he claimed, were reaping "the great benefits that properly belong to the Russian throne and its subjects."

Instead, Catherine fitted out a major scientific exploring expedition under the English Captain Joseph Billings, to bring back a firsthand report of her operations in the northern sea. At Kodiak, Martin Sauer, secretary to the Expedition, described the empire Baranov was shortly to take charge of:

"This and the nearer islands are inhabited by about 1300 grown males, and

Alexander Baranov

1200 youths, with about the same number of females, according to the register kept by Shelikoff's Establishment, now under the direction of Yefstrat Ivanitsh Delaroff, a Greek; who informed me, that he had now out on the chase, for the benefit of the Company, upwards of 600 double baidars [kayaks] of the natives, containing each two or three men. . . .

"About two hundred of the daughters of the chiefs are kept at the Russian habitations near our anchoring place, as hostages for the obedience of the natives; and, as far as I could learn, they were perfectly well satisfied; and, at the first arrival of the Russians, seemed inclined to oppose their residing on the island; but Shelikoff, surprising their women collecting of berries, carried them prisoners to his habitation, and kept them as hostages for the peaceable behaviour of the men."

With or without state sanction, Baranov began at once to transform Shelikov's dream into fact. While shipwrecked at Unalaska he had put his tireless energy to work learning the language and ways of the Aleuts, who in their tiny skin boats would shortly complete hunting the seas clean of the otter. In spite of the rigors, the raids of rival fur trading companies, the lack of equipment and supplies, and the disease and lonely hardships of win-

ter, the operation never ceased. During the first nine years of the colony's precarious existence, ships of the Shelikov-Golikov Company carried out fur cargoes valued then at a million and a half rubles.

In a single summer Baranov's Aleut fleets made journeys of hundreds of miles, traveling as much as seven miles in an hour. When the fleet was large, a line of five or six hundred kayaks might extend for miles out to sea, dividing as it moved into smaller hunting parties of six or eight boats. Any sea otter lifting his head for air was doomed, for a hunter cast an arrow, shouted and aimed at the spot where the otter dove. The other hunters formed a circle and waited until the otter surfaced. The lethal chase continued until a lucky arrow pierced the valued pelt, which went to the hunter who struck nearest the head.

All Aleut men over eighteen and under fifty years old were subject to call, each working on shares that entitled him to half his catch. In the beginning years as many as one thousand would appear, dressed in water-proof kamlikas, as the shirts made of sea-lion intestines were called, which they lashed tightly around the hatches of their one- and two-man kayaks. In these light, skin-covered canoes, the Aleut fleets paddled thousands of miles scanning the seas for the otter.

They lashed their hunting instruments—bows and arrows, throwing sticks with arrows, and hunting spears—to the bows of the kayaks. The paddles were double bladed and dipped deftly from side to side. Secure inside, the man and his craft became an inseparable, marine unit, ideally matched to his marine prey.

Before leaving Kodiak the fleets drew up along the beach. The hunters were blessed by the priest, who passed through their ranks sprinkling holy water. The Aleuts crossed themselves, took their places in the small boats, lashed themselves in, and pushed out to sea, their departure signalled by the roar of cannon firing a farewell salute.

Awaiting Baranov on the American mainland was a far different native stock, hostile and warlike, whose friendship the Russians during their long rule, could not command and whose will they could not break. Kolosh was the Russian name for all of the Indians of the Pacific Northwest Coast, derived from their word for labret.

Baranov first encountered the Tlingit in 1792, when he crossed with a small group of Aleuts to explore hunting possibilities on Prince William Sound. His party was surprised at night by a band of Yakutat Tlingit on the warpath against the Chugach of the region, and before the savage attack was routed, two Russians and nine Aleuts lay dead.

"The Kolushans wore their armor which consisted of wooden rods bound together with leather thongs," wrote Kyrill Khlebnikov, Baranov's friend and biographer. "Their faces were protected with masks which represented the heads of bears, dogfish and other animals and gave a frightening appearance. On their heads they wore large wooden hats which were fastened to the rest of their armor with thongs. Their weapons consisted of lances, bows, and two pointed daggers. The Russians aimed directly at their heads, but the bullets did not penetrate the thick head covering. The more intense the fire of the Russians became, the more vigorous was the storming of new hordes of attackers."

Although the Russians fought off the Kolosh, who retreated to their canoes, dragging their dead and wounded with them, the attack discouraged ideas of immediate settlement on the mainland.

Yet as his kayak fleets scoured the seas for the sooty head of the otter, Baranov's observant eyes noted the steady intrusion of foreign ships. Particularly disturbing were the Yankees, whose competition among themselves had sent prices sky high among the Kolosh. The Boston men's wealth of trade goods and particu-

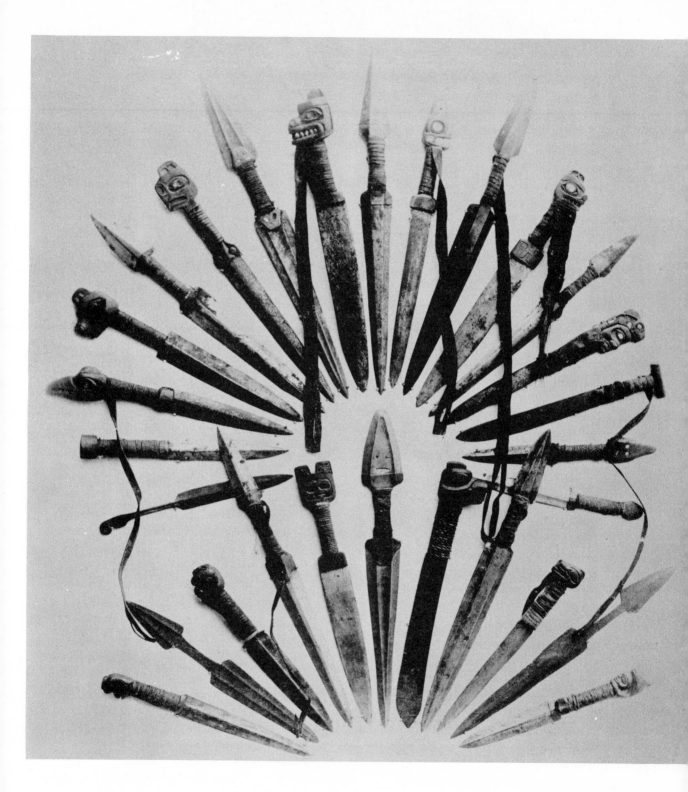

larly guns and ammunition, bought cheaply after the Revolutionary War, posed an urgent problem to Baranov, whose trade resources were poor and whose vulnerability to armed native attack was very great.

From his own explorations and a chance conversation with the Yankee captain of the *Phoenix*, Baranov decided that the most advantageous point from which to dominate the entire north Pacific coast was Norfolk Sound, the present site of Sitka, in the very heartland of the warlike Tlingit. He made his move in the spring of 1799 and with a massive flotilla of over three hundred kayaks under protection of two Russian ships, set his course southward along the treacherous coast. As they rounded Kayak Island, which Steller had observed so minutely before Bering ordered him back to the ship, a giant wave swallowed up thirty of the small boats, each manned by two Aleuts.

"While we were still mourning the loss of our hunters," Baranov wrote the Greek Delarov, "night came on, and as I saw further indications of storm, I ordered all the canoes to make for the shore. . . . when we at last reached the sandy beach, exhausted from continued paddling, we threw ourselves upon the sand over-shadowed by dense forests. No sooner had we closed our eyes, than the dreaded war-cry of the Kolosh brought us again to our feet. . . . The greatest consternation prevailed among the naturally timid Aleuts, who were filled with such dread of the well-known enemy as to think it useless to make any resistance. Many of them rushed into the forest, into the very hands of their assailants. I had only two Russians

with me, and we fired our guns into the darkness. . . . What saved us from total destruction was the intervening darkness which prevented our assailants from distinguishing friends from enemies. After an unequal contest, lasting over an hour, the Kolosh retired to the woods, while I and my assistants endeavored to rally our scattered men. By shouting to them in the Aleutian tongue, we succeeded in gathering the survivors . . . and before morning departed from the inhospitable beach, leaving thirteen canoes, the owners of which had been killed or carried into captivity. . . ."

Baranov pushed forward, traveling now at night. His arrival at Sitka Sound was watched by a large crowd of Kolosh who were gathered around their chief, Skayeutlelt. Baranov bargained for land upon which to build a post, and even before all of the small kayaks had landed, Russians began felling trees for a fort and half the men were employed in building. The other half Baranov sent out to hunt sea otter, which still swam freely in waters around the fort he named Arch-angel Michael.

The Sitka Tlingit, among whom Bar-anov set down the furthermost outpost of the Russian empire, is one of thirteen subdivisions of the Tlingit stock. These sub-divisions, all speaking the Tlingit lan-guage, were called variously quans, kwans or tribes, although their composition was not strictly tribal in nature. To the north, adjoining the Chugach Eskimo territory on Prince William Sound were the Yakutat Tlingit and to the far south, the Tongass. On the Islands of the Alexander Archipel-ago in between were villages of the Chil-kat, Auk, Hoonah, Hootznahoo, Sitka, Kake, Taku, Kuiu, Stikine, Henya and Sanya. They were all Kolosh to the Russians.

Even though they ceded to the Rus-sians a plot of land on which to erect a fort, the Sitka Indians remained aloof, treacherous. Baranov's audacity more than superiority of numbers or arms secured title to the Russian site. To force the re-lease of an interpreter captured by the Kolosh, Baranov led a small group of his men into the very center of their village, which was situated on the highest point of land, overlooking the entire region around it. The Indian warriors, possessed of guns and bullets, outnumbered Bara-nov's men twenty to one. The advancing Russians passed by the painted fronts of the long wooden houses.

"Over three hundred armed men sur-rounded us," Baranov wrote to his agent at Unalaska, "but we marched directly to the house where the prisoner was reported to be. We fired a few blank volleys to keep the crowd in awe, and seized a few men who seemed inclined to offer resistance.

Our determined attitude held the people in check, and when we had accomplished our object and released the prisoner, they began to ridicule the affair, bandying words with our men, and offering them food. I rejoiced in having accomplished my end without bloodshed, and made up my mind not to allow the slightest offence on their part to pass unnoticed in the future.

"Concerning the new settlement at Sitka," Baranov wrote, "I thought there would be no danger with proper protec-

Katlean's helmet

tion from the larger vessels, though the natives there possess large quantities of fire-arms and all kinds of ammunition, re-ceiving new supplies annually from the English and from the republicans of Bos-ton and America, whose object is not per-manent settlement on these shores, but who have been in the habit of making trading trips to these regions."

Before his departure from Sitka the next spring, Yankee traders began to put in to Sitka. Baranov met them all and talked with them on board their trim, well-equipped ships. As he watched the Yankee traders outbid each other to obtain two-thousand sea otter skins, offering cloth worth twenty-eight rubles for a single skin, an idea began to germinate in his mind, a plan of action that revolutionized the coasting trade and made Baranov's name known around the world.

Baranov left a garrison of four hundred and fifty at his Archangel fort. Four hundred were Aleut hunters, twenty were Aleut wives, and thirty were Russians, the most seasoned and trusted of Baranov's men, enjoined to maintain friendly relations with the Yankee traders and strictest vigilance at all times with the natives.

His return to Kodiak was a chronical of cumulative disasters. Within the first day out, two hundred of his returning Aleut hunters died in agony from eating a strange black mussel. The narrow passage of water where the tragedy occurred is still today called Peril Strait and is part

of present Alaska's great marine highway. Arriving at the post at Nucheck, he learned that his ship *Eagle* had gone down, carrying to their deaths eight of his best trained sailors and a cargo in furs worth 22,000 rubles. As he neared Kodiak, bits of wreckage carried eastward by the Japanese Current told of another shipwreck, his beloved *Phoenix,* modeled after the Yankee ship, the first Russian ship built in America, which was due into Kodiak from Kamchatka with desperately needed provisions.

Back at Kodiak he found that a Russian priest, Father Nektar, had been preaching insurrection. Incensed at Baranov's liaison with the Kenaitz Indian girl, Anna, Father Nektar had gone about, drawing pledges from the Aleut elders to withhold hunters from Baranov the next spring.

The lowest ebb came when two silent Aleuts brought into Baranov's presence the still body of his four-year old son, Antipatr. Distraught beyond reason by Father Nektar's incessant reproachments for her sinfulness, Anna, the common-law Kenaitz Indian wife of Baranov, had cast the boy from a rocky shore into the sea. The boy lived, but Baranov's heart was hardened against the monks, who had given him only trouble since their arrival. He gave an order to round them up. He told them to stop interfering in secular affairs. Father Nektar suspended Mass so long as Baranov was present. Baranov put the priests in the stockade. The year 1800 dragged into 1801; Baranov was ill-provisioned and ill-tempered, the future of his colony in doubt.

Resolution of the desperate impasse

was born of luck, audacity, and genius. On May sixth the Yankee ship *Enterprise* sailed into St. Paul Harbor at Kodiak. On board as mate to Captain Ezekial Hubbel was an Irishman from Boston, Joseph O'Cain, whom Baranov had met nine years before when O'Cain had sailed as mate on the *Phoenix*. They remembered each other well.

O'Cain recalled also the poverty of Baranov's operations and knew that Russia's involvement at home with Napoleon's invasion had for three years prevented her sending transports to her needy outpost in America. O'Cain entertained the notion that he could trade his cargo of food and supplies for Russian furs and be off to China a full two months before others arrived to depress prices.

Furs, indeed, Baranov had on hand. In a letter to his friend Larinov at Unalaska, he had written two months earlier, "The All-creator of the world, in his infinite mercy, has overlooked and forgiven our sins, and tempered the cruel blows of misfortune with success in sea-otter hunting. In the three years which have elapsed since the arrival of the last transport, we have collected over 4,000 skins of sea-otters—males, females, and yearlings, besides cubs. The skins secured at Nuchek and Sitka will probably amount to nearly 4,000, with the help of God."

Baranov had no authority to trade Russian furs for Yankee goods, but without food and supplies and goods to pay off his hunters, he feared for the colony's survival. For the Yankee's cargo of molasses, rum, sugar, tobacco, canvas, guns, and other necessities, Baranov bargained only over the type of furs to exchange in

payment. He offered 2,000 prime red and silver fox skins. O'Cain and Hubbel demanded sea otter pelts. According to the legend that surrounds the deal, they drank it out. When Baranov stood up after O'Cain and his captain had passed out, payment was made in fox.

The contract marked a turning point in Baranov's rule,, providing the key to political domination as well as physical survival. No longer was he entirely dependent for provisions upon the infrequent and unpredictable arrival of Company supply ships. The following spring brought additional news to strengthen his position. Through the tireless efforts of Shelikov's widow and his courtier son-in-law, Count Nikolai Rezanov, the long sought monopoly had finally been granted by Czar Alexander, who established the Russian American Company on a twenty-year charter.

Ivan Banner, a former government official, now in the service of the new company, arrived at Kodiak to read the new charter to a crowded bunkhouse and to tell Baranov that he was now a share holder as well as the chief manager. Banner placed around Baranov's neck the gold medal of the Order of St. Vladimir and read the Czar's citation, "For faithful service in hardship and want and for unremitting loyalty."

The honor greatly moved Baranov. "The undeserved favors which our great monarch has thus showered upon me almost overwhelmed me," he said. But in actual fact, Baranov had long exercised the authority that was at last royally conferred.

Between Baranov and his undisputed claim to Alaska lay one more harrowing disaster. In an armed uprising, planned surreptitiously and simultaneously through the entire Tlingit territory, the dreaded Kolosh struck. They massacred the garrison at Sitka. Conspirators included Haida chiefs from the Queen Charlotte Islands, as well as Tlingit chiefs of the Stikines, Kakes, Hootznahoos, Auks and Chilkats who met at Angoon to press the overfriendly Sitkas into rising against their Russian masters. Katlean, nephew of Skayeutlelt, aroused the Sitkas to rise. Out of the four hundred and fifty people, only forty-two survived to tell of the terrifying day in June of 1802.

Despite the chief manager's warning, wrote Khlebnikov of the holocaust, the fort commander, Medvednikov, had relaxed vigilance and on a Sunday afternoon as men went off fishing and berry picking, the Kolosh "suddenly emerged noiselessly from the shelter of the impenetrable forests, armed with guns, spears, and daggers. Their faces were covered with masks representing the heads of animals, and smeared with red and other paint; their hair was tied up and powdered with eagle down. Some of the masks were shaped in imitation of ferocious animals with gleaming teeth and of monstrous beings. They were not observed until they were close to the barracks; and the people lounging about the door had barely time to rally and run into the building when the savages, surrounding them in a moment with wild and savage yells, opened a heavy fire from their guns at the windows. A terrific uproar was continued in imitation of the cries of the animals represented by their masks, with the object of inspiring greater terror.

"Medvednikof had only time to hurry down from the upper story, and bravely attempted to repulse the sudden attack with the twelve men at his disposal. But the wailing of the women, and the frightened cries of the children, added to the confusion, and at the same time nerved the defenders to do their utmost. . . . Finally the last door of the barracks was broken in, the last weak barrier which protected the besieged, and in the savages poured. . . . The bold defenders Medvednikof, Tumakof, and Shashin were killed, and others dangerously wounded. The women in the upper story, crazed by fright, crowded with their children to the trap-door over the stairway. Another cannon-shot was heard, and the trap-door gave way. The women were precipitated into the street and in a moment were seized and carried off to the boats.

"Skayeutlelt, the false friend of Baranov, stood at the time of the attack upon a knoll opposite the agent's house, and having given the signal for the attack, shouted to the canoes with terrible yells to hasten to the slaughter. . . . The number of assailants may be estimated, without exaggeration, at over a thousand, and the few brave defenders could not long hold out against them. They fell, struck with bullets, daggers, and lances, amid the flames and in torture, but with honor. They were sacrificed for their country."

Of his attributes, the one least possessed by Baranov was patience. To retake Sitka became his obsession, and although he had not the means then, he began to plan. A young midshipman in the Russian navy wrote of the Baranov of this period: "He has lived for years among

savage tribes, surrounded by continual danger, struggling against the innate depravity of the kind of Russian sent to this country, suffering endless privations and hardships—even hunger—unable to depend on a single man for the furtherance of his plans. . . . I have the feeling he would, in time, have found some means of establishing this huge enterprise all by himself, if he had been forced to. . . ."

Baranov retook Sitka in 1804. In the meantime he solved his urgent problem of supply by a new arrangement with the Yankee O'Cain who sailed in as captain of the *O'Cain* in partnership with Boston's eminent Winship family. Having just sent the Company 17,000 sea otter skins, he had none to trade. Instead, he lent

O'Cain kayaks, gear and sixty Aleut hunters to poach in the poorly patrolled waters of Spanish California. On his return four months later, O'Cain turned over a thousand skins representing a gross profit of $80,000. Out of this Baranov bought O'Cain's cargo of foodstuffs, placed an order for more, and sent his own furs along with O'Cain to sell under the American flag at Canton.

The chief manager also bought O'Cain's armament and installed it on his own two crude ships. He began mobilizing his depleted forces. By summer he left Kodiak with a fleet of three hundred kayaks, eight hundred Aleut hunters, one hundred and twenty Russians, and four small ships, paused at Yakutat for reinforcements, and swept south to Sitka where his incredible flotilla of human paddlers beached their skin craft on the shores of the Kolosh.

As Baranov sailed into Sitka Sound a great ship greeted his eyes. The *Neva* under command of Urey Lisiansky was not only the decisive factor in the retaking of Sitka, but it symbolized the new, elevated status of Russian America. For the first time in its nearly eighty years of involvement with "Alaksu" of Northwest America, the Russian government sent a warship to protect the imperial interest.

Intimidation rather than massacre retook Sitka as the canny Tlingit were well aware that the big guns of the *Neva* could level their wooden structures. The Kolosh repulsed one effort to storm their fortifications, killing two Russians and wounding others, including Baranov. The next four days were consumed by delaying tactics of the Sitkas who, amid promises to evacuate their fort, sent hostages to the *Neva*.

"I recommenced my fire," Lisiansky wrote, "believing they were merely protracting the time till a reinforcement should arrive. I ordered also a float or raft to be made, on which our guns could be conveyed quite close under the fort. During the day we took two large canoes, one of which belonged to the old man, who, like another Charon (a name by which we called him), had in general brought the hostages to us. Shortly after, he came himself on board to demand his canoe, assuring me that just as he was quitting the fort, it had accidentally got loose and floated away. Knowing that he was telling me a falsehood, I refused his demand, and advised him to go back and persuade his countrymen to evacuate the fort as soon as possible, if they valued their safety. He consented to this; and added, that if they complied with our wishes, it would be made known to us in the night, by their singing out, Oo, oo, oo!

"About eight o'clock in the evening our ears were saluted with this cry, which we immediately answered with an hurrah; after which followed, on the part of the savages, a song, expressing that now only the Sitka people could reckon themselves free from danger.

"When morning came, I observed a great number of crows hovering about the settlement. I sent on shore to ascertain the cause of this; and the messenger returned with the news that the natives had quitted the fort during the night, leaving in it, alive, only two old women and a little boy. It appears that, judging of us by themselves, they imagined that we were capable of the same perfidiousness and cruelty; and that if they had come out openly in their boats, as had been proposed, we should have fallen upon them in revenge for their past behaviour. They had therefore preferred running into the woods, leaving many things behind, which, from their haste, they had not been able to take away. By this unexpected flight we obtained a supply of provisions for our hunters, and upwards of twenty large canoes, many of which were quite new. Mr. Baranoff ordered the fort to be completely destroyed; to effect which, three hundred men were sent on shore . . . under an officer from my ship.

"It was on the 8th that the fate of Sitca Fort was decided. After every thing that could be of use was removed out of it, it was burned to the ground. Upon my entering it, before it was set on fire, what anguish did I feel, when I saw, like a second massacre of innocents, numbers of young children lying together murdered, lest their cries, if they had been borne away with their cruel parents, should have led to a discovery of the retreat to which they were flying! There were also several dogs, that, for the same reason, had experienced the same fate. —O man, man! of what cruelties is not thy nature, civilised or uncivilised, capable?"

Baranov buried the dead and again raised the Russian flag over Sitka. He

called the new fort which he erected on the vanquished Indians' stronghold, New Archangel. The Russians and their Aleuts settled down to the worst winter of their co-existence, plagued by scurvy, starvation and marauding Tlingit.

Baranov eked out an existence by sending his little sloop *Yermak* to King Kamehameha in Hawaii, whose reply was a gift of pigs, taro, bananas, yams and cocoanuts for his brother monarch, Baranov. Over the years a deep friendship developed between these two natural leaders whose domains were linked by the Northwest Coast fur trade.

Spring came and with it the Yankee trader O'Cain's brother-in-law, Oliver Kimball, arrived in the *Peacock*. Again Baranov lent out his Aleuts to poach California waters. Kimball brought back skins worth $30,000. When the *Neva* pulled up anchor to complete her round-the-world voyage, back to Russia, she carried nearly half a million rubles in furs: 3,000 sea otter pelts and 150,000 smaller skins.

As the second winter began to close in on the establishment at Sitka, a person of great importance stepped off the brig *Maria*, visiting for the first time the posts of the Russian American Company he had helped create. The visitor was Nikolai Rezanov, now His High Excellency, Grand Chamberlain Rezanov. Dressed in the attire of the court's ranking nobleman, he arrived at the crude, pioneer outpost of rough hewn, wooden structures along streets of mud.

He had lost the wife he loved deeply. Shelikov's daughter died unexpectedly after childbirth. To forget, Rezanov joined

"The next day Mr. Baranoff paid me a vist on board the Neva, bringing with him a number of masks, very ingeniously cut in wood, and painted with different colours (See Plate I. fig. b). He had found them in the habitations he had destroyed. These masks were formerly worn by the Colushes in battle, but are now used chiefly on festivals. They are placed on a neck-piece of wood (Plate I. Fig. c), that extends from the lower part of the neck to the eyes, with indentations, o, at the edge, to see through, and fastens behind. Some of them represent heads of beasts, others of birds, and others of imaginary beings. They are so thick, that a musket-ball, fired at a moderate distance, can hardly penetrate them. Mr. Baranoff brought with him also two other curiosities; one of which was a thin plate, made of virgin copper, found on the Copper River, to the north of Sitca (Plate I. Fig. f): it was three feet in length, and twenty-two inches in breadth at one end, and eleven inches at the other, and on one side various figures were painted. These plates are only possessed by the rich, who give for one of them from twenty to thirty sea-otter skins. They are carried by the servants before their master on different occasions of ceremony, and are beaten upon, so as to serve as a musical instrument. The value of the plate depends, it seems, in its being made of virgin copper; for the common copper ones do not bear a higher price than a single skin. The other curiosity was a rattle (Plate I. Fig. e), which is used in dancing, and was very well finished, both as to sculpture and painting." Captain Urey Lisiansky—A Voyage Around the World, 1814

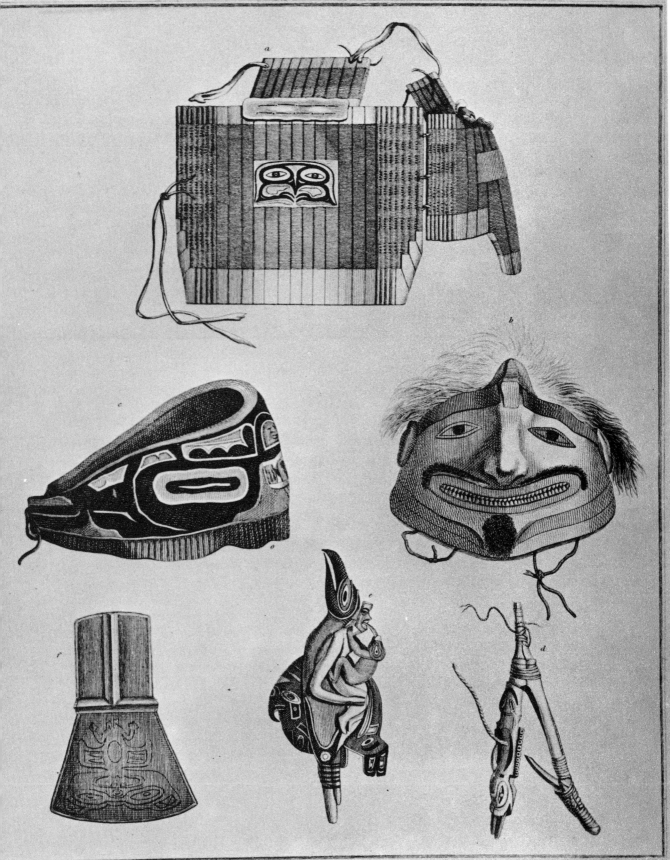

the celebrated Russian global voyage, and, after a disappointing state visit in Japan, made his way to Sitka along the island posts of the Russian American Company.

His dismay on seeing Russia's American capital was less at the disparity between the fiction he'd been led to believe and the facts of existence than at the anarchy he found everywhere. On his very first stop he observed the wanton destruction of fur seals on the Pribilof Islands, as many as 30,000 killed for their flesh, the skins left to rot on the shore.

"The multitude of seals in which St. Paul abounds is incredible; the shores are covered with them," he wrote Czar Alexander. "They are easily caught, and as we were short of provisions, eighteen were killed for us in half an hour. But at the same time we were informed that they had decreased in number ninety per cent since earlier times. . . . As over a million had already been killed, I gave orders to stop the slaughter at once, in order to prevent their total extermination, and to employ the men in collecting walrus tusks, as there is a small island near St. Paul covered with walrus."

Rezanov's orders were not long heeded. Some years later even the most hardened profiteer recognized the critical depletion of the seals and, during the administration of Baron Ferdinand von Wrangell, killing was for a time stopped. But not until 1911 was an international treaty signed to insure survival of the species. The walrus fared less well, succumbing before the end of the century to the guns of whalers who took them for their tusks.

To Rezanov's physician, Georg Heinrich von Langsdorff, conditions at Sitka were little better. He admired Baranov, but could not stomach the desperate cruelty that passed for life. Of the Aleuts, who far outnumbered their Russian masters, he wrote, "They are at present so completely the slaves of the company, that they hold of them their baidars, their clothing, and even the bone with which their javelins are pointed, and the whole produce of their hunting parties is entirely at their disposal. . . . The Russian promyshleniks are not in a much better situation. They are extremely ill-treated, and kept at their work till their strength is entirely exhausted; if they are ill, they must never hope for medical assistance or support in any other way; while as little attention at the same time is paid to their minds as to their bodies."

Apprehension pervaded the entire atmosphere. "Our cannon are always loaded," wrote Rezanov, "and not only are sentries with loaded guns placed everywhere but arms are our chief ornaments. After sundown, all night long, signals are given every few minutes from the parapets and the watchword passed until daybreak. Baranov maintains strict military discipline and we are always ready to repulse another savage attack."

As a nobleman used to luxury Rezanov did not let the crudities of New Archangel blind him to where fault lay. He blamed officers of the Company and Government who accepted the lucrative return, leaving to shift for himself the man who despite incredible obstacles kept things going and miraculously made profits besides.

"We all live poorly," Rezanov wrote in his first report to the comfortable St. Petersburg stock holders, "but worse than all lives the founder of this place, in a miserable hut, so damp that the floor is always wet, and during the constant heavy rains the place leaks like a sieve. Wonderful man! He only cares for the comfort of others, and is very neglectful of himself. Once I found his bed floating in the water, and asked him whether the wind had not torn off a board somewhere from the side of the hut. 'No,' he answered quietly, 'it is only the old leak.' . . . I tell you, gentlemen, that Baranof is an original, and at the same time a very happy production of nature. His name is heard on the whole western coast, down to California. The Bostonians esteem him and respect him, and the savage tribes, in their dread of him, offer their friendship from the most distant regions."

For his own part, Baranov improvised answers to crises as they arose. Each setback only strengthened his resolve, and the setbacks of the bleak winter were unusually bitter. The brig *Elizabeth* which he had sent to Kodiak for supplies, was wrecked during a heavy storm. New Russia, the sorry colony of serfs he had settled at Yakutat, was reduced to ashes and the heads of the victims were impaled on sticks lining the beach. Fleeing the scene of the massacre, the promyshlennik Demianenkov and two hundred Aleut hunters perished at sea. By the end of 1806 over sixty of the one hundred and ninety-two at Sitka were incapacitated by scurvy and eight were dead.

Relief tantamount to salvation came yet a third time from Boston. Sailing into Sitka Sound on the *Juno* after a success-

ful summer's trading, twenty-four-year-old Captain John D'Wolf said he was "received by Governor Baranov with that kind and obliging hospitality which made him loved and respected by every visitor." The tough old Russian and young captain of the *Juno* discussed poaching possibilities off California, but the unexpected arrival of Rezanov's entourage made immediate procurement of foodstuffs imperative. As a careful housekeeper, Langsdorff observed, "Baranoff was put to no small embarrassment by the wholly unexpected arrival of so large a train of visitors."

Baranov's answer was to buy the *Juno* outright, paying $300 in cash, five hundred and seventy-two sea-otter skins, a draft of $54,638 on the Russian American Company at St. Petersburg and, in addition, turned over to D'Wolf the small Russian brig *Yermak*. The *Juno's* cargo of salt beef, sugar, molasses and flour, Baranov transferred to his own sparse cupboard. The act was well approved all around.

"By this purchase," observed Langsdorff, "the Russian American Company obtained an excellent swift-sailing vessel, with a rich lading of useful supplies for trading with the natives of the northwest coast, consisting of a great quantity of linen and woollen cloth, kitchen utensils, knives, axes, hatchets, firearms, etc. But particularly a large supply of excellent provisions was got, by which all fears of the probable famine were removed. In fact, it was principally for the sake of this supply that the purchase was made."

To the consternation of those at the fort, young D'Wolf and Langsdorff announced plans to visit a village of the Sitka Tlingit some distance north on Peril Strait.

"As these were the very Indians who had recently been so roughly handled by the Russians," D'Wolf wrote, "it was considered by the Governor and other friends to be a rather perilous adventure. . . . We relied a good deal on our not being Russians, and upon the fact that I had been among them during the previous summer from a people with whom they were on friendly terms." Baranov equipped the adventurous souls with kayaks, supplies, two Aleuts and an Indian woman as an interpreter.

"By nightfall of the third day we had nearly reached the place of our destination," wrote D'Wolf, "but owing to a strong wind and tide, which were directly against us, we had the mortification of seeing the sun go down before the whole distance was accomplished. . . . Suddenly, some hundred naked Indians, armed with muskets, and holding firebrands in their hands, thronged to the water's edge. No sooner had we made known who we were, and approached the shore, than we were surrounded in a tumultuous manner by the Kaluschians, who dragged us towards their fortress. . . .

"We were hurried over a rather fatiguing road to the top of a high rock, on which stood the fortress, and were immediately introduced into the very spacious habitation of the chief Dlchaetin, the father of our interpreter. He assigned us a place directly opposite the entrance, where we spread a carpet, and, by the light of a very large fire on a raised hearth in the centre of the room, were subjected to the gaze of some hundreds of the natives. Shortly after, to our great astonishment, our packages were brought to us from our baidarkas, not the smallest trifle being withheld. . . .

"We had scarcely refreshed ourselves with a dish of tea and a glass of punch, when we were invited by the eldest and most distinguished of the chiefs, the commandant of the fortress, to come and visit him. He received us with much kindness, and presented me with a sea-otter's skin, and Dr. Langsdorff with a beautiful sea-otter's tail. Much fatigued, and in need of rest, we returned to the habitation of our host; but we found ourselves in too exciting a scene to permit of sleep.

"While eating a very good dish of fish and rice prepared by him, we were entertained with a lively and pleasing melody, sung by a number of men seated round the fire, which had been piled up to a great height. Though the night was cold and windy, the savages went barefoot to the neighboring forest, and brought home large blocks of wood upon their

some ribbon, and some glass beads. As soon as we had performed these necessary ceremonies, we were permitted to walk about wherever we chose, without the trouble of guides. Dr. Langsdorff even shot some birds close to the fortress without attracting any attention.

"The natives of the Northwest Coast of America are called by the Russians Kaluschians, but this people call themselves Schitchachon, or inhabitants of Sitcha. Expelled from Norfolk Sound, they had fortified themselves here, upon a rock which rose perpendicularly to the height of several hundred feet above the water's edge. . . . A natural wall of earth beyond the palisading on the side towards the sea, conceals the habitations so effectually, that they cannot be discerned from a ship.

"The houses within the fortress were placed in regular rows, and built of thick planks, fastened to posts which formed the framework, and covered at the top with bark. The entrance was at the gable end, and was often stained with different colored earths. The interiors of their dwellings were indescribably filthy, filled with smoke, and perfumed with decayed fish and train-oil. The men painted their faces, and, as well as the women, delighted in profuse ornaments; like other savages, they were particularly pleased with glittering trinkets, or European garments. The women on the coast had one very strange fashion, which I think is peculiar to this part of the world. At the age of fourteen or fifteen, they make a hole in their under lip and insert a small piece of wood like a button. This in increased in size as they advance in age, until it is three or four inches long, and one or two wide. I saw

naked shoulders, and heaped them on the hearth. It was incomprehensible how the roof, covered as it was merely with bark, was not entirely consumed. Once it did take fire; but a boy ran like a mouse up the side of the wall, and extinguished it. . . .

"On the morning of the next day we carried to the commandant from whom we had received the presents the evening before the counter presents due to him. At the same time, we made the proper tribute of presents to the parents of our interpreter, the latter having given us to understand that the sooner it was done, the greater would be their esteem for us. To her father we gave some ells of woollen cloth, a large knife, some fish-hooks, and some pounds of tobacco; to her mother a shift, some needles, a small looking-glass,

one old woman, the wife of a chief, whose lip ornament was so large, that, by a peculiar motion of her under lip, she could almost conceal her whole face with it. . . .

"The occupations of the Sitcha Indians, beside hunting and fishing, appeared to be making canoes, fishing-lines and hooks, and wooden ware. The women manufacture a kind of carpet out of the wool of wild sheep, and are very expert in wicker-work; some of their baskets are so closely woven as to hold water. Both sexes are expert in the use of firearms, and are excellent judges of their quality. I could not find that they had any organized government. Success in fishing and in the chase constitutes the source of their wealth, and consequently of their influence. . . ."

Despite the show of hospitality accorded D'Wolf and Langsdorff, Tlingit hostility never wholly abated. Unwary hunters were ambushed. As Yankee trade tactics became more abusive, the retalia-tory unrest spread up and down the coast. Avenging bands of Tlingit, Haida and Nootka boarded vessels and massacred the crews. The Chilkat Tlingit of Lynn Canal were regarded as particularly war-like.

"A more hideous set of beings, in the form of men and women, I had never seen before," wrote the Yankee Captain Richard Cleveland, who found his vessel surrounded by their war canoes. "The fantastic manner in which many of the faces of the men were painted, was probably intended to give them a ferocious appearance; and some groups looked really as if they had escaped from the dominions of Satan himself. One had a perpendicular line dividing the two sides of the face; one side of which was painted red, the other, black. . . . Another had the face divided with a horizontal line in the middle and painted black and white. The visage of a third was painted in checkers."

Caution was the watchword along the

entire coast and traders bargained from behind boarding nets from well-armed ships, never knowing when trade overtures might turn into attack.

A decade after D'Wolf's intrepid visit in 1818, a hunting expedition fitted out at Sitka for Camille de Roquefeuil, a Frenchman searching out trade opportunities, was attacked in the waters of the Alexander Archipelago. Returning to Sitka after the disaster in which twenty-three Aleuts lost their lives, he found the settlement in a state of alarm. Kolosh had killed two Russians within plain sight of the fort.

"Mr. Hagemeister spoke to me," Roquefeuil wrote of the new manager sent to replace Baranov, "of the hostility of the Indians who seldom let the fine season pass, without giving reasons for alarm." The French captain did not find Hagemeister's gloomy bias to be entirely true. In two seasons on the coast he met many of the Indian chiefs, including Maquinna and Wicananish, with whom he relived the early days of the fur trade. The roving Roquefeuil recorded significant changes worked by the years of white contact.

The Indians were far more knowledgeable about the ways of white men. In the Queen Charlottes, Roquefeuil noted the caution of Itemtchou, chief of Masset, indicating that the distrust so often expressed by the traders went both ways. "Itemtchou, the head chief of Masset, came in a handsome canoe, accompanied by his three wives. His face is long, a little morose and savage, and has something of the Swiss character. A zig-zag red line on his forehead, was continued to part of his nose. He wore, by way of a mantle, a white blanket, with a blue stripe at the extremities, open before, and fastened by a cord: his hat was in the form of a truncated cone, in the Chinese fashion. He would not come on board, till we had promised that an officer should remain as a hostage in his boat. We received him in the best manner, and made some presents, both to him and to his wives. . . . We conversed," Roquefeuil wrote, "by means of an Indian of Skitigates, named Intchortage." Roquefeuil said the Indian interpreter "piqued himself not only on speaking English well, but also on his polished manners; of which he endeavoured to persuade us by saying frequently, 'Me all the sames Boston gentleman.'

"The Indians gave us no cause of

alarm," Roquefeuil said of his Masset hosts. "They are the finest men on the north-west coast; they seem better fed, stronger, and much cleaner than the others. In their persons, and in every thing belonging to them, there is an appearance of opulence and comparative cleanliness, superior to all that we had before observed. As far as we could judge, the huts composing the four villages, on the two sides of the entrance, are better built, and in better order, than those of the north. There is something picturesque in the whole appearance of this large village; it is particularly remarkable for the monstrous and colossal figures which decorate the houses of the principal inhabitants, and the wide gaping mouths of which serve as a door."

Further north near present-day Angoon in Alaskan waters, Roquefeuil met a canoe. "An Indian [Youtchkitan] of a ferocious countenance, but dressed with a degree of pomp, came on board. He said he was a chief of Houtsnau, and had made several cruises on the coast, with the Americans. He seemed to be intelligent, and to have a knowledge of the trade and navigation of the Straits. Thinking that he might be useful to us, I gave

him the permission which he had desired, to remain on board. He immediately sent away his boat, and made me a present of an otter skin, and a beaver skin, in return for which I gave him, also as a present, some powder and a sword which had attracted his attention."

Youtchkitan guided Roquefeuil's ship to villages along Chatham Strait, Cross Sound and up Lynn Canal, "having assured me I should find furs as cheap again as at Houtsnau." On coming abreast of a village, said Roquefeuil, they frequently "hoisted American colors, these being the best known by the savages of this coast."

Wherever Roquefeuil went, the Indians had guns. This was the most fundamental change introduced by Yankee traders. The old eagerness for iron, so marked during the early years, now manifested itself in the desire for firearms. At Houtsnau, "as many as eleven canoes came out, one of them manned with thirteen men, another with seven, and the others with a smaller number, most of them armed with muskets.

"These two days had procured us forty-five otter skins, besides other furs of less value. The greater part was paid for in powder, at the rate of 12 lbs. for one otter skin. Here, as at Nootka, the Indians found our woollen goods very bad; as for the muskets, there were some among those of the French manufacture which suited them, but they would not take the Spanish muskets at any price. At this rate the powder which we had remaining would not be sufficient to procure more than about two hundred otter skins."

At a village in Chatham Strait, "a great number of Indians, with furs, came on the 22d, but we had no dealings with them, the only article which they demanded being powder, and I would not give the same quantity as I had done before, Youtchkitan having given me to understand, that the rate was too high."

The most noticeable difference of all was the decline in skins. The waters teemed with sea otters in the time of Dixon and his contemporaries so that they could be "scooped up like salmon"; their pelts were now offered by hard bargaining natives, one or two at a time.

At Masset, Roquefeuil wrote, "several canoes came on, but they had few otter skins." In Chatham Strait "the canoes came at ten o'clock, but in small numbers and with few skins." In the same area he met up with the *Brutus*, commanded by Captain Nye. "He had just gone round Admiralty Island, and had got only a single fur." Three decades of relentless pursuit by the traders from Boston and Baranov's hunters had taken heavy toll.

By the time of Roquefeuil's voyage few Yankee ships took on Aleuts to poach Spanish waters. When he stopped at San Francisco, the aggravated Spaniards gave the Frenchman an idea of the magnitude of Baranov's illegal expeditions: "In the

years 1809, 1810, and 1811, these intrepid fishermen came . . . in divisions of thirty or forty boats, each with two men. They entered, keeping along the north coast of the inlet; when they had once got in they were masters of this gulf, in which the Spaniards had not a single boat. The otters, which till then had nothing to fear but the attacks of the Indians of the country, were now pursued by the most intrepid and experienced enemy; it was estimated that about 8,000 were destroyed in the three years that they repeated their incursions."

The year of Roquefeuil's visit was the year the Russian American Company replaced Baranov with a Navy man, Lieutenant Leontii Hagemeister. During the years between Rezanov's visit and his replacement, Baranov lived with his legend, his word the sole law over the vast coastal arc of the North Pacific.

Except for hunting expeditions under

Russian license, no foreign vessel sailed the waters above Sitka. In California, the agricultural colony he had founded at Fort Ross helped supply Russian America with food. Trade arrangements with the Yankees brought the benefits of the China Trade. Overtures from the United States fur baron, John Jacob Astor, to split the coastal fur trade between them, foundered not for want of Russian power, but because England took Astoria from the Yankee nation as spoils in the War of 1812.

To the world Baranov was bigger than life, a self-made czar whose port at Sitka dominated the commercial life of the Pacific. Even captains who had no business to transact made it a port of call out of respect. Baranov's twenty-seven-year rule set the character of Russian control over Alaska, a control which, said Roquefeuil, was "the most absolute monopoly . . . in this part of the world."

Now, in the year 1818, the year of Baranov's replacement, both Shelikov and Rezanov were dead. Of the triumvirate whose merchant's vision, noble zeal and practical genius had made Russia a factor in the Pacific, only Baranov was left.

The years had greatly drained the emotional Baranov. He was pressed from above by an arrogant Russian Navy, wishing to control the empire he had created. From below, unruly new recruits plotted against him. He suffered the agonies of arthritis. His eyesight was failing. He was getting old.

Upon the departure of Nanuk, as Baranov was known in America, even the Kolosh came to pay their respects to the one man whose strength over the years had earned their respect, and in an ambiva-

lence born of prolonged contact, even a fierce sort of love. The beach was lined with the long wooden canoes of the Tlingit Indians: Chilkats, Stikines, Auks, Kakes, Hootznahoos, whose chiefs, their faces savagely painted with totemic designs, had come to bid their old enemy farewell.

Katlean, successor to his uncle Skayeutlelt, instigator of the Sitka massacre and now chief of the Sitkas, came with the Auk chief to say good-bye. He recalled to Baranov the years of violence and ven-

geance. "Now we are old men together and about to die," Katlean said. "Let us be brothers."

Baranov's gift to the Auk chief was a wry symbol of the relationship that had grown up during his rule. He gave the Indian the shirt of chain mail he had worn for many years after retaking Sitka. The Auks kept the steel shirt until their last chief died, at which time—well into the 1900's—a Russian priest secured it from them and presented it to the United States National Museum. Here it disappeared until 1966 when a young ethnologist stumbled upon it in a storage box and resurrected it.

Baranov set sail from Sitka in November, 1818, in the *Kutuzov*, commanded by Hagemeister. He had the satisfaction before he left of seeing his lovely daughter, Irina, married to Lieutenant Semyon Yanovsky, Hagemeister's second in command. The young lieutenant and Baranov's daughter, who was loved by everyone in the colony, remained in charge at Sitka. An old and broken man, torn from the context he had written, Baranov died on the long voyage. On April 12, 1819, in an irony of geography, his body was slipped to rest into the waters of the Indian Ocean.

Yanovsky did not long stay in command at Sitka. The Imperial Navy, staffed by members of the Russian nobility, had always chafed under the rudities of the merchant Baranov's rule. The alliance between the young Navy man and Nanuk's daughter came as an opportune transition from the lusty improvisations of Baranov to respectability, protocol, and order.

With his young bride, Yanovsky

toured the posts of the Company, inspecting conditions at the twenty-four stations, including Kodiak, Unalaska and the Pribilof Islands, and taking a careful census. The figures he sent the Company's board of directors revealed the truly phenomenal accomplishment of the man the Navy had dismissed. Russian America was controlled by three hundred and ninety-nine Russians. The largest number, one hundred and ninety-eight men and eleven women, were at Sitka. Seventy-three manned the posts on Kodiak. Some stations had twenty men, others but two or three. Creoles, Aleuts, Chugach and Kenaitz Indians comprised the balance of the "Russian" population. Over the Kolosh, or "wild tribes" the Company exercised no control.

Whether myth or miracle, Baranov's fur-gathering structure continued for a half century more to funnel furs to Russia. A full decade after Baranov's death, a Russian ship commander, Fedor Lutke, observed at Sitka, "The soul of this remarkable man guards, it appears, even now over the establishment, by him founded."

The chief managers who followed Baranov rode the crest of the wave he had set in motion. Each year saw an increase in pomp and ceremony inaugurated by the influx of high ranking naval officers. As time went on, the heightened, court-like atmosphere was matched by a corresponding decrease in take of furs and profits; but through the administrations of Baron von Wrangell in the 1830's and Adolf Karlovich Etolin a decade later, this discrepancy was noticed only by the most sharp-eyed observers.

During his voyage around the world to survey trading stations of his own pow-

Baranov's chain mail.

erful fur empire, Sir George Simpson, head of England's Hudson's Bay Company, visited Sitka at what seemed the very pinnacle of its golden age.

"New Archangel, notwithstanding its isolated position," he wrote, "is a very gay place—much of the time of its inhabitants is devoted to festivity; dinners and balls run a perpetual round, and are managed in a style which, in this part of the world, may be deemed extravagant." At the same time his practical Scottish mind noted tersely that "for the amount of business done here, the men, as well as the officers, appear to be unnecessarily numerous."

The turning point of the top-heavy Russian kingdom had come a good fifteen years prior to Simpson's visit. In renewing the Russian American Company charter in 1821, the Imperial Government tried to extend the southern limits of her New World territory to 51 degrees North latitude, just above Vancouver Island.

The new boundary might have stood had not Russia banned, also, all foreign trade in her territorial waters. Yankee shipmasters, whose trade revenues to 1811 alone came to $6,000,000, were adamant. President James Monroe and his Secretary of State, John Quincy Adams, led the protest for the United States, applying the principles of free trade embodied in the Monroe Doctrine to Pacific as well as Atlantic shores. Settlement of the controversy established the boundary lines that prevail today. The United States and Russia signed a treaty in 1824 that raised Russia's southern limits to 54 degrees 40 minutes North latitude, the boundary now of the State of Alaska.

A year later England negotiated a treaty that limited Russia's eastward expansion as well, drawing the north-south line that cuts the coast from mainland Canada to form the panhandle of Southeastern Alaska. This narrow coastal strip, approximately thirty miles wide, from Yakutat to Prince of Wales Island, embraces all the territories of the Tlingit and the Kaigani, or Alaskan Haida.

During her century-and-a-quarter-long harvest of America's wealth in furs the Russian American Company concerned itself very little with the well-being of the "wild" tribes. Contact between the Kolosh and Russian ranged from armed conflict to cold war. To protect his rebuilt fort-settlement at New Archangel, Baranov banished the Sitka Tlingit from their former homesite. Out of the same concern for Russian security, Captain Matvei Murariev, who succeeded Yanovsky, called them back to rebuild their village, reasoning that they would be less dangerous within reach of Russian guns. The uneasy atmosphere that pervaded life during these years is made plain by Captain Edward Belcher, sent by England in the 1830's on Hudson's Bay Company business, who wrote:

"The establishment at Sitka is situated on a broad flat delta. . . . It is about sixty feet above the sea-level, and completely commands all the anchorages in the immediate neighbourhood . . . the longest base of this delta, is protected by a heavy line of picketted logs . . . flanked at the angles, within musket-shot of each other, by small block-house redoubts, loopholed and furnished with small guns and swivels. . . . This cuts off all connexion with the natives, but through a portcullis door, admitting into a railed yard those bringing goods to market. This door is closely watched by two or three guards, who, upon the least noise or dispute in the market, drop the portcullis, and proceed summarily with the delinquents."

The adjacent Indian village became known as the Ranche, and its colorful family and clan houses, painted with totemic clan insignia, where in later years the delight of the annual crop of summer tourists.

Under Russian rule the railed yard of the fort became a busy market center where the Indians came to trade game, fish, furs, and even their own unusual masks, hats, blankets and other handicrafts for Russian tobacco, iron cooking pots, glassware, fabric, potatoes, and other goods, all pegged at company rates of exchange.

On one commodity, however, the Indians set the price. "I had the opportunity here," Belcher wrote, "of viewing some of the skins, particularly the sea otter, which they purchase from the natives, and was not a little surprised to find how completely they have arrived at their standard value, which is a very high price. A moderately good sea otter skin will fetch from six to seven blankets, increasing to thirteen for the best . . . In money they frequently ask forty dollars; on the coast of California, at San Francisco and Monterey, as much as eighty to a hundred."

The Kolosh all along the coast were sharp traders and full of tricks. On his first run up to Sitka, Simpson stopped along the way to trade with the Kwakiutl: "The natives, now that they no longer dare to employ force against the whites, still occasionally resort to fraud, practising every trick and devise to cheat their trader. One favourite artifice is to stretch the tails of land-otters into those of sea otters. Again, when a skin is rejected as being deficient in size, or defective in quality, it is immediately, according to circumstances, enlarged, or coloured, or pressed to order, and is then submitted, as a virgin article, to the buyer's criticism by a different customer. In short, these artists of the north-west could dye a horse with any jockey in the civilized world, or 'freshen up' a faded sole with the most ingenious and unscrupulous of fishmongers."

Except for one uncommon Russian, a Russian Orthodox priest whose studies anticipated the anthropologists and have come down via their reports, the Tlingit nation under Russia is presented largely as a savage backdrop for white history. To experience the variety and power of their vivid tribal culture, one must come as a visitor, as did the English representatives of the Hudson's Bay Company, Captain Belcher who visited Sitka in the *Sulphur*, during Ivan Kupreanov's admin-

istration, and Sir George Simpson, who came during Governor Adolf Etolin's term a few years later in the Hudson's Bay Company's *Beaver*.

These were the peak years of the Russian American Company's domination of the North Pacific and the years of greatest tranquility between the Russians and the Indians. Turbulence attending colonization had quieted, broken only at intervals by usually traceable provocation. During Wrangell's administration as many as a thousand Indians visited markets held at Sitka to trade goods which ran in value one year to eight hundred rubles.

A culmination was reached during

Harbor of New Archangel, in Sitka or Norfolk Sound

Governor Etolin's administration in a trade fair to which some five hundred important Tlingit came from as far north as Yakutat and as far south as Tongass territory bordering Portland Canal, bringing pelts of beaver, mink, martin, and otter, the proceeds of which they spent staging potlatches that became increasingly lavish. Etolin envisioned the fair as an annual event, but after his administration there is no further mention of it.

The natives during this period pursued a schizoid existence, presenting alternately their civilized and savage countenance. As the *Sulphur* lay at anchor in Sitka Sound, Belcher played host to a delegation of Sitka Tlingit whose native distrust of white men could not check their curiosity.

"The chiefs having pestered the Governor to ask permission to visit the *Sulphur* . . . observed great ceremony in their approach, and were dressed in the most fantastic garb imaginable, being generally painted with scores of vermillion, in some instances not devoid of taste. Some had helmets of wood, carved in imitation of frogs, seals, fish, or birds' heads. Others wore the very sensible plain conical hat without rim, which serves effectually to ward off sun or rain, and the generality wore, or carried with them, their native shawl, which is very laboriously worked into carpet figures, from the wool of some animal which I could not ascertain. . . .

"The canoes were as fantastic as their occupants. They were carved in grotesque figures, and remarkably well handled. After encircling the ship, singing, and gesticulating, as if she was to become a good prize, they at length came on board,

and were severally presented by the Governor—not omitting their virtues or vice versa, when they possessed sufficient notoriety. I observed that those who had become (nominally) Christians were entitled to precedence, but no particular virtues were enumerated as their especial property.

"A feast, as it is termed here, of rice and molasses, had been provided, on tables ranged on the maindeck. Instead of the proposed thirty-seven, I think one hundred might be nearer their number. After one good feed they were served with previously diluted grog; (mixed to Sitka proof, about four to one;) then a second dose of rice and molasses, followed by the grog, and then a third, finished that of the meal; the ladies quietly bagging the remains in order, I presume, to prevent their soiling our maindeck. One or two ludicrous dances followed, to their own music,—a species of tambourine, clapping, yelling, etc., and a new musical instrument, composed of three hoops with a cross in the centre, the circumferences being closely strung with the beaks of the Alca arctica. This being held by the centre of the cross from below, and given a short vibratory motion, similar to the escapement of a watch, produced not a bad accompaniment.

"I was heartily glad when they decamped, as they began to be noisy, wanted more lumme (rum), and thought they had not been treated well,—being as yet only half-seas over, it was too apparent what a pest they might have turned out had I indulged them further!"

In line of duty as governor of the Hudson's Bay Company, Simpson twice steamed up the inland passage to check

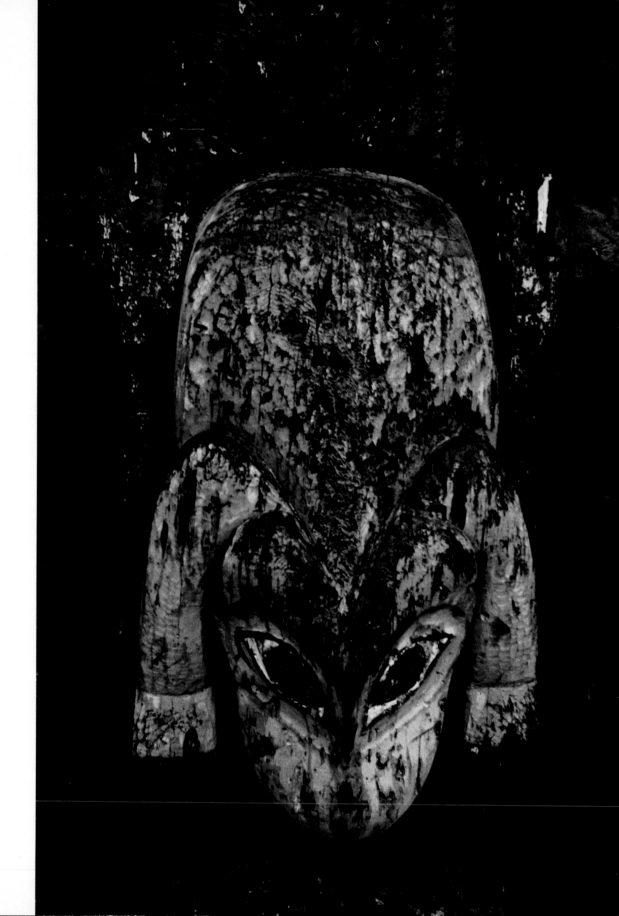

on his newly negotiated Fort Stikine, leased to the British by the Russians in 1839 for 2,000 land otter skins a year. Simpson was curious about everything.

"While I was at New Archangel, a funeral took place among the Kaluscians. . . . The body, arrayed in the gayest apparel of the deceased, lay in state for two or three days, which were spent by the relatives in fastings and lamentations. At the end of this period, it was placed on a funereal pile, round which the mourners ranged themselves, their faces painted black, their hair clipped short, and their heads covered with eagle's down. The pipe was next passed round two or three times; and then, at some secret signal, the fire was kindled in several places, while a discord of drumming and wailing deafened one till the pile was consumed. Lastly, the ashes were collected into an ornamented box, which was ultimately to be elevated on a scaffold, or on the top of a pole. On the side of a neighbouring hill we saw a vast number of these monuments, which presented a very curious appearance."

Simpson also watched a fight of Tlingit against Tlingit that exemplified the Northwest Coast Indians' demand for redress of wrongs.

"Soon after my return from the baths, I witnessed an Indian scene, which surpassed in wildness any thing of the kind that I had ever seen. In the native village, which lies under the guns of the fort, two savages, the one a high chief, and the other a man of some consequence, but still inferior in rank to his companion, had quarrelled over their cups; and, in the scuffle that ensued, the former had slain

the latter, by stabbing him through the lungs with his dagger. The party of the deceased, to the number of about a thousand men, immediately turned out, with horrible yells, to revenge his death, painted in the most hideous manner, and armed with all sorts of weapons, such as spears, bludgeons, dirks, and firearms; while the women, more ferocious, if possible, than the warriors themselves, were exciting the tumultuary band to actual violence by

the most fiendish screams and gestures. From the battery, where we had all taken our stand to watch the proceedings, Governor Etholine endeavoured, but in vain, to appease the fury of the mob; happily, however, the approach of night prevented the immediate commencement of the civil war.

"By six in the morning, I was roused from my bed by information that, with a new day before them, the friends of the deceased were determined to carry their threats of the preceding afternoon into execution. The scene, when we were all again collected on the battery, would beggar description—(The combatants wore, as defensive armour, leathern jerkins and wooden cuirasses, which protected the body, down to the knees)—several thousands of all ages, and both sexes, unaccustomed at any time to put the slightest restraint on their passions, and now maddened into demons, partly by their own vindictiveness, and partly by the exhortations of their schamans, or priests. The chief's life was demanded as an atonement, but refused by his party, as being of more value than that of the person slain. At this point, the Governor and the Bishop interposed on behalf of the chief, as being a baptized member of the church; while, by way of backing the remonstrance, the guns of the battery, already pointed in the right direction, were made ready for action. This strong hint in favour of a compromise was not lost. The parties met with a loud warwhoop; for a minute or two a clashing of arms was heard; and when both sides simultaneously receded from the spot, we beheld the bodies of two slaves that had been sacrificed in lieu of the chief. The ignoble blood of the unfortunate substitutes—quantity making up for quality—was accepted as a satisfactory adjustment of the feud, and the village again resumed its wonted appearance."

A few weeks earlier Simpson had checked an attack on his Fort Stikine post, where savages were "assembled round it to the number of about two thousand. This scene of violence, and the recent tragedy at Stikine, both events being clearly the result of drinking to intoxication," Simpson wrote, "determined Governor Etholine and myself, on behalf of our respective companies, to discontinue the use of spirituous liquors in tradng wth the natives of this coast; and we immediately entered into an agreement to that effect."

When Etolin departed in 1845 and the friendly overtures of Wrangell and Etolin were reversed, relations between the Indians and Russians deteriorated rapidly. By the mid-1850's sporadic outbursts had become full scale war. Tribal feuds, which had never ceased, now boiled over to include violence against the Russians, when, in full view of the Russians, who did nothing to stop them, the Sitka Tlingit massacred a party of Stikines whom they had invited to a potlatch. In revenge, the frustrated Stikines sent a war party to destroy the Russian hospital at a much frequented hot spring a few miles south of Sitka.

During these years of violence, individuals were ambushed and Russian forts were attacked. The terror came to a head when a Sitka Tlingit stabbed a Russian sentry in an argument over firewood. Threats on both sides erupted into action. Spread with war paint and armed with muskets, the Sitka Tlingit swarmed from

Bishop Ivan Veniaminov

their village toward the fort. For two hours they held their ground against superior fire. Sixty Tlingit were killed and in the end they were beaten.

The date of the battle, 1855, is cited as the last outburst against Russian rule. The reason given for Russian victory is the technical superiority of her resources. If the Indians had been in possession of a few pieces of cannon, one early historian has said, it is not improbable that there might have been a repetition of the Sitka massacre.

Perhaps, but the fifty years of Russian presence among the Indians of Southeastern Alaska, the debilitating effects of the Hudson's Bay Company post on the Stikine, complicated by the free trading Yankees with their guns and spirits, had eaten deeply into the cohesiveness and strength of the native culture and eroded the spontaneous unity that could prompt villages from Yakutat south to the Queen Charlottes to rise with their kin at Sitka against Baranov's crude fort.

Overshadowing these contributing demoralizing factors was the paramount disaster of death from disease. In 1836, two decades before the date of the cited Indian defeat, a smallpox epidemic swept through Southeastern Alaska, virulent and unchecked, although some efforts were made to vaccinate the natives. The Sitka quan alone lost four hundred adults, half the population of their village.

The epidemic wreaked its horrors and destruction first on the populous and warlike Tongass Tlingit, whose territory adjoined British possessions, from whence the sickness came. As it raged north through the Alexander Archipelago, whole villages were wiped out. Those who miraculously survived, fled, leaving the corpses to rot in abandoned ghost sites. A doctor of the Company said 3,000 natives died before any vaccination was attempted, and at first all efforts at vaccination were rejected. Resistance was finally overcome by the one man in all Russian America to whom the Indians would listen.

This man was a giant, spiritually and physically, a Russian priest Ivan Veniaminov, brought by Wrangell to Sitka to work with the Tlingit as he had worked with the Aleuts. "When he preached the word of God," an aged Aleut of Unalaska recalled, "all the people listened, and listened without moving, until he stopped. Nobody thought of fishing or hunting while he spoke; nobody felt hungry or thirsty as long as he was speaking, not even little children."

Veniaminov was the first white man to show concern for Indian welfare. He studied the character and customs of the Tlingit, collected their myths, identified their villages, learned their language. The wealth of anthropological information in his studies and letters is the bedrock upon which later students based their work. Yet even Veniaminov could not at once overcome the years of mistrust and hatred:

"In spite of how well I became acquainted with the Tlingit and how friendly our intercourse was, a long period of time passed before they were satisfied as to my knowledge and ability. After I had been there three years, in 1834, I tried without success to persuade them to use smallpox vaccine. In 1835 the smallpox epidemic came and decreased their population by almost half, and while the

William Seward

Tlingit, knowing it to be contagious, wished that the Russians would also get it, not one Russian succumbed to the disease. Now they saw that the Russians had greater knowledge than they, and their own cures of ice and snow and the shaman's practice had not helped them, so they flocked in droves and from great distances to the Russian doctor in order that he might vaccinate them and their children. In one year two hundred and fifty Tlingit were vaccinated."

Prior to the epidemic Veniaminov estimated the Tlingit and Haida to be 10,000 persons. The first United States census, gave in 1880, the figure of 6,763.

But statistics conceal the human disaster that overtook those who survived. Heads of family had been swept away. Family units, the basis of their society, were in fragments. Women, children, orphans, men without women and women without men were left to cope with the problem of survival. The abandoned home

sites of once populous villages and the reduced numbers in numerous others testify to the magnitude of the catastrophe and the long shadow of its consequence. If the Tlingit lost their battle with the Russians in 1855, they lost the war to disease during the dread epidemic of the thirties.

Now, it was not Kolosh, but finances and politics that dominated Russian thinking during the final years of her rule. Profits were down. Expenses were up and, despite some efforts to establish a method of conservation, revenue from the seemingly inexhaustible supply of fur bearing mammals had withered. In 1804 a single hunting party had taken 2,000 sea otters on a quick run from Cross Sound to Chatham Strait. In the last two decades, the total sea otter catch in all Russian waters was less than 1,000 annually.

Russia's sale of Alaska to the United States was prompted partially by the Crimean War, which led to her expansion southward in Siberia to the Amur River, a territory long tied by treaty to China. In Imperial circles the argument ran that Russia should rid herself of the American liability in order to concentrate on the rich potential of the Amur. A second reason was the growing warmth in relations between the United States and Russia during the young republic's trials of Civil War. But in truth, Russia was receptive to relinquishing her American possession because, after fifty years riding the wave's crest, the momentum generated by Baranov had run down.

In the end, two small and zealous cliques, one ranking high in the Imperial Government, and the other in the United

States, led by Secretary of State William Seward, maneuvered over a period of years to achieve title transfer of a property that Russia did not in her heart wish to sell, to a nation that did not wish to buy.

October 18, 1867, was the day of transfer. The gracious ceremonies Seward had planned became in fact a blunt militaristic exercise that turned over a proud, self-sufficient and properous colonial community of 2,500 people, many of whom were second and third generation residents of Sitka, to a career soldier, Jeff Davis, who had been called back for the assignment from the Wild West, where he had gone after the Civil War to fight Indians.

The Tlingit and Haida of Alaska were not permitted into Sitka to watch transfer of their land from the Slav, whose ways they had grown to know, to the Yankees, whose actions had earned their distrust. Attired in the clan regalia that characterized their unbroken native culture, they stood silently beside their hand-hewn, fiercely decorated canoes lining the beach to watch the ceremony described by a naval officer of the U.S.S. *Ossipee*, which had conveyed United States Commissioner Lovell H. Rousseau to Sitka:

"Captain Petchouroff ordered the Russian flag hauled down, and thereby, with brief declaration, transferred and delivered the territory of Alaska to the United States; the garrisons presented arms, and the Russian batteries and our men of war fired the international salute; a brief reply of acceptance was made as the stars and stripes were run up and similarly saluted, and we stood upon the soil of the United States."

"In This Place Sitka, Russian Territory Became American." Painting by Harry Wood

Chapter VI

AMERICA'S
NEGLECTED BARGAIN

As they lined the beach watching the perfunctory transfer of their land from Russia to the United States, the Tlingit chiefs of Southeastern Alaska did not dream that the cannon's boom sounded also the termination of their own native culture. For nearly one hundred years they had swapped the skins of the sea otter for trade goods of the merchant mariners of Spain, France, England, the United States, and the Russian intruder. Rather than changing their ways, the new wealth and coveted iron accrued from the fur trade had quickened the pace of their affluent, showy culture, intensifying its characteristics, not ending them.

A marine people, they undertook long coastal voyages in their remarkably crafted canoes, visiting friend and foe in villages tucked among the coves and inlets of their island dominion to trade, wage war, and attend the potlatches that held together the Pacific Northwest Coast Indian culture.

For food the Indians harvested the abundant wealth of the Pacific west coast land and sea. With the approach of spring, winter villages emptied as their people, grouped in family units, loaded their belongings into canoes and went to the special fishing sites held by each lineage from time immemorial, to catch in a few weeks—from the incredible annual run of salmon on their way upstream to spawn—their basic food for the winter. Also staple were halibut, herring, shellfish and the important *olachen* or "candlefish," rich in oil and an essential ingredient of the daily diet. Fruit from the high, lush summer growth of huckleberries, currants, salmonberries and other plants completed their table.

The majestic and lush abundance of environment gave the Tlingit and his coastal neighbors an opportunity—rare among any people—to satisfy their material needs easily and within the few short months of summer. This left the long winter hours free for enjoyment of a highly sociable existence filled with story telling, songs, dancing, and intricate ceremonies, all heightened and embellished by fanciful and frightening masks, headgear, rattles, costumes and other paraphernalia pertinent to each of the many impersonations and performances. All of this the children absorbed as they grew. This was their heritage, and each generation in turn passed it on to the next.

Into this balance struck with nature "flocked in amplest proportion, a herd of all sorts and conditions of men—Alaskan pioneers, aspirants for colonial emoluments and honors." The Navy man, C. D. Bloodgood, who reported the transfer, stayed on eight months more to watch the scramble for spoils. "Before our first sunset gun was fired, their preempting stakes dotted the ground, and ere long they had framed a city charter, devised laws and remunerative offices, and by an election, at which less than one hundred votes were mustered, gave publicity to, and inaugurated their schemes. Their squatter claims were confirmed and recorded. Some such a course, perhaps, is unavoidable in the incipiency of colonization, though it reflects humiliatingly upon the nationality of those concerned."

Stores, restaurants, bowling alleys, and saloons opened. Trade and shipping were brisk. Within the first year some seventy ships entered Sitka's harbor bringing trade estimated at $400,000. Enterprising California merchants bought out Russian holdings at token prices. A flotilla of unrestrained fur hunters cleared harbor for the Seal Islands to begin a slaughter that in the single year of 1868 took the lives of 240,000 fur seals. Yet despite the disorderly frontier atmosphere, pioneer prospects looked promising.

The bubble burst early. The new Alaskans soon found that they had no government through which to order their affairs. Nor could they form one. Two pieces of legislation—all that would be passed for the next seventeen years—stuck in the pin and transformed dream into nightmare. The Customs Act of 1868 put Alaska in custody of a customs collector who was granted neither means to patrol his 26,000 mile coastline, nor au-

thority to prosecute, if by some miracle he caught an offender. The only regulations extended by the act were over navigation and commerce and the prohibition on sale and import of firearms and distilled liquor.

The rightful essentials of civilized life, so complacently taken for granted, were denied. No Alaskan could acquire land, clear any portion of forest, deed property, transfer it, or build a house with any assurance that it would not be seized. Legally he could not be born, marry, die, or will his possessions. Crime could not be punished. Wrongs could not be adjudicated. Attempts at popular government broke down because there were no laws to enforce compliance.

Immediately Alaskans began pleading with Congress far away in Washington to give them a structure of government. A detailing of this long drawn out, frustrated supplication comprises classic Alaskan history. The beginning "era of total neglect," said former Governor Ernest Gruening, now Senator, was followed by fourteen years more in which neglect was "fragrant." The sorry saga is usually told without reference to affairs in the States, making the territory's plight more outrageous because it seems unaccountable.

Lawless Alaska had its counterpart in a frontier America that itself gave only token observance to law during the last half of the nineteenth century. The lowest ebb in American political history came during the three decades that followed the Civil War, a period of governmental corruption and frontier anarchy that coincide with the first thirty years of Alaska's struggle for a civil government. Ulysses S. Grant became President in 1869. Of his administration the historian Henry Adams said, "No period so thoroughly ordinary had been known in America politics since Christopher Columbus first disturbed the balance of American society."

Graft, bribery, and pay-offs were a commonplace. Senators, cabinet members and even the Vice-President used their offices of public trust for private gain. Like a fat goose up for plucking, the still virgin land of America was exploited through lavish susidies, charter grants, open-end contracts and protective tariffs by the new men in Congress, who often held stocks in the same enterprises that they aided by their own, unashamed legislation.

Said James Russell Lowell, succinctly, "Men buy their way into the Senate, and of course, expect a profit on their investment."

From these ruthless, aggressive, acquisitive years emerged modern America, rising in concord with the modern world, distinguished from its predecessor by decisive technological advances that put human beings in control of vast natural energies. Transportation, communication, industrial production came into a new high level during the last half of the nineteenth century.

These decades that triggered America's rise to economic and political greatness were the same that saw the buffalo swept from the western plains, minerals torn from the hills, the forest cut down, and the Indian tribes, which once roamed free, packed off to reservations. This is the period that coincides also with Alaska's long neglect, overlooked, or more aptly, looked over by its own counterpart of the wire-pulling commercial interests who directed politics in Washington.

To the congressional mind, and in the mind of the executive branch as well, Alaska was synonymous with the two small

fog-bound islands of St. Paul and St. George in the South Bering Sea. To these tiny, remote spots of land three million fur seals migrated every summer to bear their young, a natural phenomenon which resulted in the largest aggregate of seals at one time, any place in the world. In its second piece of legislation Congress handed them over on a twenty-year lease to a California combine, the Alaska Commercial Company, for $55,000 a year and a royalty of $2.62 per skin on a permitted annual take of 100,000 seals. In its first year of sealing, after paying off a capital investment of $1.75 million, the Company declared a $200,000 dividend to its sixteen stockholders.

To look after its interests the Treasury Department sent special agents to the Pribilofs, who came back impressed, and frequently on the Alaska Commercial Company's payroll, to write glowing accounts of the operation. "Ever since the transfer," said Alaska's second governor, Alfred P. Swineford, in his report to Congress, "a studied and determined effort has been made to imbue the general public, as well as the government, with the belief that there is nothing of value in Alaska save its fur-bearing animals. Agents of the government, sent out to examine and report upon its resources, instead of honestly performing the service for which they were paid, have, in the interest of a corporation into whose service they have drifted . . . broadcast statements concerning the climate and undeveloped resources of Alaska which they knew were utterly false, but which, according with a preconceived public opinion born of ignorance, were generally accepted as true."

With the Army in charge of the people, a commercial company in control of Alaska's vast fur resources, and the lawmakers in Washington preoccupied with their own state side wheeling and dealing, the United States' misrule of the future forty-ninth state was thus begun.

To the natives of Alaska the anarchy that passed for military rule cut more deeply than the denial of political rights of which they as yet had no concept. To them came demoralization, disease, and death.

"The sending of the soldiers to this country was the greatest piece of folly of which a government could be guilty," wrote John G. Brady, head of the Presbyterian Mission to a treasury agent, William Gouverneur Morris. "Surveying ten years of havoc wrought by the military," he said, "it will require twenty years to wipe out the evils which were brought to the natives. They knew nothing of syphilis, nor did they know how to make an intoxicating liquor from molasses; but now they are dying from these two things."

In his report to the Secretary of the Treasury, John Sherman, Morris described the devastating drink and its effect:

"Previous to the arrival of the military its manufacture was unknown to the Indians, but no sooner had the soldiers made their appearance in Alaska than the detestable traffic commenced. And from the first sergeant of a company down to the drummer-boy, it may be safely said, a large number were either directly or indirectly interested in some soul-destroying still.

"Molasses rum, or hootzenoo is made by the whites and Indians in Alaska in an

empty five-gallon coal-oil can . . . by the following recipe: One gallon of molasses, five pounds of flour, one half box of yeast-powder; add sufficient water to make a thin batter, place the mixture alongside a fire, and when it has fomented and become sour, fill the can three parts full and begin boiling. The worm [a six-foot tin pipe] being fitted to the nozzle of the can, then passes through a barrel of cold water, and the steam from the boiling mixture passing through the pipe or worm, on reaching the cold pipe in the barrel, condenses and appears again at the end of the worm beyond the barrel in drops, and which the Indians drink while warm. One gallon of the mixture will make three-fourths of a gallon of hootzenoo, and the three-fourths of a gallon will craze the brains of ten Indians. This is about the most infernal decoction ever invented, producing intoxication, debauchery, insanity, and death."

"I am compelled to say," wrote Sitka's first customs director, William S. Dodge, "that the conduct of certain military and naval officers and soldiers has been bad and demoralizing in the extreme; not only contaminating the Indians, but in fact demoralizing and making the inhabitants of Sitka what Dante characterized Italy: 'A grand house of ill-fame.' . . . Many is the night I have been called upon after midnight by men and women, Russian and Aleutian, in their nightclothes, to protect them against the malice of soldiers. . . . Within six months after the arrival of the troops at Sitka, the medical director informed me that nearly the whole of the Sitka tribe, some twelve hundred in number, were suffering from venereal diseases. Many have died. . . .

"For a long time some of the officers drank immoderately of liquor, and it is telling the simple truth when I say that one or two of them have been drunk for a week at a time. The soldiers saw this, the Indians saw it; and as 'Ayas Tyhus' or 'big chiefs,' as they call the officers, drank, they thought that they too must get intoxicated. Then came the distrust of American justice when they found themselves in the guardhouse, but never saw the officers in when in a like condition."

Dodge addressed his remarks to Vincent Colyer, who as Special Indian Agent for the United States visited Alaska in 1869. Colyer was not *sent* by the Indian Board of Commissioners, which did not list Alaska as Indian Territory nor include the Tlingit and Haida among Indian tribes over which the government exercised authority. Colyer went to Alaska on his own initiative. "I had already visited the Indians in Eastern Kansas, Indian territory, Northern Texas, New Mexico, North-eastern Arizona and Southern Colorado," he wrote the Secretary of the Interior. Despite the fact that the Territory of Alaska was not included in the commission's program, "I thought it clearly my duty to visit Alaska."

Like the curious and observant Sir George Simpson, whose route he followed up the inside passage, Colyer was intrigued by the unique Northwest Coast culture, so different from anything he had observed among Indians of the States.

As he passed through the Strait of Juan de Fuca, where less than a hundred years before, Tatooche had terrorized the traders who rendezvoused at Nootka, Colyer wrote, "The morning was clear and mild and the Indians were out in wooden canoes fishing. . . . The men were dressed like our fishermen, with the exception of the hat, which has a broad brim, running down in one unbroken convex sweep from the flat top to the outer rim.

"The first place at which we stopped in the Territory of Alaska was Tongas, an old Indian village, near which the United States government has built a new post. It is located on one of the islands on the coast, near Portland Channel, the boundary line of British Columbia.

"I regret that we cannot engrave the picture of this Indian village at Tongas. The village contains about sixteen houses, which are well built of hewn plank, one story high, and have both doors and windows, the latter of glass, the sashes and glass for which are obtained from white people trading on the coast. . . ."

Known as Captain Ebbetts since Baranov's time, when he exchanged names with the Yankee commander of Astor's ship, *Enterprise,* the chief of the Tongass, Colyer wrote, "is an intelligent and kind hearted old man. As we were leaving his house, the daughters called to him as 'he was going with the Boston men,' as they call all Americans, 'not to drink any whisky.' This warning proved plainly enough that the Indian women like our own poor wives and daughters, fully appreciate the curse of strong drink."

Before his death Chief Ebbetts commissioned the famous Abraham Lincoln totem pole. Ebbetts was of Raven lineage. For years a militant confederacy of Eagle clans had made war on his people, pursuing them from haven to haven, until the United States assigned the revenue cutter *Lincoln* to Tongass Island. Chief Ebbetts gathered his people under the protection

A recarved Lincoln replaces ruined Tongass pole now in Alaska State Museum.

of her guns to avoid the dreadful choice of extermination or slavery, and in tribute to the Great Emancipator, whose protection insured his own people's freedom, he erected—higher than all the other poles of the village—the statute of Lincoln.

Colyer arrived next at the explosive Stikine Tlingit stronghold of Wrangell, ruled over since earliest Russian days by Chief Shakes and two lesser but notable chiefs, Toyatte and Shustaks. "There are thirty-two houses in the village," he wrote, "located on a tongue of land and curve in the shore of Wrangel Island. On the opposite side of this curve . . . the government post is located, about five hundred yards distance, with the guns commanding the village."

Colyer noted the ornamented house fronts and elaborately carved totem poles marking important clan houses and, in particular, the three poles of the notorious Shakes that today stand in replica in front of a reproduction of Shakes house. "On [house] no. 5 are some very curious colossal frogs, a bear, war-chief, with his 'big medicine-dance hat' on," Colyer wrote. The Shakes of Colyer's day was the last "savage" to hold the celebrated title which was perpetuated into the 1940's.

The Indian village, or Ranche, at Sitka, impressed Colyer less favorably than the vigorous Stikine community at Wrangell. Its proximity over the years to civilized settlement facilitated the absorption of white man's vices without prompting the adoption of his virtues. From the medical report made to him by the Army post surgeon, Colyer learned that 1,251 Tlingit lived at the Sitka Ranche in forty-four plank houses. "Cleanliness and neatness is generally wanting in their abodes, although there are a few who in both respects are excellent models for the rest. . . .

"The diseases most common among them are syphilis, rheumatism, and conjunctivitis. The first is much aggravated and diffused by unrestrained intercourse with the troops, and affects both sexes equally. . . . Their moral condition is low, and rendered worse by the proximity of the whites, as evidenced by the superiority

of the tribes in other parts of the Territory whose relations have been less intimate with us."

At Sitka Colyer began collecting data in earnest. His report is largely a list of punishments meted out by the Army for Indian unruliness provoked by its own men, which in the absence of other narratives, has by default taken its place as the earliest chapter in Alaska's history under United States rule. Colyer gathered his information from Army, customs and medical personnel, traders and Indian chiefs themselves, and reached the inescapable conclusion that second only to "hooch" as a cause of Indian hostility, was the arrogant stupidity of the military forces in charge. Army philosophy held that the best way to rectify an error was to compound it.

Such thinking set off a widening circle of reprisals between Indians and whites, that smoldered on for many years. It began with an insult to a proud Chilkat chief named Colcheka. Colcheka visited Sitka from the Chilkat village of Klukwan. When William Seward visited Alaska, he and Klukwan's ranking chief, Shotridge (Chartridge, Shathitch, Kloh-Kutz) had fêted Seward, General Davis, and Professor George Davidson of the United States

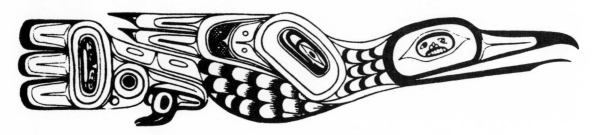

Coast and Geodetic Survey. Colcheka was, in other words, no unknown savage, but a sub-chief of sufficient rank to receive the man who as United States Secretary of State had promoted the Alaskan purchase.

"The Kake War arose out of a pure case of drunkenness," said Sitka's Customs Collector William Dodge. As Colcheka left "General Davis's house" where he had been "potlatched to a bottle of whisky," a soldier kicked him. Colcheka grabbed the soldier's gun. A ruckus arose. Colcheka fled to the Ranche. The general issued an order restricting all Indians to the Ranche until Colcheka surrendered, which he did the following day. The matter was deemed settled and the restriction on movement was rescinded.

"The post commander, who was drunk," said Dodge, "did not promulgate the order. . . . the next morning a canoe with some Indians started to leave the village to go wood-chopping, and the sentry on the wharf killed two of them [a Kake and a Chilkat]. I do not know if the military reports of General Davis detailed these facts as I have stated them," Dodge said, "but the officer responsible boasts 'that there is not power enough to dismiss him from the army.'"

In revenge, the Kakes killed two chance prospectors. To avenge the killing of the two white men, General Davis ordered an armed force to proceed aboard the U.S.S. *Saginaw* to Kake Island, where they bombarded and destroyed the sixteen houses of Old Kake Village and two other villages of the Kake quan of the Tlingit. In his report General Davis did not mention the shelling, only that the *Saginaw* "rendered all the assistance which I desired." Nor did he say he had destroyed the Kake's winter food supply and their canoes, their only transportation.

The post-trader at Sitka, Frank K. Louthan, understood Tlingit concepts of justice far better than General Davis. "The failure to promptly pay for a real or supposed injury is at once the signal for retaliation," he told Colyer. For the Kake Indian killed by the the sentry, "The Kakes very promptly sought the usual remedy, 'an eye for an eye, a tooth for a tooth'; Meeting two white men near their village, promptly dispatched them and thereby lost all of their village, burned by order of the general commanding.

"I can but look with great favor upon the system on the part of the government adapting itself to the one idea of 'immediate settlement' with their people for

all wrongs of magnitude, (whether on the part of the military or the individual) entirely upon estimated value. This is the time-honored custom of the red man in Alaska."

The destruction of the village was supposed to have ended the so-called Kake War. Yet five months afterwards, Louthan told Colyer, "No coast or interior Indian appeared among us, to the great detriment of trade, the Chilkats especially keeping themselves aloof from us all winter."

Finally, Louthan himself took on the responsibility of settling the Army's badly managed affairs:

"Well knowing the chief and most of his people, I determined to pay them a visit for purpose of trade and to restore friendly relations. First, a small schooner reached their village in May last, and found them sullen and listless. . . . At the end of the fourth day our little vessel was suddenly boarded by about seventy-five well-armed men, bent on satisfaction either in property or life, for the man killed at Sitka nearly five months previous. The exigencies of my situation required prompt and immediate action. . . . I stepped out among them with my interpreter, an Indian, and whilst protesting against their wish that I should pay for what had been done by our military chief at Sitka, satisfied them by giving them a letter to the general commanding, asking him, for the sake of trade and security to life, to pay for the man killed, giving my promise to the Indians to pay for the dead man if the general refused.

"The general refused to listen to the delegation waiting on him with my letter.

I returned with my vessel again to Sitka and to Chilkaht, when I promptly paid the price asked—thirteen blankets and one coat, amounting in value, all told, to about fifty dollars, coin. I feel quite sure that in this simple settlement I arrested serious trouble to myself and probably to the government."

In the laconic reports of Davis and the other military and naval men who

"governed" Alaska in these early days—reports now filed away by document numbers in thick volumes comprising United States congressional archives, there is no evidence to suggest acceptance of indemnity payments for wrongs, real or imagined. The military, and the Navy afterwards, held to force as a punishment, administering bombardments like righteous spankings, despite the proven contention of Louthan and all other students of the Tlingit that prompt material settlement of wrongs or injuries "will always keep the Indian peaceable and friendly."

The Indian village of Wrangell also met the fate of bombardment, stemming from an incident originating with "the vile hoochenoo." The Army's report is a model of brevity:

> Post Hospital, Fort Wrangel,
> Wrangel Island, Alaska Territory,
> December 29, 1869
>
> Sir: I have the honor to report as the result of the late Indian trouble:
>
> One (1) white man, Mr. Leon Smith, killed.
> One (1) Indian killed.
> One (1) white woman, company laundress, finger bitten off.
> One (1) Indian severely wounded, by gunshot fracture of the right humerus.
> One (1) Indian hung.
>
> H. M. Kirke,
> Acting Assistant Surgeon
> United States Army,
> In charge of Post Hospital

Rumors and reports filtering back to Washington raised no blood pressure in Congress. It may safely be said that Colyer's documentary on these early years has subsequently received far more attention from outraged historians than ever it got from his congressional contemporaries.

Ten years passed before another special agent was dispatched to check on the nation's custom district of Alaska. Like Colyer, William Gouverneur Morris emphasized the urgent need for a civil government, proper patrol ships, and the replacement by a licensing system of the prohibition on liquor, a ban that was openly violated, and even worse, stimulated the manufacture of hoochinoo from molasses, the import of which was not prohibited.

Morris offered to present Alaska's plight to Congress. Secretary John Sherman, into whose Treasury poured over a quarter million dollars annual seal fishery royalties wrote back, "I have given the subject-matter of your letter due consideration and can see no practical good to be accomplished by your personal visit."

The government finally recognized the absurdity of trying to patrol a 26,000 mile coastline with land-bound soldiers at Sitka, Wrangell and other island posts. Withdrawal of the military in 1877 brought home to the less than five hundred white residents of Alaska that no semblance of government or show of force protected them from some seven thousand Tlingit and Haida. They looked with alarm on what they regarded as a precarious position, their anxiety generated in part by a sense of guilt over the many abuses inflicted on the native population.

Katlean, descendent of the Chief Katlean who led the Sitka Tlingit against Baranov's fort at New Archangel, vowed vengence for the burning of Old Kake and other outrages. He was opposed by another chief, Annahootz, who defeated him before arrival of a United States warship.

The white population were nevertheless certain that they would be massacred to a man, and were relieved beyond measure when H.M.S. *Osprey* answered their pleas and arrived from British Columbia to protect them until their own government could be persuaded to send help.

The American ship finally stationed in Alaskan waters to begin the five-year period known as "Navy rule," was the U.S.S. *Jamestown* under command of Captain L. A. Beardslee, who, upon his arrival in June of 1879, began directing his capable energies to improving the demoralized situation.

"I do not believe that, uninflamed by drink, the Indians would assault the whites, but they will be crazy with rum (and that they will so be is almost entirely due to the fault of our government)," he wrote the Secretary of the Navy.

"There is absolutely no danger to the settlement at the present time. In fall, when the hunters and fishermen return, there will be; their return will be celebrated by a series of 'pot-a-latches' (tremendous drunks), which will culminate, unless precautions are taken to keep them under control, in a very probable assault upon the settlement, as the grudge excited by the events of last winter is as yet a cause for anticipation of trouble."

Beardslee's answer was to appoint as native policemen Annahootz, Sitka Jack, and eventually even the troublemaker Katlean, all of whom "control large numbers, responsible for the preservation of order and peace."

"However pure may have been the motives of most of those who called for protection," observed Beardslee, "I am fully convinced that some of them valued at a far higher figure this ship as a means of money-making, through our disbursements of several thousand dollars monthly, than they do for the protection she affords."

Like Colyer and Morris before him, Beardslee urged the government in Washington to provide Alaska with a government, primarily to provide order among the white population, and a court of law with powers to arrest and punish crime. As before, the recommendation went unheeded. A new element stepped into the void. It was small in numbers, but its presence was as influential in molding internal Alaskan life as was the influence exercised by the California seal monopoly.

A first inkling of this revolutionizing force appeared in the Puget Sound *Argus* of November 1877, which carried the plea of three of the Stikine chiefs, Shakes, Toyatte and Shustaks, the same trio whose truculence ten years before brought bombardment of their village at Wrangell:

"For many years we have been desirous of having schools and churches established among us. With the coming of the military among us came a big church 'tyhee,' who told us that the soldiers were come to protect us, and that he would have schools established and churches built for us. Time passed; no schools were established and no churches built, and, instead of soldiers being any protection to us, they sought to debase and demoralize us. Liquor they sold us that crazed the brain. . . ."

The *Argus* correspondent was Wrangell's deputy customs collector, I. C. Dennis. "Our Indians here are not a band of cut-throats and pirates that require bayonets and brass guns to keep them in subjugation," Dennis wrote.

"Here at Wrangel, the Indians, although greatly demoralized, are somewhat civilized, and after many efforts a school has been established on a permanent basis at this place. The Presbyterian Board of Missions having taken the matter in hand, a lady by the name of McFarland has been sent here, and she has now a daily attendance at school of about sixty Indians, old and young, most of whom have mastered the alphabet and many of whom can read sentences composed of words of one syllable."

The "lady by the name of McFarland" was brought to Wrangell on August 10, 1877, by the Reverend Sheldon Jackson, another of the larger-than-life figures whose crucial role at a critical moment helped shape Alaska's destiny. Armanda McFarland was a missionary who, until her husband's death the preceding year, had worked among the Indians of the West. Sheldon Jackson was the Presbyterian Superintendent of Missions for the Western States who heeded the pleas of native Alaskans and whose name, even today, is synonymous with education in the state.

Awaiting Jackson and Mrs. McFarland at Fort Wrangell was a third re-markable person, a Tsimshian Indian named Clah who had migrated north from Fort Simpson. Known also by his Christian name, Philip McKay, Clah had with seven other Tsimshian Indians begun the nucleus of a mission, the first in Tlingit territory.

Jackson left Mrs. McFarland in charge of the school as teacher. He returned to the States to raise funds and recruit graduates from theological seminaries for missionary work in Alaska. Reverend S. Hall Young came the next year to head the mission at Wrangell, and Reverend John G. Brady took the post at Sitka, remaining on in Alaska to become, some twenty years later, the territory's fifth governor.

Until his premature death from tu-

Portrait of young Chief Shakes painted during the period of Russian rule

berculosis the next year, Clah was Mrs. McFarland's assistant. A Christian Tongass Indian named Mrs. Sarah Dickinson served the mission school as interpreter. Mrs. Dickinson "was a hundred miles up the Stickeen River gathering her winter supply of berries," Jackson wrote. "Learning from a passing steamer that the missionaries had come, she placed her children, bedding, and provisions in her canoe, and paddled home, against heavy head winds, to give us a welcome." Three years later she went among the Chilkats to found the mission at Haines.

As she built the day school at Wrangell, simultaneously laying plans for a girls' boarding school, Mrs. McFarland kept Jackson advised of her progress in bringing the village Indians into the church.

"Dear Brother," she wrote, "I went into the school room the morning after you left. . . . It now averages thirty scholars. I have had as high as thirty-eight some days. They all seem very anxious to learn. . . . They study reading, spelling, geography and writing. I go at nine o'clock and remain until one. Then Clah has a short session in the afternoon. I am teaching the whole school the multiplication table in unison. . . .

"Several chiefs have been to see me. They are all very anxious to have a 'white man preacher come,' and to have a 'church house like Fort Simpson.'

"Our school-room has been rented for a dance house, and will be taken from us by the 15th of the month. . . ."

"Dear Brother," Mrs. McFarland wrote in January, "Although we have commenced a new year, we feel sadly broken up and discouraged, for God has taken away our beloved Philip [Clah]. He passed away very peacefully, on Friday, December 28, 1877.

"I went up to see him on Thursday. He talked very cheerfully. Said he thought he had only a few hours to live. I asked him how death seemed to him. He replied, 'As earth fades away, heaven grows brighter.'

"My school is very full. . . ."

"I am rejoiced to report that we are back with the school and church into the dance-house. The dance business did not seem to be profitable, so they closed the house. . . .

"I must describe to you how the natives observed Christmas. Between twelve and one o'clock Christmas morning I was awakened by hearing persons coming up to my house. I arose, and from my window saw about sixty of my Indians standing in a double row in front of my house, with their lanterns and umbrellas, for it was raining heavily. Just as I looked out they commenced singing, 'While shepherds watched their flocks by night.' They sung that and another hymn, and then went quietly away. . . . About nine o'clock in the morning I saw a large procession filing into my yard. First came the son of one of our prominent men, a boy about thirteen, carrying a large British flag. Perhaps some Sabbath-school class of boys would be willing to present our mission with an American flag, the Stars and Stripes. Next came the Christian chief, Toy-a-att. Then came all the leading men; then their wives, then my school. They walked in single file. I stood in my door, and as they walked past each one shook hands with me and wished me 'A Merry Christmas.' The old chief took my hand and said, 'A Merry Christmas,' and 'God bless you, dear teacher,' and, much to my surprise, leaned forward and kissed me on the cheek."

Despite Mrs. McFarland's civilizing influence, trouble boiled over during the Christmas holiday. As reported in the *Argus*, "One John Petelin, a Russian, and distiller of poison, sold to an Indian some of his manufacture, which caused a drunken row in the ranch and in which several Indians got seriously hurt. . . . Consequently the church party [Indians] concluded it was time to make an example of somebody in order to convince white men that whisky-selling by them to Indians would be no longer tolerated. A score of Indians therefore marched to the Russian's house, seized his 'still' and liquor, and with him in custody started for the ranch. Arriving at Toy-ah-att's residence a council was held, and the decision was that the Russian should be tied to a post for one hour. This sentence was carried out, and the culprit's 'still' and 'mash-tub' were placed alongside of him, that all passers-by might know why such punishment was inflicted. A portion of our white population (those who hesitate not in violating the laws of the country) set up an ignominious howl over the occurrence, claiming that if Indians were permitted and tolerated to perpetrate acts like this they would become emboldened, and no white man would be safe. Many talked loudly of marching to the rescue of the Russian while under sentence, but, as is generally the case, talk was cheap, and none cared to act. Others, who are possessed with more brass than brains, commenced defining other men's duties, never once considering that their duties, as law-abiding citizens, demand that they shall discountenance and endeavor to suppress the liquor traffic in Alaska. And, again, there were a few of another class, of the 'cut and shoot' stamp, who howled loudly of individual rights and self-protection. . . . Here, law-makers of Washington, was a scene to be carefully considered by you.

Here were three hundred white men greatly agitated over an act perpetrated by a few law-abiding Indians!"

In a final effort to bring order out of the unholy chaos at Wrangell, several hundred white citizens and Indians convened for a constitutional convention. "The school-house was packed full," Mrs. McFarland wrote Jackson. The rules of conduct which were adopted have long since faded away. But the great speech made by Chief Toyatte, addressed pointedly to the white members of the crowded audience, has lived on:

"My Brothers and Friends: I come before you today to talk a little, and I hope that you will listen to what I say, and not laugh at me because I am an Indian. I am getting old and have not many summers yet to live on this earth. . . . In ages past, before white men came among us, the Indians of Alaska were barbarous, with brutish instincts. Tribal wars were continual, bloodshed and murder of daily occurrence, and superstition controlled our whole movements and our hearts. The white man's God we knew not of. Nature showed to us that there was a first great cause; beyond that all was blank. Our god was created by us; that is, we selected animals and birds, the images of which we revered as gods.

"Natural instincts taught us to supply our wants from that which we beheld around us. If we wanted food, the waters gave us fish; and if we wanted raiment, the wild animals of the woods gave us skins, which we converted to us. Implements of warfare and tools to work with we constructed rudely from stone and wood. These we used in the place of the saws, axes, hammers, guns and knives of the present time. Fire we discovered by friction.

"In the course of time a change came over the spirit of our dreams. We became aware of the fact that we were not the only beings in the shape of man that inhabited this earth. White men appeared before us on the surface of the great waters in large ships which we called canoes. Where they came from we knew not, but supposed that they dropped from the clouds. The ship's sails we took for wings, and concluded that, like the birds of the air, they could fly as well as swim. As time advanced, the white men who visited our country introduced among us every thing that is produced by nature and the arts of man. They also told us of a God, a superior being, who created all things, even us the Indians . . . and that all mankind were His children. . . . We are not the same people that we were a hundred years ago. Contact and association with the white man have created a change in our habits and customs. We have seen and heard of the wonderful works of the white man. His ingenuity and skill have produced steamships, railroads, telegraphs and thousands of other things. His mind is far-reaching; whatever he desires he produces. His wonderful sciences enable him to understand nature and her laws. Whatever she produces he improves upon and makes useful.

"Each day the white man becomes more perfect in the arts and sciences, while the Indian is at a stand-still. Why is this? Is it because the God you have told us of is a white God, and that you, being of His color, have been favored by Him?

"Why, brothers, look at our skin; we are dark, we are not of your color, hence you call us Indians. Is this the reason that we are ignorant; is this the cause of our not knowing our Creator?

"My brothers, a change is coming. We have seen and heard of the wonderful things of this world, and we desire to understand what we see and what we hear. We desire light. We want our eyes to become open. We have been in the dark too long, and we appeal to you, my brothers, to help us.

"But how can this be done? Listen to me. Although I have been a bad Indian, I can see the right road and I desire to follow it. I have changed for the better. I have done away with all Indian superstitious habits. I am in my old age becoming civilized. I have learned to know Jesus and I desire to know more of Him. I de-sire education, in order that I may be able to read the Holy Bible. . . .

"We have been told that the President of the United States has control over all the people, both whites and Indians. We have been told how he came to be our great chief. He purchased this country from Russia, and in purchasing it he purchased us. We had no choice or say in change of masters. The change has been made and we are content. All we ask is justice.

"We ask of our father at Washington that we be recognized as a people. . . .

"We ask that we be civilized, Christianized and educated. . . . And now, my brothers, to you I appeal. Help us in our efforts to do right. If you don't want to come to our church, don't laugh and make fun of us because we sing and pray.

"Many of you have Indian women living with you. I ask you to send them to school and church, where, they will learn to become good women. Don't, my

brothers, let them go to the dance-houses, for there they will learn to be bad and learn to drink whisky.

"Now that I see you are getting tired of listening to me, I will finish by asking you again to help us in trying to do right. If one of us should be led astray from the right path, point out to us our error and assist us in trying to reform. If you will all assist us in doing good and quit selling whisky, we will soon make Fort Wrangell a quiet place, and the Stickeen Indians will become a happy people. I now thank you all for your kind attention. Good-by."

Toyatte's plea, too, went unheeded. Before the next year was out, he was dead. He was shot by a member of the neighboring Hootznahoo Tlingit as he stood, unarmed, before his own Stikine warriors, trying to settle peacefully a conflict that arose over the manufacture of hoochinoo. The long-forgotten stone marking his grave is overgrown by brush in the abandoned native graveyard at Shustaks Point outside Wrangell.

The famous naturalist, John Muir, wrote of this Stikine chief, "In all his gestures, and in the language in which he expressed himself, there was a noble simplicity and earnestness and majestic bearing which made the sermons and behavior of the three distinguished divinity doctors present seem commonplace in comparison."

Having heard of Alaska's great natural beauty, Muir came up on the steamer in 1879 to explore glaciers, many of which he discovered and named. Muir chose Toyatte for his guide, "not only because he owned the canoe, but for his

skill in woodcraft and seamanship." Replicas of totem poles carved by this wise and gentle man, stand today at Wrangell.

Reverend Young seized the opportunity to accompany Muir on a journey that would permit him to bring God's message to remote Tlingit villages. Muir was more interested in their pagan ways.

"I greatly enjoyed the Indian's campfire talk on their ancient customs," Muir wrote, "how they were taught by their parents ere the whites came among them, their religion, ideas connected with the next world, the stars, plants, the behavior and language of animals. When our talk was interrupted by the howling of a wolf, Kadachan puzzled the minister with the question, 'Have wolves souls?' The Indians believe that they have, giving as foundation for their belief that they are wise creatures who know how to catch seals and salmon by swimming slyly upon them with their heads hidden in a mouthful of grass, hunt deer in company, and always bring forth their young at the same and most favorable time of the year. I inquired how it was that with enemies so wise and powerful the deer were not all killed. Kadachan replied that wolves knew better than to kill them all and thus cut off their most important food supply.

"We arrived at one of the Kupreanof Kake villages, just as a funeral party was breaking up. The body had been burned and gifts were being distributed—bits of calico, handkerchiefs, blankets, etc., according to the rank and wealth of the deceased. The death ceremonies of chiefs and head men, Mr. Young told me, are very weird and imposing, with wild feasting, dancing, and singing. At this little place there are some eight totem poles of bold and intricate design, well executed, but smaller than those of the Stikeens. As elsewhere throughout the archipelago, the bear, raven, eagle, salmon, and porpoise are the chief figures. Some of the poles have square cavities, mortised into the back, which are said to contain the ashes of members of the family. These recesses are closed by a plug. I noticed one that was calked with a rag where the joint was imperfect.

"It was at the northmost of the Kupreanof Kake villages that Mr. Young held his first missionary meeting, singing hymns, praying, and preaching. . . . Neither here nor in any of the other villages of the different tribes that we visited was there anything like a distinct refusal to receive school teachers or ministers. On the contrary, with but one or two exceptions, all with apparent good faith declared their willingness to receive them. . . .

"At a Hootznahoo village on Admiralty Island," said Muir, "Men, women, and children made haste to the beach to meet us, the children staring as if they had never before seen a Boston man. The chief, a remarkably good-looking and intelligent fellow, stepped forward, shook hands with us Boston fashion, and invited us to his house."

The next morning as they made their way toward the main village of Killisnoo (Angoon), "We heard sounds I had never before heard—a storm of strange howls, yells, and screams rising from a base of gasping, bellowing grunts and groans. Had I been alone, I should have fled as from a pack of fiends, but our Indians quietly recognized this awful sound, if such stuff could be called sound, simply as the 'whisky howl' and pushed quietly on . . . As for preaching one might as well try to preach in Tophet. The whole village was afire with bad whisky. This was the first time in my life that I learned the meaning of the phrase of 'a howling drunk.' "

Muir and Young landed and "cautiously strolled up the hill to the main row of houses, now a chain of alcoholic

volcanoes." Here and there a few blackened faces appeared in the round doorways. Some of the Indians ventured out to stare and to call their companions "and we began to fear that like the Alloway Kirk witches the whole legion was about to sally forth. But instead, those outside suddenly crawled and tumbled in again. We were thus allowed to take a general view of the place and return to our canoes unmolested."

"On the south side of Icy Strait," continued Muir, "we ran into a picturesque bay to visit the main village of the Hoona tribe. . . . While we were yet half a mile off, we saw a flag unfurled on a tall mast in front of the chief's house. Toy-a-tte hoisted his United States flag in reply, and thus arrayed we made for the landing. Here we were met and received by the chief, Kashoto, who stood close to the water's edge, barefooted and bareheaded, but wearing so fine a robe and standing so grave, erect, and serene, his dignity was complete."

"The climax of the trip, so far as the missionary interests were concerned," wrote the Reverend Young, "was our visit to the Chilcat and Chilcoot natives on Lynn Canal, the most northern tribes of the Alexandrian Archipelago. Here reigned the proudest and worst old savage of Alaska, Chief Shathitch. His wealth was very great in Indian treasures, and he was reputed to have cached away in different places several houses full of blankets, guns, boxes of beads, ancient carved pipes, spears, knives and other valued heirlooms. He was said to have stored away over one hundred of the elegant Chilcat blankets woven by hand from the hair of the mountain goat. His tribe was rich and unscrupulous. Its members were the middle-men between the whites and the Indians of the Interior. They did not allow these Indians to come to the coast, but took over the mountain articles purchased from the whites—guns, ammunition, blankets, knives and so forth—and bartered them for furs. It was said that they claimed to be the manufacturers of these wares and so charged for them what prices they pleased. They had these Indians of the Interior in a bondage of fear, and would not allow them to trade directly with the white men. Thus they carried out literally the story told of Hudson Bay traffic,—piling beaver skins to the height of a ten-dollar Hudson Bay musket as the price of the musket. They were the most quarrelsome and warlike of the tribes of Alaska, and their villages were full of slaves procured by forays upon the coasts of Vancouver Island, Puget Sound, and as far south as the mouth of the Columbia River. I was eager to visit these large and untaught tribes, and establish a mission among them.

"About the first of November we came in sight of the long, low-built village of Yin-des-tuk-ki. As we paddled up the winding channel of the Chilcat River we saw great excitement in the town. We had hoisted the American flag, as was our custom, and had put on our best apparel for the occasion. When we got within long musket-shot of the village we saw the native men come rushing from their houses with their guns in their hands and mass in front of the largest house upon the beach. Then we were greeted by what seemed rather too warm a reception—a shower of bullets falling unpleasantly around us. Instinctively Muir and I ceased to paddle, but Tow-a-att commanded, 'Ut-ha-, ut-ha! pull, pull!' and slowly, amid dropping bullets, we zigzagged our way up the channel towards the village. As we drew near the shore a line of runners extended down the beach to us, keeping within shouting distance of each other. Then came the questions like bullets—'Gusu-wa-eh? —Who are you? Whence do you come? What is your business here?' and Stickeen John shouted back the reply:

"'A great preacher-chief and a great ice-chief have come to bring you a good message.'

"The answer was shouted back along the line, and then returned a message of greeting and welcome. We were to be the guests of the chief of Yin-des-tuk-ki, old Don-na-wuk (Silver Eye), so called because he was in the habit of wearing on all state occasions a huge pair of silver-bowed spectacles which a Russian officer had given him. He confessed he could not see through them, but thought they lent dignity to his countenance. We paddled slowly up to the village, and Muir and I, watching with interest, saw the warriors all disappear. As our prow touched the sand, however, here they came, forty or fifty of them, without their guns this time, but charging down upon us with war-cries, 'Hoo-hooh, hoo-hooh,' as if they were going to take us prisoners. Dashing into the water they ranged themselves along each side of the canoe; then lifting up our canoe with us in it they rushed with excited cries up the bank to the chief's house and set us down at his door. It was the Thlinget way of paying us honor as great guests.

"Then we were solemnly ushered into the presence of Don-na-wuk. His house was large, covering about fifty by sixty feet of ground. The interior was built in the usual fashion of a chief's house—carved corner posts . . . a platform of some six feet in width running clear around

the room . . . and a high platform, where the chieftain's household goods were stowed. . . . A brisk fire was burning in the middle of the room; and after a short palaver, with gifts of tobacco and rice to the chief, it was announced that he would pay us the distinguished honor of feasting us first.

"It was a never-to-be-forgotten banquet . . . before Muir and me were placed huge washbowls of blue Hudson Bay ware,

Before each of our native attendants was placed a great carved wooden trough. . . . We had learned enough of Indian etiquette to know that at each course our respective vessels were to be filled full of food, and we were expected to carry off what we could not devour. It was indeed a 'feast of fat things.' The first course was what, for the Indian, takes the place of bread among the whites,—dried salmon. It was served, a whole washbowlful for each of us, with a dressing of seal-grease. Muir and I adroitly manoeuvred so as to get our salmon and seal-grease served separately; for our stomachs had not been sufficiently trained to endure that rancid grease. This course finished, what was left was dumped into receptacles in our canoe and guarded from the dogs by young men especially appointed for that purpose. Our washbowls were cleansed and the second course brought on. This consisted of the back fat of the deer, great, long hunks of it, served with a gravy of seal-grease. The third course was little Russian potatoes about the size of walnuts, dished out to us, a washbowlful, with a dressing of seal-grease. The final course was the only berry then in season, the long fleshy apple of the wild rose mellowed with frost, served to us in the usual quantity with the invariable sauce of seal-grease.

"'Mon, mon!' said Muir aside to me, 'I'm fashed we'll be floppin' aboot i' the sea, whiles, wi' flippers an' forked tails.'

"When we had partaken of as much of this feast of fat things as our civilized stomachs would stand, it was suddenly announced that we were about to receive a visit from the great chief of the Chilcats and the Chilcoots, old Chief Shathitch (Hard-to-Kill). In order to properly receive His Majesty, Muir and I and our two chiefs were each given a whole bale of Hudson Bay blankets for a couch. Shathitch made us wait a long time, doubtless to impress us with his dignity as supreme chief.

"The heat of the fire after the wind and cold of the day made us very drowsy. We fought off sleep, however, and at last in came stalking the biggest chief of all Alaska, clothed in his robe of state, which was an elegant chinchilla blanket; and upon its yellow surface, as the chief slowly turned about to show us what was written thereon, we were astonished to see printed in black letters these words. 'To Chief Shathitch, from his friend, William H. Seward!'"

Here, to an enormous gathering of the Chilkat-Tlingit, Young delivered his Christian message, spelled by Toyatte,

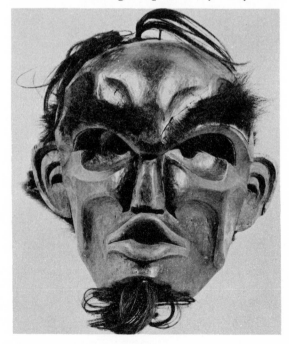

Kadachan and even the "ice-chief" when Young's voice ran out.

"At the last meeting," Muir wrote, an old white-haired shaman of grave and venerable aspect, with a high wrinkled forehead, big, strong Roman nose and light-colored skin, slowly and with great dignity arose and spoke for the first time.

"'I am an old man,' he said, 'but I am glad to listen to those strange things you tell, and they may well be true, for what is more wonderful than the flight of birds in the air? I remember the first white man I ever saw. Since that long, long-ago time I have seen many, but never until now have I ever truly known and felt a white man's heart. All the white men I have heretofore met wanted to get something from us. They wanted furs and they wished to pay for them as small a price as possible. They all seemed to be seeking their own good—not our good. I might say that through all my long life I have never until now heard a white man speak. It has always seemed to me while trying to speak to traders and those seeking gold-mines that it was like speaking to a person across a broad stream that was running fast over stones and making so loud a noise that scarce a single word could be heard. But now, for the first time, the Indian and the white man are on the same side of the river, eye to eye, heart to heart. I have always loved my people. I have taught them and ministered to them as well as I could. Hereafter, I will keep silent and listen to the good words of the missionaries, who know God and the places we go to when we die so much better than I do.'"

More typically, shamans obstructed ef-

forts to replace native customs with the circumspect garb of Christianity. Veniaminov had regarded the shaman, or medicine man, as the primary perpetuator of ignorance, superstition and savagery, and felt a possible positive aspect of the smallpox epidemic had been the value of innoculation in undermining the Indians' faith in their power.

Among the generation of chiefs in power at the time of the purchase, only some accepted the new way. Said old Chief Shakes at Wrangell, "I am too old to learn a new religion, and besides, many of my people who have died were bad and foolish people, and if this word the missionary has brought us is true, and I think it is, many of my people must be in that bad country the missionary calls 'Hell,' and I must go there also, for a Stickeen chief never deserts his people in time of trouble."

When Shakes died, he lay in state surrounded by the ceremonial regalia of his high office. "On Saturday they sent for me to decide whether they should burn or bury the body," Mrs. McFarland wrote Jackson. "Of course I decided that it was better to bury it. . . . On Sabbath they sent for me to take charge of the funeral, saying 'they wanted me to come and pray like white people.' . . . They seemed very much pleased. None of Shakes' people have ever attended church."

Although Chief Shustaks turned his back on the mission, he sent his daughter to Mrs. McFarland, saying that he "was a wicked old man, but he wanted his little girl to be good. . . ."

"On Saturday," she wrote, "I talked with the new chief, Shakes' brother. He promised me that he would attend church." Of the three generations, one remained with the past. One was propelled into the future. The middle man, in transition, had a place in neither.

By the mid-1880's, a varied and articulate stream of visitors began taking the Pacific Coast Steamship Company's "elegant steamers" up from San Francisco or Portland. Round-trip fare including berth and meals came to $135. Easterners who took advantage of excursion rates on the Northern Pacific Railroad, traveling in parties of ten at $165 per head, from St. Paul, Minneapolis, Duluth, Superior, or Fargo to Portland, saved forty dollars on the fare to Sitka.

Books and articles of the more observant helped dispel some of the acid ignorance about Seward's "ice box," his "polar bear treaty," the watery waste, a northern land of perennial ice and snow. An Alaskan chaffing under these indignities told one author, "If those Senators and Congressmen don't know any more about the tariff, and the other things they help to discuss, than they do about Alaska, the Lord help the rest of the United States." In the absence of more orderly methods of collecting data, the travel narratives of the eighties and nineties—like those of the first visitors to the Northwest Coast—preserve valuable glimpses into the swift acculturation overtaking traditional native life.

If the military and naval authorities saw the Indians as bad children—and the missionaries regarded them as pagan souls to be saved—the deck-chair tourists looked upon them as curiosities. By 1886 these excursions were so popular that the steamship company doubled its service during summer to accommodate the new segment of frontier America who could visit exotic, faraway places as sightseers instead of as pioneers.

Shortly after crossing the famous 54 degrees 40 minutes boundary in Dixon Entrance, the steamer put in at Tongass to look at the salmon cannery owned by Astoria packers and to bargain with the Tongass Tlingit who caught and packed the firm, shining fish.

"Owing to the good salmon season and the steady employment given them at the cannery, the Indians held their things so high that even the most insatiate and abandoned curio-buyers made no purchases, although there has been regret ever since at the thought of the wide old bracelets and the finely-woven hats that they let escape them."

With this amused observation Eliza Ruhamah Scidmore, an irreverent but astute writer for the St. Louis *Globe Demo-*

crat, the *New York Times* and other journals, took note of two powerful elements that were wooing the Indian away from his past—commercial fishing and the bottomless new market for his handcraft. Miss Scidmore became a veteran traveler on the steamer, took the 1890 census in southeastern Alaska, and later published a guide book that remains serviceable to this day. In 1883 she was among one of the earliest boatloads of tourists and in her *Journeys to Alaska* gives an astringent appraisal of both the visitor and visited, backed by the lore and knowledge of the day.

"The thrifty Siwash, which is the generic and common name for these people, and a corruption of the old French voyagers *sauvage,*" wrote Miss Scidmore, "keeps his valuables stored in heavy cedar chests. . . . At the first sound of the steamer's paddle-wheels—and they can be heard for miles in these fiords,—the Indians rummage their houses and chests and sort out their valuable things, and when the first ardent curio-seeker rushed through the packing houses and out toward the bark huts, their wares were all displayed. The Haida are famous as the best carvers, silversmiths, and workers on the coast; and there are some of their best artists in this little band on Kasa-an Bay. An old blind man, with a battered hat on his head and a dirty white blanket wrapped around him, sat before one bark hut, with a large wooden bowl filled with carved spoons made from the horns of the mountain goat. These spoons, once in common use among all these people, are now disappearing, as the rage for the tin and pewter utensils in the traders' stores increases, although many of them have the handles polished and the bowls worn by the daily usage of generations. The horn is naturally black, and constant handling and soaking in seal oil gives them a jetty lustre that adds much to the really fine carvings on the handles.

"Silver bracelets pounded out of coin, and ornamented with traceries and chasings by the hand of 'Kasa-an John,' the famous jeweller of the tribe, were the pieces eagerly sought and contended for by the ladies. The bangle mania rages among the Haida maids and matrons as fiercely as on civilized shores, and dusky wrists were outstretched on which from three to nine bracelets lay in shining lines like jointed mail. Anciently they pounded a single heavy bracelet from a silver dollar piece, and ornamented the broad two-inch band with heraldic carvings of the crow, the bear, the raven, the whale, and other emblematic beasts of their strangely mixed mythology. Latterly they have become corrupted by civilized fashions, and they have taken to narrow bands, hammered from half dollars and carved with scrolls, conventional eagles copied from coins, and geometrical designs.

"In one house an enlightened and non-skeptical Indian was driving sharp bargains in the sale of medicine-men's rattles and charms, and kindred relics of a departed faith. His scoffing and irreverent air would have made his ancestors' dust shake, but he pocketed the chickamin, or money, without even a superstitious shudder.

"The amateur curio-buyers found themselves worsted and outgeneralled on every side in this rich market of Kasa-an

by a Juneau trader, who gathered up the things by wholesale, and, carrying them on board, disposed of them at a stupendous advance.

"Dance blankets from the white, and yellow wool, spun from the fleece of the mountain goat, was paraded by the anxious owners, and the strangers elbowed one another, stepped on the dogs, and rubbed the oil from the dripping salmon overhead in the smoky huts, in order to see and buy all of these things."

In the few short years that had seen the defiant town of Wrangell yield to Mrs. McFarland and mining enthusiasm shift from the Cassier to Juneau, Wrangell had blossomed and gone dead. "The 'miners' Palace Restaurant, and other high sounding signs, remain as relics of the livelier days, and listless Indian women sit in rows and groups on the unpainted porches of the trading stores. They are a quiet, rather languid lot of klootchmans," siad journalist Scidmore, "slow and deliberate of speech, and not at all glamorous for customers, as they squat or lie face downward, like so many seals, before their baskets of wild berries. In the stores, the curio departments are well stocked with elaborately carved spoons made of the black horns of the mountain goat; with curiously fashioned halibut hooks and halibut clubs; with carved wooden trays and bowls, in which oil, fish, berries, and food have been mixed for years. . . .

"The houses of the Indian village string along the beach in a disconnected way, all of them low and square, built of rough hewn cedar and pine planks, and roofed over with large planks resting on heavy log beams. . . . Heraldic devices in outline sometimes ornament the gable front of the house, but no paint is wasted on the interior, where smoke darkens everything. . . . Before many of the houses are tall cedar posts and poles, carved with faces of men and beasts, representing events in their genealogy and mythology. These tall totems are the shrines and show places of Fort Wrangell, and on seeing them all the ship's company made the hopeless plunge into Tlingit mythology and there floundered aimlessly until the end of the trip."

On this subject, Miss Scidmore issued a warning made by other lay students of Tlingit lore. "There is nothing more flexible or susceptible of interpretations than Indian traditions, and the Siwash himself enjoys nothing so much as misleading and fooling the curious white man in these matters," she wrote. "The truth about these totems and their carvings never will be quite known until their innate humor is civilized out of the natives, but meanwhile the white man vexes himself with ethnological theories and suppositions."

At Sitka tourists of the day met one of the most enterprising Indian characters in all of southeastern Alaska, a commercial phenomenon named Mrs. Tom, "a character, a celebrity, and a person of great authority among her Siwash neighbors. . . . Even savage people bow down to wealth," noted Miss Scidmore, "and Mrs. Tom is the reputed possessor of $10,-000, accumulated by her own energy and shrewdness. . . . Like all the Indians she puts her faith mostly in blankets, and her house is a magazine of such units of currency, while deep in her cedar boxes she has fur robes of the rarest quality.

"Mrs. Tom has acquired her fortune by her own ability in legitimate trade, and each spring and fall she loads up her long canoe and goes off on a great journey through the islands, trading with her people. On her return she trades with the traders of Sitka, and always comes out with a fine profit."

Fifteen years later a prospering Princess Tom was again encountered by Miss Scidmore who blasted the myth built up during the intervening years. In her remarkably comprehensive guide for Appleton in 1899, she wrote, "Mrs. Tom, who is not a princess, but of commonest Yakutat stock and of an inferior totem, is possessed of great wealth in silver dollars, and is one of the shrewdest and largest traders in the Territory, owning schooners and branch stores. Extensive advertising has made her famous and raised the price of her goods, but few of the romantic histories current have any foundation in truth."

A new and unexpected reference to Mrs. Tom's industry appeared as late as

February of 1965 in—of all places—the Alumni Journal of Princeton University in an article on "Tlingit Treasures, How an Important Collection came to Princeton."

Back in Grover Cleveland's time, in 1886, during the first flush of the steamer tourist trade, Princeton and the *New York Times* co-sponsored an expedition to climb Mount St. Elias, the lofty landmark of Bering and Cook. Princeton Professor William Libby accompanied the expedition which was headed by bluff, burly writer-explorer Lieutenant Frederick Schwatka who sent back breezy dispatches for *Times*' readers. They did not quite scale Mount St. Elias, but at Yakutat they vied with each other and with their gunboat captain, a young Navy lieutenant named George Thornton Emmons in collecting Yakutat masks, rattles, hats, bowls, and other examples of these northerly Tlingits' work.

They were surprised to find items that were obviously made for the tourist trade. The answer, they found, was the enterprising Mrs. Tom who made the rounds in her great Haida war canoe to collect the pieces, bracelets mostly, that she had ordered for her fast-growing business at Sitka.

Another personality of renown was Sitka Jack, esteemed as a silversmith, and revered for a spectacular potlatch given in 1877 as a mammoth housewarming at which he gave away over five hundred blankets. Even in a culture based upon the surprising custom of giving to denote wealth, Sitka Jack so outdid his contemporaries that his gala was noted in government reports and continued to be a colorful topic of conversation among the tourists who bought his bracelets. Some of his finest bracelets were collected by Lieutenant Emmons and can be seen today at the United States National Museum in Washington and American Museum of Natural History in New York.

Most of the villages touched by the tourist steamer were Tlingit: the Stikines at Wrangell, Auk and Taku at Juneau and Sitka at the district's capital, but in its commercial mission it threaded among the islands, touching at infant settlements and trading posts of the Kakes, Hootznahoos, the Hoonahs whose "women weave baskets from the fine bark of the cedar and from split spruce roots, and ornament them with geometrical patterns in brilliant colors."

Rounding the southern end of Prince of Wales Island on the return run, Miss Scidmore noted differences in the village and people of the Kaigani Haida. The village of Howkan [called Kaigani by the early traders], "fronts on two crescent beaches. . . . A fleet of graceful Haida canoes was drawn up on the first and larger beach, all of them carefully filled with grass and covered over. . . . The houses at Howkan are large and well built, and the village is remarkably clean. Some of the chiefs have weather-boarded their houses and put in glass windows and hinged doors, but before or beside nearly every house rises the tall ancestral totem poles that constitute the glory of the place. . . .

"Back in the dense undergrowth rise the mortuary poles, the carved totems that mark the graves of dead and gone Haida. (The chief) Skolka's father and uncles have fine images over their burial boxes, and from the head of the Eagle on one of these mortuary columns, a small fire-tree, taking root, has grown to a height of eight or ten feet. In this burying ground there are large boxes filled with the bones and ashes of those said to have died when the great epidemics raged among the islands a half century ago.

"Like all of their tribe, these Kaigahnee Haida are an intelligent and superior people, skilled in the arts of war and the crafts of peace, and their carvers have wrought matchless totem poles, canoes, bows, spoons, halibut clubs and hooks. Their carvings show finer work, and in silver work they quite surpass the rest of the Thlinkets. . . .

"We found the Howkan shipyard under a large shed, and the canoe builder showed us two cedar canoes that were nearly completed. The high-beaked Haida canoes are slender and graceful as gon-dolas, and the small, light canoes that they use in hunting sea otter were marvels of boat building."

The Haida canoe was the most sought on the Coast and was purchased by the Tlingit, primarily from the Queen Charlotte Island Haida, for blankets and trade goods amounting to hundred of dollars. The young Chief Shakes, whom Mrs. McFarland hoped would join her church at Wrangell, had acquired two Haida canoes, and when the historian William Woollen retraced Vancouver's historic voyage in 1913, he met Shakes, old now and a self-appointed proprietor of his own "museum of Indian curiosities." "He took me to his canoe shed," Woollen wrote, "and showed me his two large canoes. They were the finest that I had ever seen. . . . He told me that the largest one of them was fifty feet long and would hold fifty passengers,

and that he had bought both of them in Queen Charlotte Sound for five hundred dollars each. . . . Shakes was very proud of them and regretfully spoke of the fact that the use of canoes was fast being supplanted by gasoline launches."

This and other far reaching changes were overtaking native life. Wrote Miss Scidmore, "As late as 1883 a forest of totem poles rose by the great lodges of the Stikines' village. In 1893, only a half dozen

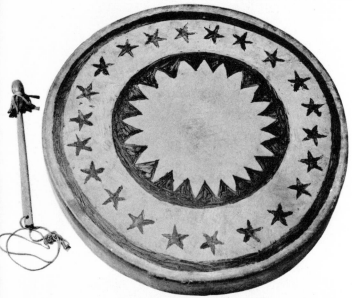

remained and the show pair guard a bay windowed cottage which replaces the ancestral lodge." Old village sites were abandoned as the once independent Indians moved en masse to live in squalid clusters around the white man's canneries and mining centers.

Not only were villages transplanted. Many of them, as during the smallpox epidemic of the thirties, simply expired. Between the population count of 1880 and 1890 an entire Chilkat village—one of four in which the Chilkat people lived—

was wiped out by flu. Vanishing along with their ancient traditions was life itself. During the eighties and nineties the native population of Alaska drastically declined.

The great Chilkat people numbered over 2,000 when their chief Kloh-Kutz, or Shotridge, entertained Seward shortly after the transfer. In 1880 their number was given as 988. Enumerators in 1890 counted 811 Chilkats in three villages along the Chilkat River.

Figures for the Tlingit and Haida as a whole showed a similar decline. Petroff's estimate for the 1880 census was 6,763 Tlingit. By 1890 the count was 4,737. The Haida dropped from 788 to 391 in the same period. The prime cause of death was disease, most varieties of which were unknown prior to the coming of the whites: tuberculosis, smallpox, diphtheria, venereal diseases, influenza, measles. Some effort was made locally to help the natives, but not until 1916 did Congress appropriate money—$25,000—for their medical assistance.

During the desperate decades before the turn of the century, the United States Government ignored the needs and pleas of the native population. Under Grover Cleveland's administration, in 1899 the Department of Interior published a major survey entitled "Statistics of Indian Tribes," examining over three hundred tribes from Apache to Yuma in the States and Territories. The report did not even mention the Indians of southeastern Alaska, or their comrades in despair, the Aleuts, Eskimos and Athapascans of the interior.

Exemplifying the congressional mind was the appropriation in 1887 of $25,500 for the entire operation of Alaska's civil government and $43,350 for the Seal Islands, the lease for which, despite warnings of serious depletion, it renewed in 1890 for another twenty years. Native needs were not even considered.

In 1891 Congress passed the Trade and Mining Sites Act, which, said Governor Alfred P. Swineford, was enacted strictly for the benefit of the salmon canning companies who sought to own all the best harbors and fishing grounds. By this time thirty-seven canneries owned by absentee California capital and estimated in value at $2,786,929 were operating with illegal barricades and traps along river mouths and passages that seasonally ran rich with salmon. Yield at this time from the Treadway Mine on Douglas Island—also California owned—was over $3,000,-000 a year.

Passage of the Homestead Act in 1898 aroused hope among white residents of Alaska for an end to their transient status, until they discovered that no provision was included for the surveying of land, and claims surveyed and filed at their own expense were only provisional.

The following year brought the long called for end to the unenforceable prohibition on liquor in favor of a licensing law, the first taxation levied in the district, and at long last, enactment of a criminal code.

The only solace in all this to the native Alaskan was that he could not actually be deprived of land which he occupied. The Organic Act of 1884 provided "that the Indians or other persons . . . shall not be disturbed in the possession of any lands actually in their use or occu-

pation or now claimed by them." Failure to clarify native land status, however, hampered economic development, desired by Indians as well as whites, and in the 1940's exploded into complex litigation described by the Solicitor General before a House hearing as "unmitigated chaos in native land claims."

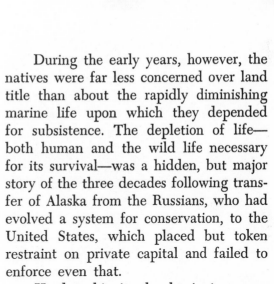

During the early years, however, the natives were far less concerned over land title than about the rapidly diminishing marine life upon which they depended for subsistence. The depletion of life—both human and the wild life necessary for its survival—was a hidden, but major story of the three decades following transfer of Alaska from the Russians, who had evolved a system for conservation, to the United States, which placed but token restraint on private capital and failed to enforce even that.

Hardest hit in the beginning were the Eskimos and Aleuts whose fur fisheries were invaded earlier than the salmon fishing preserves of the Tlingit and Haida. In 1890 Sheldon Jackson described to his superiors in the Interior Department the epic disaster that had overwhelmed the human population of the Arctic.

"I would like to call your attention to the starving condition of the Eskimo on the Arctic coast, as learned during my late visit," said Jackson. "From time immemorial they have lived upon the whale, the walrus, and the seal of their coasts, the fish and aquatic birds of their rivers, and the caribou or wild reindeer of their vast inland plains.

"The supply of these in years past was abundant and furnished ample food for all the people. But fifty years ago American whalers, having largely exhausted the supply in other waters, found their way into the North Pacific Ocean. Then commenced for that section the slaughter and destruction of whales, that went steadily forward at the rate of hundreds and thousands annually, until they were destroyed and driven out of the Pacific Ocean. They were then followed into Behring Sea and the slaughter went on. The whales took refuge among the ice fields of the Arctic Ocean, and thither the whalers followed. In this relentless hunt the remnant have been driven still farther into the inaccessible regions around the North Pole, and are no longer within the reach of the natives.

"As the great herds of buffalo that once roamed the western prairies have been exterminated for their pelts, so the whales have been sacrificed for the fat that encased their bodies and the bone that hung in their mouths. With the destruction of the whale one large source of food supply for the natives has been cut off.

"Another large supply was derived from the walrus, which once swarmed in great numbers in those northern seas.

"But commerce wanted more ivory, and the whalers turned their attention to the walrus, and thousands were annually destroyed for the sake of their tusks. Where a few years ago they were so numerous that their bellowings were heard above the roar of the waves and the grinding and crashing of the ice-fields, this year I cruised for weeks without seeing or hearing one. The walrus as a source of food supply is already practically extinct.

"The seal and sea lion once so common in Behring Sea are now becoming so scarce that it is with difficulty that the natives procure sufficient number of skins to cover their boats, and their flesh on account of its rarity has become a luxury.

"In the past the natives with tireless industry caught and cured for use in their long winters great quantities of fish, but American canneries have already come to some of their streams and will soon be found upon all of them, both carrying the food out of the country and by their wasteful methods destroying the future supply. Five million cans of salmon annually shipped away from Alaska, and the business still in its infancy, means starvation to the native races in the near future.

"With the advent of improved breech-loading fire arms the wild reindeer are both being killed off and frightened away to the remote and more inaccessible regions of the interior, and another source of food supply is diminishing.

"Thus the support of the people is largely gone, and the process of slow starvation and extermination has commenced along the whole Arctic coast of Alaska. Villages that once numbered thousands have been reduced to hundreds; of some tribes but two or three families remain.

"On the island of Attou, once famous for the number of its sea-otter skins, the catch for the past nine years has averaged but three sea otter and twenty-five fox skins, an annual income of about $2 for each person."

To save the sea otter, whale and walrus, Jackson's disclosures came too late. By the end of the century all had been hunted to commercial extinction. Despite more recent international treaties for its protection, the whale, found predominately now in Antarctic waters, faces biological extinction as well.

Arctic Ocean. The ship *Mercury* killed two thousand whales in 1877. Between 1870 and 1880 the estimated kill was one hundred thousand animals.

By 1910 only seven ships hunted whales in the North Pacific. That same year the total sea-otter take in all Alaskan waters was twenty-nine.

Although Alaska's salmon story more properly belongs to the twentieth century, it began in 1879 with the opening of the first canneries at Kodiak and Klawock. Few familiar with the story speak of it without indignation. In his *History*

The whaling industry's golden age peaked between 1835, when Captain Folger in the bark *Ganges* struck the first right whale off Kodiak, and 1855, when the bow-head was being taken in great numbers. In 1846 the number of ships leaving United States whaling ports was 735. The use of steam vessels in the 1880's eliminated the last of the romance and enabled the whalers to systematically clean out remnants of once mighty herds which rolled in coves past Point Barrow in the

of Alaska, Henry W. Clark declared: "The history of Alaskan fishing from 1890 down to 1922 is a story of senseless exploitation by private interests running rampant." No regeneration occurred in the ranks of the absentee packers, who for the better part of a century curbed and circumvented all legislative restraints on their operations and made a mockery of the Government's feeble efforts at conservation.

The first of these efforts was made in 1889 with a ban on "the erection of dams, barricades or other obstructions in any of the rivers of Alaska, with the purpose of preventing or impeding the ascent of salmon . . . to their spawning grounds." Characteristically, Congress passed no appropriation for enforcement. Evidence of how much attention the canners paid to this and subsequent restrictions is apparent in a bulletin published thirty years later by the governor's office:

"That the future of Alaska's greatest industry and her greatest source of revenue, that of fishing, is threatened, there is no gainsaying. The falling off is not due to fewer concerns engaged in the business, but to fewer fish returning from the mighty ocean to the spawning grounds, which condition has been brought about by the inordinate greed of trappers, seiners and trollers who for years have plied their methods for taking fish so close to the mouths of spawning streams . . . until depletion is not only threatened, but imminent."

Thus, during the first half century of United States rule the Federal Government ignored pleas of the whites in Alaska for a workable civil government. It ignored the needs of the native population—did not, indeed, take note of its existence. Beyond enabling provisions of the Organic Act authorizing Sheldon Jackson to promote schools, no governmental attention was paid to health, education or welfare of any Alaskan subject. Congress passed only a slap on the wrist to halt exhaustion of the greatest salmon fishery known to the world.

Only in one area did the government concern itself. "From 1867 until 1896 the hundred square miles of Pribilofs and

their seals," declared Governor Gruening, "received many times more governmental attention than did the rest of Alaska's 586,000 square miles and its people." The greater the attention, the fewer the seals. By 1890, when the Alaska Commercial Company relinquished its monopoly to the North American Commercial Company, having netted for its stockholders $18 million over the twenty-year lease, Treasury Agent Charles Goff warned depletion was so great as to require that "there be no killing of fur seals . . . for an indefinite number of years."

These great strides toward exhausting Alaska's human and animal population would appear impressive enough. Yet before the turn of the century, still one final assault was to be made on the territory's unbelievable reserve of natural wealth.

In July of 1897 the steamer *Portland* docked at Seattle, carrying about $700,000 in gold. The Seattle *Post-Intelligencer's* headline proclaiming that a "ton of gold" had been brought out of the Klondike flashed around the world and the stampede was on. Men came by the thousands, drawn by tales of rich strikes and the well-calculated advertising campaigns of San Francisco, Portland, Seattle, Victoria, and Vancouver, each of which advertised itself as the take-off point for gold. In February of 1898 a throng of five thousand prospectors, mostly ill-informed and poorly equipped, were dropped by steamer at tidewater at Dyea and Skagway, new boom cities, at the head of Lynn Canal. From these brawling, lawless, frontier towns two passes led through Chilkat country over the mountains to Dawson. An estimated twenty-eight thousand people beat their way up the trails that year. Altogether some fifty thousand reached the interior of Alaska and Canada to scratch for gold in the frozen shafts of their claims in the Klondike.

Some made it. Some returned in defeat. Some pushed on to Seward Peninsula, joined by thousands more, to mine the "golden sands of Nome." A frozen waste five years before, Nome counted by 1900 some eighteen thousand people who sank prospect holes everywhere, mining the very sands of the beach to take out millions in dust before moving on to Fairbanks where the creeks yielded up another million more. "Out of the Yukon Basin where, at the time congressmen orated in invectives against Seward's Icebox, not a dollar was known to be," wrote historian Andrews, "there have been taken $171,-938,900 of the lifeblood of commerce to the close of 1935."

The spectacular nature of Alaska's gold rush, heightened by revolutionizing improvements in communication, transportation, and advertising techniques, accomplished what all the previous efforts had failed to do toward awakening federal interest in the district. The discovery of gold in the Klondike brought with it national discovery of Alaska to the States. Politically, economically, numerically, the rush days lifted Alaska over the threshold and into the twentieth century.

Chapter VII

FROM POTLATCH
TO POLITICS

In 1899 the railroad magnate Edward Harriman could charter a holiday ship, fill it with famous writers, artists and naturalists of the day, and cruise the scenic wonders of Alaska's inland passage to visit villages consisting of "ten, fifteen or twenty large houses . . . with totem poles, some of which are fifty or sixty feet high . . . elaborately carved with figures of men, frogs, birds and various mammals."

In less than a generation most of these tribal houses, except for one or two owned by enterprising Tlingit who turned them into museums, had been replaced by conventional structures. The Indians worked and fished for the canneries, voted in Territorial elections, and had elected the first of many of their members to the Territorial legislature.

The transition from potlatch to politics took a mere quarter century, a time span in which the infant becomes a man. Within this remarkably brief time the In-

dian shed his exotic plumage and donned the work pants and civilian dress of his white brother. The tourist of the 1920's found him working, voting and competing, on terms laid down by the exigencies of our modern world. During these crucial years, the fortuitous accident of governmental inattention saved the Alaskan Indian from sharing the tragic fate of his State-side brothers.

"The Interior Department in those times," wrote Commissioner of Indian Affairs John Collier, appointed by Franklin D. Roosevelt "was the agency of Congress in the liquidation of the American national estate—in the turning over to individuals, at the lowest possible price, public lands, including their timber and minerals. The Interior Department assimilated the Indians, their lands, societies, communities, families, personalities and very souls, into its 'liquidation' preoccupation and technique. It transformed the Army's unproclaimed policy and strategy of tribal dissolution from an unformalized, somewhat episodic practice to a proclaimed policy, even into a kind of religious, fanatical progression. Elaborately implemented, followed through amid financial corruption with compulsive ruthlessness, the Interior Department prosecuted 'Indian Liquidation' right on into the dawn of the 1930's."

The Organic Act protected Alaska's Tlingit and Haida from a similar destiny. Instead, they were left—along with the white population—to shift for themselves, consigned, although not confined, to their predominately native villages on the islands of Alaska's great marine highway. Except for the thin trickle of educational funds elicited by the efforts of Sheldon

Jackson, they were officially neither helped nor hindered, but, like the white man, left to make the most of a situation in which almost all of the laws were drawn up to prevent local civic action.

Legally, neither white nor native could claim title to land, but in practice the new Alaskans and absentee commercial salmon canners simply took possession on the basis of squatter's claims. They were popularly regarded as binding and came to be regarded as law by the natives who were thenceforth forbidden entry. In consequence, although they were not moved off their land, they no longer had full use of it.

Building the canneries at sites of the most abundant salmon runs meant that the natives, who depended for the entire year on their seasonal catch, could no longer fish their own waters. They could starve or enter the service of the cannery, a course which, once embarked upon, broke forever the tie with a life based on seasonal accord with the environment and committed them to a commercial existence dependent upon the white man's economy.

The Indians of Alaska were fully aware of this fateful choice. As early as 1899 Chief Johnson, a Tlingit of Taku lineage, used the white man's methods and addressed himself to the white man's institution, to plead for protection of this basic source of livelihood:

"I have come a long way from my home in Alaska to see you and tell you of the condition of my people," he told Chairman John M. Thurston of the Senate Committee on Indian Affairs. "I was sent here by the chiefs of the principle tribes to represent them, and have brought with me a petition signed by them.

"We find our country Alaska overrun by white men who have crowded or driven the Indians from their fishing grounds, hunting grounds, and the places where their fathers and grandfathers have lived and been buried. . . . We do not ask anything unreasonable of the U.S. government," said Chief Johnson. Then he made the following points on which the Indians desired help.

"1st.   That the fishing and hunting grounds of their Fathers be reserved for them and their children, and that the whites who have driven them off of the same be ordered by the government to leave them. The Indians' chief method of support is by fishing and hunting and that is the only way that most of them can live, as only a small number are educated sufficiently to go out in the towns of the land and compete with the whites.

"2nd. The Indians of Alaska pray that the U.S. government will set apart certain reservations for them and their children where they and their children can each have a home allotted to them, the same privileges as the Indians of the United States enjoy. We ask this in return for all of Alaska which has passed into the hands of the whites, without a murmur from us. We have given up a great deal and now only ask the great and good Father at Washington to give us back a little of the land, in return for the much we gave him, and protect us from the encroachments of greedy white men who would drive us into the Sea in order to advance their own interests. . . .

"Therefore I have come to Washington to speak and to lay our case before

the Congressmen of the government, to implore their aid in giving the Alaska Indians homes and schools, and protecting them by law from the encroachment of avaricious white men."

Congressional apathy spared Chief Johnson's people the privileges of the reservation, but it also did nothing to help them cope with their changing world. And so, they went to work for the salmon canners, the men hiring out to fish, the women working inside, cleaning and packing the gold of Alaskan waters. Along the mainland they hunted and trapped lynx, fox, otter and beaver for furs to sell, first at local trading posts and later, as they became more sophisticated, for shipment to markets at St. Louis, Chicago, and Seattle. Others carved curios for the tourist trade, or sold piece-by-piece their carved family heirlooms.

After 1880 when Commander Beardslee negotiated with Chief Shotridge to allow the passage of miners through Chilkat territory to prospect for gold in the interior, Chilkats began earning good money packing loads up the steep passes for the prospectors, explorers and adventurers who came to Alaska.

In 1883 Lieutenant Schwatke made his first trip to Alaska to explore the Yukon River for the *New York Times* and posterity. At Klukwan, he said, "some boys, eight or ten, came forward to solicit a share in the arduous labor, and one little urchin of not over fourteen, a son of the Chilkat chief, Shot-rich, manfully assumed the responsibility of a sixty-eight pound box, the distance he had to carry it being about thirty miles, but thirty miles equal to any one hundred and thirty on the good roads of a civilized Country." A generation later the grandson of Shot-rich, Louis Shotridge, returned to Klukwan on an assignment from the University Museum of the University of Pennsylvania to collect examples of his ancestors' disappearing art.

"When I carried the object (a rare Shark helmet) out of its place no one intervened," said Louis Shotridge, "but if only one of the true warriors of that clan had been alive the removal of it would never have been possible. I took it in the presence of aged women, the only survivors in the house where the old object was kept, and they could do nothing more than weep when the once highly esteemed object was being taken away to its last resting place.

"It is true that the modernized part of me rejoiced over my success in obtaining this important ethnological specimen for the Museum, but, as one who had been trained to be a true Kaguanton, in my heart I cannot help but have the feeling of a traitor who has betrayed confidence."

This transition, so swift on history's time line, came more slowly to those who experienced it. To the native Alaskan, it was predicated always on white disregard for Indian rights and welfare. With simple-minded self-interest, white Alaska stepped up its pressure for self-government, its target primarily the absentee canning and mining interests who blocked territorial status. Native needs were not considered.

The first national figure to concern himself with the plight of Alaska's native population was Theodore Roosevelt. Rough

Rider, conservationist, trust-buster, and builder of the Panama Canal, Theodore Roosevelt was an already controversial personage when he assumed the presidency in 1901 after the assassination of William McKinley. A heroic figure in an age urgently in need of heroes, Roosevelt set for himself the prodigious task of securing the subservience of great business combines to government and law, and retrieving from "the robber barons" some portion of the market they had cornered on the nation's natural wealth.

Roosevelt first turned his attention to

Chief Anatlash of the Taku Tlingit was a rich and influential chief at the turn of the century. In 1907 he gave this spruce-root Swan Hat to Judge James Wickersham, who was made "Chief" of their tribe.

Alaska in regard to the crisis over pelagic sealing, the taking of seals in the open sea as they migrated to their rookeries in the Pribilof Islands. As they surfaced to breathe, seals were shot indiscriminately, females with pups as well as bachelors and bulls, and more sank and were lost than were retrieved by gaffing. Even more damaging and wasteful, hunters cruised off shore of the islands, shooting females, again pregnant and in search of food for their newly born pups on the islands. Death of the mother took the life of the unborn pup and left the pup on shore to starve also as each seal nurses only its own offspring. By 1909, the herd of three million seals was reduced to a scant 100,000.

Presidents Harrison, Cleveland and McKinley had dealt inconclusively with the issue. Theodore Roosevelt's administration worked out an international treaty banning the catastrophic practice, which was signed by the United States, Great Britain, Japan, and Russia in 1911 under Taft. Final settlement of the long standing dispute between Canada and the United States over the boundary line between British Columbia and southeastern Alaska was also settled during Roosevelt's administration in 1903.

Roosevelt extended his conservationist policies to Alaska, setting off the giant reserves of the Chugach National Forest on Prince William Sound and Kenai Peninsula, homeland of Baranov's native wife, and the Tongass National Forest which embraces the wooded homeland of the Tlingit and Haida along the panhandle of southeastern Alaska.

Most important to Alaska's political future was the passage during Roosevelt's administration of the Nelson Act in 1905, the first break in the district's long campaign for a voice in Washington. It permitted Alaskans to elect a delegate to sit in Congress. The delegate had no vote, but for the first time an Alaskan could be present in Congress.

Three years later James Wickersham, who had in 1900 been appointed to a district judgeship by McKinley, campaigned vigorously for the post against the fishing-mining combine. His election as delegate polarized the two factions that would thenceforth vie for the Congressional ear —the white resident population of Alaska against the absentee, wire-pulling interests of the mining syndicate and salmon canners. In effect, Wickersham took over the torch from Sheldon Jackson to press in the new century for a more sophisticated set of political demands. Jackson was removed from his office as Education Agent in 1906, a date generally regarded as marking Alaska's transition from Pres-

byterian paternalism to partisan politics.

Eight presidents had come and gone since the purchase of Alaska. Roosevelt was the first to inquire into the needs of the Indians. He assigned the job to Lieutenant George Thornton Emmons whose long tour of Navy duty and serious ethnological bent had given him a scholar's knowledge of the Indian culture and a deep compassion for their situation. The message Emmons brought Roosevelt has taken its place alongside the earlier appeal of Jackson as an enduring statement on human rights.

"Forty-four years have elapsed since we acquired Alaska," Emmons said, "and yet the legal status of the Native remains undetermined. He is not recognized as an Indian for he has no reservation of land nor receives any gratuity from the Government; however intelligent and educated he may be he is denied citizenship, so he can neither acquire land, locate mineral claims, nor take out a license as master, pilot or engineer of his own craft."

Emmons divided the natives of Alaska into two groups; "those who are self-sustaining and need only supervision, education and moral support; and those who have been deprived of their natural means of living by the opening up of the country and need material assistance to bridge them over this period of transition." In

this second group he put "the Aleut, the Athapascan, and the Eskimo, the bulk of the native population of Alaska, occupying the vast interior and extended coast line of the Pacific west."

These people "who heretofore have lived undisturbed in primitive simplicity, are being rudely awakened by in the inrush of strangers. Their country is being

overrun; their natural food supply, never overabundant in this northland, is being taken from them; the large game is being slaughtered and driven to a distance, and the waters depleted of fish, the woodlands burnt over, and fatal diseases hitherto unknown brought to their midst, to spread distress and death far and wide. All of these conditions they are of themselves helpless to meet. Grown up children, in their ignorance and simplicity, they look with wonder on the coming of the white man, and his methods of business and means of living they are wholly unable to comprehend.

"This first contact has proved very fatal; already thousands have succumbed, and education, looking to self support and independence, is a question of Territorial

importance, which asks shall they become a burden on the white settlers in this new country, or shall they be transformed into a working force, assisting in the advancement and the development of the country?"

The Indians of southeastern Alaska, Lieutenant Emmons said are an entirely different people.

"The Tlingit, Haidas, and Tsimsheans, who occupy the narrow continental shore and adjacent islands," he said, "number some 6,000 souls and live in comparative comfort under very favorable condition in large, well-built villages along the coast and channel ways. Here the climate is mild and healthful, wood and water are on every hand, fish life is abundant, and game is more than sufficient for their wants. They are intelligent, honest, and good workers; an accumulative, thrifty people, quick to learn, and anxious to improve their condition."

But their longer contact with civilization has "so changed their manner of life that our system of living, food and clothing have become acceptable to their wellbeing. In short," said Emmons, "they have passed through that most trying period of contact, the initial stage . . . wholly through their own exertions and industry, without any material assistance from the General Government, [they] have established themselves as an independent, selfsupporting population, fully capable of rendering such labor as the conditions of the country demand.

"Still these people have their limitations and the fact that their improvement has come from within instead of from without, and that they have advanced their own interests unaided, does not mean that they have no needs, nor that the Government can through persistent neglect gain immunity from the fulfillment of its moral obligations.

"Summed up in a few words, the natives of Southeastern Alaska ask for simple justice in the execution of the law—the same educational advantages that are given to all others in the land, protection in their rights to hold property and to locate mineral lands, citizenship when qualified, and the establishment of hospitals at central points. In short, they ask only the rights that are accorded to every stranger who comes to this country to make a home, while they, the children of the soil, can know no other."

Roosevelt urged Congress to act on Emmons' recommendations, but even his forcefulness could not awaken in that body a spirit of humanity. The $25,000 it appropriated for native medical aid in 1916, seven years after Theodore Roosevelt's Presidency, Governor John F. A. Strong called "a drop in the bucket."

Nor did much humane spirit exist within Alaska. One of the few who worked to improve native health, education and living standards was Judge Wickersham, in both personal contact with the Indian community and as a delegate. Throughout his vigorous public career, Wickersham privately conducted ethnological studies into the language, customs, art, and origins of the Tlingit and the Haida. The bulk of this valuable data is still in manuscript.

The single channel through which tangible help came continued to be the life line of education, secured by Sheldon

Jackson before the turn of the century. The intimate reports of teachers, employed on the slim funds allotted to the Bureau of Education, tell of the irrevocable change that was occurring.

"The monthly report cards forwarded by the teachers in the 14 schools in the district," declared School Superintendent Charles Hawksworth, in 1917, "show that we have administered to the educational, social, economic and moral needs of 3,335 natives of Southeastern Alaska. These are listed in tribes as follows: Thlingets, 2,467; Tsimpsean, 534; Hydas, 334." A third of the total population, 1,050 Indians, were formally enrolled as students.

At Hydaburg, a village created to consolidate the Alaska Haida, 103 out of the community's 334 total census were enrolled. They were also involved in numerous construction projects: a church belonging entirely to the people, a teachers' residence, a new dock, and the framework for a cannery. Hydaburg's sawmill cut 300,000 feet of lumber, part of which was used and the balance sold for $3,800.

At Klawock, site of the first commercial cannery in southeastern Alaska,

school did not begin until the first of October "on account of the Lateness of the canning season." Klawock's teacher, Charles Hibbs said his "pupils have become very efficient in their ability to prepare reading lessons unassisted and also in reading them. . . . The pupils enjoyed this work very much, for most of them have enough of an English vocabulary to understand the stories and data given them . . . I believe the grades here will fall very little below the respective grades in the States."

Klawock's Commercial Company, one of the cooperatives stores financed by natives and conducted by them under supervision of the local school teacher, issued a twelve per cent dividend and put two per cent back into the business. "The towns of Hoonah and Kake, which have been more steeped in tribal customs than most of the other towns of the district, are manifesting a worthy pride," Superintendent Hawksworth reported. "They have cooperated and plan to join the Forest Service in surveying the towns and building roads. Both are almost a mile from their canneries, and both have agreed to furnish

the labor to build the proposed roadways if the Forest Service would furnish the material. Tribal homes along the water front are customary in Kake and Hoonah. There are no lots surveyed behind these shore lines, consequently the people, of necessity, are forced to live in houses consisting of one big room, in which are some eight beds in full view of all in the room . . . I am looking for great progress at both Kake and Hoonah."

Even Klukwan, home of the proud Chilkat, one of the last communities to cast off the traditions of native life, did "over $10,000 worth of business" in its cooperative store "with a profit of fifteen per cent to the stockholders. . . . Some of the older natives were not satisfied with the profits," said Klukwan's teacher Fay Shaver, "because they had dropped off from those of preceding years."

More than elsewhere, the old ways still held powerfully to Chilkat outlook and habit. "In connection with the store I might add that the credits are a great drawback," Miss Shaver said. "There is generally one of two causes for them. It is very seldom that the party asking credit has no money, but because a certain amount has been laid away for the big potlatch. This is never touched, even though the family is in want. The other reason, which is the cause of most of the credits, and which is being overcome gradually, is the fact that the native must see and handle the money on a transaction to know the profit made."

In contrast, some of the Klukwan natives were sufficient masters of white techniques to ship their furs to competitive markets in Chicago, St. Louis, and Seattle.

With the assistance of the Bureau of Education, Alaskan Indians were beginning to avail themselves of banking facilities in Seattle, primarily to set up credits on the sale of furs for use in purchasing supplies. "In the past year approximately $20,000 was handled in this manner," Alaska's Governor John F. A. Strong reported. The financial acumen of the Pacific Northwest Coast natives had been noted by the earlier merchant-explorers.

But cultural hangovers persisted, especially in native social life for which no satisfactory substitute had been offered.

Wrote Miss Shaver: "The big potlatch was held at Yendistuckie, where the feasting lasted for two weeks. This village is about 19 miles from Klukwan. Most of the people from our village and Haines were there. The only ones not going, I think, were those not invited. I have not been able to find out just how the potlatch was conducted . . .One native gave away $1,000 in addition to the food he furnished. This must have been an unusual amount of money, as there was lots of talk about it. They had the whiteman's dance every afternoon and evening. There was one day when they did not let the whites in. I was not able to find out what took place at that time. When the people returned they said they did not know that it was to be an old-custom affair, but that when they got there they could not get away. The truth is that this feasting will fill many an evening with gossip, and they would not have missed it for anything."

At Metlakatla—the Tsimshian mission community moved by Dr. William Duncan from British Columbia to Alaska in 1887—a saw mill was in use, a new salmon cannery was under construction and the Metlakatla Commercial Company store had paid up capital stock of more than $7,000. In addition a school fair was held there during the year at which students from Hydaburg and Klawock participated in a contest of oratory.

"I have seldom, if ever," Superintendent Hawkesworth wrote, "heard Lincoln's Gettysburg Address, or the great speech of Patrick Henry, given with more convincing power than when those orations were delivered by boys from Metlakatla."

While the meagerly financed government schools brought education and the rudiments of business procedure to native villages, a far more potent educational force was at work in Sitka. Begun in the 1880's as the Sitka Industrial and Training School, it was enlarged in 1911 and its name changed to the Sheldon Jackson School. What the school lacked in numbers, was made up for in fervor, as it taught not only academic and technical skills, but imbued its students with hope.

In 1917 six boys and nine girls were graduated from the eighth grade of the Sheldon Jackson School at Sitka. "In all the history of the school work among the native people of Alaska," stated the school newspaper, "there has never been a result so encouraging as this year's eighth grade class in the Sheldon Jackson School. These fifteen young people, having widely dif-

ferent tastes and diversity of interest, are representative of the native people along the coast. They are from eight different native villages. It is of special interest that two of the boys are carpenters, one a skilled worker in metals, one a machinist, and two are studying to be printers. Of the girls one is a musician, two plan nurses' training; all are capable housekeepers and seamstresses." That same year Sheldon Jackson marked another milestone by organizing a high school class of five boys and four girls.

The school, which today is both a high school and a junior college, opened its doors April 17th, 1878. As he had inspired Mrs. McFarland to come to Wrangell, so had Sheldon Jackson directed the course of a newly graduated divinity student, John G. Brady, to Sitka. Of that day Brady wrote Jackson:

"We arrived here the night of April 11. Our first meeting occurred on Sunday in the Castle [Baranov's Castle, now old and weatherbeaten]. The day was charming, for the clouds had vanished, the sun was warm, and the scenery was all that could be asked. Far out beyond the harbor protected by innumerable green islets, lay the vast Pacific, in a sort of rolling calmness. At another point rose the funnel shaped Edgecumbe, crested with snow.

"The castle has been stripped of everything, and is in a dilapidated condition. As we began to sing some of the Moody and Sankey hymns, the Indians began to steal in and squat themselves on the floor along the back wall. Most of them had their faces black; some were black and red and a few surrounded with a coat of red. All but a few of the chiefs were in their bare feet, and wrapped in blankets of various colors.

"Sitka Jack and Annahootz, chiefs, were clad in some old suits of the naval officers who had been there . . .

"The people listened attentively to all I had to say. Then Jack broke into a gesticulating speech, telling how they were heretofore. Now they were glad that they were going to have a school, a church and people to teach them. . . . We held but one service that day, as it had lasted several hours. There were 125 persons present."

Over the years more than 13,000 students from all over Alaska—from the far islands of the Aleutians, the Eskimos of the north, and the Indians of the interior and of southeastern Alaska and, since 1942, white students—have received an education at Sheldon Jackson. Over two hundred and fifty natives and whites were enrolled during the 1965-66 school term in Sheldon Jackson High School and Junior College.

Quality, however, not quantity, gave the cutting edge to this durable school's influence. To leave their native village and

Alaska's Governor John G. Brady collected these totem poles from their tribal owners in Haida villages around Old Kasaan for the Alaska exhibit at the Louisiana Purchase Exposition (shown here) held at St. Louis in 1904, and the Lewis and Clark Exposition in Portland a year later. Afterwards, their native owners gave the poles, together with a Fog Woman pole and four house posts, to the government. They are now in Sitka National Monument.

enroll for a period of years as boarding students took will and courage. For these students, Sheldon Jackson School widened horizons and strengthened the resolve to achieve more, for themselves and for their people.

An early graduate of the school was Edward Marsden, a Tsimshian from Metlakatla, who after graduation continued his education of Mariette College in Ohio and Lane Theological Seminary. Completing the metamorphosis from aboriginal to contemporary white orientation, Marsden was ordained to the ministry, the first Protestant Alaskan Indian to achieve this status. In 1898, he established a mission at the native village of Saxman within walking distance of Ketchikan from which

Still standing on Village Island a century after her abandonment, Fog Woman holds in each hand the symbol of Alaska's well being—the salmon. "While Raven was fishing in his canoe one day, a dense fog descended and Raven lost his way. A woman appeared, took Raven's spruce-root hat and all the fog went into it. The sun shone and Raven reached the shore. Raven took Fog Woman for his wife. Later, to assuage her hunger and the hunger of Raven's slaves, she created in the waters of a spring, the first salmon. Sharing her miracle, Raven became proud and overbearing, until finally Fog Woman left her husband. All the salmon followed her. Even the dried and smoked salmon came to life and went with her into the sea. Because Fog Woman had created the first salmon in fresh spring water they return each year." *With intelligent conservation the salmon will continue their seasonal return into the next millenium. Left to the elements, Fog Woman has only a few years left. Unless help comes, she—like a last few dozen remaining old poles in deserted sites—will vanish forever.*

he visited other native communities in a thirty-six foot steam boat, imparting to them the message of God and progress.

Unlike Indians of the States, the Alaskan natives accepted this challenge of a modern future and sought to share its opportunities and benefits on an equal footing with their white neighbors. They early perceived that education was the key to this aim and looked to the educated among them for leadership. It is no coincidence that the new generation of native leaders who emerged during the first decade of the twentieth century were educated.

"Why is it we have school life?" asked student Mary R. Kadachan in a school composition. "Well, we Thlinget people never had schools among us before, and we didn't know how to live right; now we have teachers to teach us how. It is in school we are getting strong. When we grow up, we will be the leaders of our people."

By 1917, on the eve of World War I, Governor John F. A. Strong could describe the Indians of southeastern Alaska as leaning heavily toward the known marvels and unknown frustrations of a modern future. "It is remarkable to note how they have availed themselves of modern conveniences and adapted them to their needs," he said.

"In southeastern Alaska the native fishermen equipped with power boats are no small asset to the salmon industry of the Territory. Most of such boats have been built by the native owners. They not

only possess such ability to a marked degree, but the care and handling of gas engines appear natural to them.

"The fact that the Alaska natives are not a dependent people can not be over-emphasized in order to give them the credit they deserve for successfully fighting for an existence in the face of rapidly changing conditions, caused by coming in contact with the white man. Although the native has had to rearrange his mode of living and to a certain extent, his method of securing his livelihood, he has rarely been forced to ask for aid."

When Territorial status came finally with the Second Organic Act of 1912, it did not directly affect the native population. Long overdue, it provided white Alaskans at last with their own elected Territorial legislature, comprising House and Senate, and conferred upon them limited powers of self-government, subject always to Congressional approval, and reserving to Federal control the vital issues bearing on Alaska's economic development. The Territory was happy to leave jurisdiction over native welfare in the hands of the Federal Government which continued to minister to the single segment of increasing and multiple native needs—native schools.

For three decades more, until Franklin D. Roosevelt's New Deal legislation dispelled the lethargy previously shrouding native Alaskans, the Tlingit and the Haida were largely left on their own to cope with the problems of acculturation. During this time southeastern Alaska was a favorite stamping ground of anthropologists and a paradise for writers of travel literature.

Observers sent out by the Smithsonian's National Museum and the American Museum of Natural History returned to tell and re-tell the aboriginal story, piecing it together from living informants, both native and white, and the writings of their living and late anthropological predecessors.

Travel writers, too, concentrated on the past, lamenting the squalid appearance of the present as a decline brought on by native indigence; a necessary evil like highway billboards.

Also prolific during this period were the brochure writers for the Alaska Steamship Company and the curio-shop proprietors in Juneau, Wrangell, Ketchikan and the jump-off port of Seattle. Their numerous small pamphlets offered bite-sized and often inaccurate nuggets of information on Indian basket weaving, totem poles, legends and lore, to satisfy the superficial appetites of summer tourists who continued, until interrupted by World War I, to make the steamer run up the inland passage.

Living in the present, the Indians themselves looked ahead. Ignored by the scholars, inadequately helped by friends, and left to fend for themselves by unconcerned whites, they depended on their own resources.

They recognized that the ambiguity of their political status was the first handicap to their participation in the way of life that now dominated their ancestral home. Having no citizenship, they could not own or be anyone that the white man legally recognized. They still could not file on a mining claim, secure title to land, or obtain a mariner's license despite their acquaintance with native waters. Nor were they accorded equality before the law which often flimflammed them because of their naïveté.

By threading their way through an

obstacle course set up by the 1915 Territorial Legislature, a native could manage to acquire citizenship. He had to demonstrate satisfactorily that he had "severed all tribal relationship and adopted the habits of a civilized life," pass an examination given by a majority of the teachers of a federal, territorial or municipal school, and obtain endorsement of five white residents of Alaska. Accomplishing all this, he then made application for a certificate of citizenship to the district judge who held a hearing to decide whether to grant or deny it. A few natives are said to have achieved citizenship in this arduous way, but their names are nowhere noted.

Another way out of limbo was evolved by the Indians themselves. In a political leap that defied their cultural disparity, ten Tlingit, Haida, and Tsimshian Indians organized a fraternal order aimed at securing for Alaska's native population the same rights, obligations and privileges enjoyed by whites. The young men came from various native communities: Ralph Young, Paul Liberty, Frank Price, and Peter Simpson were residents of Sitka, Frank Mercer and James Watson of Juneau, Eli Katanuk of Angoon, Jim Johnson of Klawock and Seward Kuntz and George Field.

Their English names, bestowed by men who could not, or would not, bother to pronounce the strange Tlingit sounds, signified a degree of participation in the white man's world. Their Indian names they had left behind in the village of their birth. In this regard they were not typical of the native population. These young men had acquired a better education than most Indian youths. Most of them had attended the Sitka Training School, were members of Presbyterian congregations and had achieved a measure of success in their adaptation to white culture. In the language of the anthropologist, they were all "highly acculturated individuals."

The ten met at Sitka in 1912 to found an organization "to assist and encourage the native in his advancement from his native state to his place among the cultivated races of the world, to oppose, discourage, and overcome the narrow injustice of race prejudice and to aid in the development of the Territory of Alaska, and in making it worthy of a place among the States of North America." Such a statement left little question that political maturity had quickly followed the Indians' economic toe hold. They named their organization the Alaskan Native Brotherhood.

Formation into a Grand Camp and Subordinate Camps, set up as local village chapters, demonstrated that the founders had observed and learned from both their own missionary-inspired organizations and the political activities of white Alaskans who through the years formed various pressure organizations. Among these was the Arctic Brotherhood, originally a fraternal order of Klondikers, which later turned political to press Congress for self-government.

Brotherhood Camps at Sitka, Juneau and Douglas were established first. Soon after, the Alaska Native Sisterhood took its place alongside the Brotherhood Camps in the villages. By the mid-1920's the sixteen communities of Angoon, Craig, Douglas, Haines, Hoonah, Hydaburg, Juneau, Kasaan, Kake, Ketchikan, Kla-

wock, Klukwan, Saxman, Sitka, Wrangell and Yakutat had functioning Camps supported by dues-paying members of both Brotherhoods and Sisterhoods. Those who could not afford to pay dues still considered themselves to be active members.

During its early years the Brotherhood concentrated its efforts on the issues of citizenship, the right of Indian children to attend Territorial schools and the abolition of fish traps, the injurious practice which decreased native employment and depleted Alaska's salmon.

It also campaigned against old customs, the wearing of clan ceremonial crests and costumes. Particularly under their en-

Wrangell's last totem-carver, Thomas Ukas

THE VOICE OF BROTHERHOOD

Design created by Indian artist Ray Peck for masthead of A. N. B. newspaper,
Voice of Brotherhood

lightened fire was the potlatch, the very core of family and clan relationships.

In its simplest dimension the potlatch might be described as a payment party, elaborately trimmed with feasting, singing, dancing and social conviviality, called for the purpose of distributing gifts of value for services rendered. A lot of nonsense has been written about the custom, primarily by observers who saw the form but did not understand the spirit. They have described the custom as a "giant give-away" by a chief to put other chiefs down, a type of rivalry that did on occasion occur. In these descriptions, the chief is described as beggaring himself by the sumptuousness of his gifts, which tradition demanded be repaid in kind.

What these accounts leave out is the warm sociability that cemented family ties between the two mighty lineages. As seen through the eyes of the Indians themselves, a potlatch was an exciting occasion for the get-together of relatives. The wife of Louis Shotridge, writing in the 1913 *Journal* of the University Museum, explained some of the subtleties of the important institution:

"The Tlingit are separated socially into two sides. . . . One side is known as the Raven, the other as the Eagle. This division is based on ties of blood, for the members of one side are said to be kindred; therefore the Raven man marries the Eagle woman and the Eagle man marries the Raven woman, while the children always belong to the mother's side.

"Each side is subdivided into clans, the members of which are more closely related to one another than to the whole of one side. Clan with us means a collection of families under the same totem. Totem is a figure of a bird, beast or the like used to distinguished to which side a clan belongs, whether the Eagle or the Raven, for though the same totem may be used by different clans on the same side, the same totem is never used by clans on the opposite side. Finally, the clans are subdivided into families or house groups, the members of which may own one or several houses, though very few own more than one."

A potlatch celebration marked completion of an important event, such as "erection of a family house, being a monument to the family. Distinguished persons of the opposite side are called together by the chief and his relatives, and to them is assigned the supervision of the work. Posts, beams, planks and others parts are allotted to a number of men. . . . The carvings and paintings were usually done by famous artists. I have often heard my father say with pride that his house totems were painted by Shkecleka who besides being the most famous chief of the Ravens was a clever artist as well."

At the ceremony attending the opening of her own house, she said, "A long line of women dancers formed around the room and I cried to be allowed to dance with my aunt. They finally gave permission in spite of the fact that I was of the Raven side and the dancers were of my father's side, the Eagle. This was but one of the many dances which were performed during the feast which attends the opening of a family house and lasts a week."

This same principle held for all occasions requiring the performance of special labors: preparations for burial of a deceased chief, assumption to title of his successor, the carving and raising of a totem pole in his memory, that of raising a pole to commemorate some special event, or the formal presentation of an heir presumptive to the chieftainship. For each of these occasions, Ravens undertook work for Eagles, Eagles worked for Ravens, and for these labors, the head of the family paid in gifts of blankets, chief's coppers and other objects of value. Such labor was deemed a privilege. The payment, made in the pleasurable and festive form of a potlatch, was accepted as an expression of appreciation and thanks.

While no longer called a potlatch, the deeply ingrained spirit still persists. "Is old Tlingit custom," an aged Alaskan Native Brotherhood member told the authors, who on conclusion of a lengthy interview made "a contribution to the Brotherhood treasury." "Is old Tlingit custom to show appreciation by making gift."

Clothed in the garb of amiable sociability, the potlatch served economically and culturally to strengthen family ties. No birthday or Christmas was ever awaited with keener anticipation by children and adults alike than these splendid events that enlivened the long winter nights.

To discourage the potlatch, as the missionaries insisted and the Brotherhood urged, was to tear out the heart of the Tlingits' family existence. Yet the Brotherhood felt that its elimination was essential for assimilation into the white man's "cultivated" life. Even Tlingit and Haida native tongues were discouraged. "Those eligible to membership," read the Brotherhood's 1917 constitution, "shall be Eng-

lish speaking members of the Native residents of the Territory in Alaska."

The stipulation did not work in practice. The better-educated Grand Camp leadership could conduct its meeting in English. Brotherhood Camps at Kake, Angoon or other villages comprising the native majority still conducted their affairs in the language of their fathers. In a later draft of the constitution, the language requirements were not included. This contrast in use of language exemplifies the reach of the organization itself. From the most tradition-minded village Indian, steeped in the customs and superstitions of his ancestors, the Brotherhood presented at its other extreme a sophisticated leadership, capable of speaking out in forceful English on behalf of its people.

In this sense the Brotherhood came to assume the leadership function of chieftainship and often, although not always, clan chiefs and Brotherhood officials were one and the same. Most important to native welfare, the Alaskan Native Brotherhood for the first time in history united the people of all villages, regardless of their matrilineal phratry, clan or family in a common cause. In both structure and

intent the Brotherhood transcended this schism and began as well to offer the people a substitute for many of the customs that were frowned on or had lost meaning in their semi-acculturated lives. In most villages the Brotherhood hall functioned —and still functions—as a community meeting place for both business and pleasure. The Brotherhood has also involved itself directly and indirectly in labor relations, acting at one time as bargaining agent for Indian fishermen, but more usually serving Indian needs on a broader front, of which union matters form only a part.

With arrival in 1918 and 1920 of the Paul brothers, originally of Wrangell, the Brotherhood entered the courts. William Paul and his brother Louis were sons of parents of mixed blood. They grew up in the States and attended the Indian University of Carlisle. William Paul was a lawyer and, because of his admission to practice in the State of Oregon, was entitled to practice also in Alaska. The Paul brothers focused the Brotherhood's efforts on specific targets, testing in 1922 the Indians' right to vote in litigation involving the seventh holder of the Chief Shakes title, Charlie Jones.

As had been his custom, Charlie Jones appeared at the polls in Wrangell to cast his ballot and to his bewilderment was challenged. For help he turned to the mother of the Paul brothers, an educated Stikine. They were both arrested. William Paul, naturally and ideologically, came to their rescue. By winning the case for Charlie Jones, William Paul actually won *de facto* enfranchisement for Alaskan Indians in 1922, two years before Congress passed legislation extending citizenship to all Indians born within the territorial limits of the United States.

Alaska's Tlingit and Haida absorbed the benefits of this legislation immediately. They had never considered themselves wards of the government. They rejected the concept of reservations. From the beginning they had sought the advice of those Alaskans whose council they could trust. Of a Brotherhood meeting to which he was invited in 1920, Wickersham wrote in his diary, "It seems all the Indians are much opposed to reservations. . . . My talk last night was simply a plain statement of the law and the road that leads to becoming a citizen of the United States and semed very satisfactory to the Indian men."

By 1926 they had learned the ropes sufficiently to elect as their first representative to the Territorial Legislature, William Paul. Some 2,000 Indian votes decided the election, but Paul's backing by the Republican party organization indicated the change occurring in relationships between natives and whites.

By 1929 the Brotherhood felt ready to tackle the problem of discrimination. When a Juneau movie house refused a Brotherhood officer admission to the main floor, the Executive Committee notified its camps that a boycott was being called. It proved effective and movie houses in the various communities found it economically advisable to drop the offensive practice. Persistence prodded the Territorial Legislature in 1946 to enact legislation prepared by Territorial Governor Ernest Gruening providing for full and equal privileges to all citizens in public places. Dis-

criminatory hiring practices still persist, but, although laws alone cannot wipe out prejudice, they soften the ground under it.

Since the 1920's a long list of native Alaskans have served in the State Legislature and in each instance he has also been a Brotherhood member of importance. Frank Peratrovich of the fishing community of Klawock, the first native Alaskan elected to the Territorial Senate, served as ANB Grand President. Other ANB grand presidents who served in the legislature are Frank Johnson of Kake, Alfred Widmark of Klawock, Andrew Hope of Sitka, and Frank See, Mayor of Hoonah and Brotherhood Grand President for 1966.

"In this electronic age the strife of the Tlingit is for both economic freedom and freedom from bureaucratic control—this is the theme of all thoughtful Tlingit and Haida today."

Bureaucratic control is one of two rankling hangovers from the past. The mature and politically sophisticated Alaskan of Tlingit, Haida, and Tsimshian ancestry feels that he has outgrown the overly solicitous attitude of the Bureau of Indian Affairs, that he can handle his own business affairs more realistically through his own channels than through the theoretically-inclined civil service.

Second and more consuming is the issue of aboriginal land claims which has been pending since 1936. The Franklin D. Roosevelt socio-economic reform era inspired the concept of reimbursing the nation's Indians for lands taken away in settlement. The kind of dollar sign that can be put on the destruction of a way of life is a question logic cannot answer. It raises, in addition, the consideration of whether any people actually "owns" a segment of earth, or whether each successive owner is merely privileged to hold it in trust, exchanging for its use a promise to live on it in harmony, improving upon it if he can, but knowing surely that if each man destroys the usefulness of his own portion, the whole will be taken away through exhaustion.

Nor have the Indians of southeastern Alaska been all losers. The same over-solicitousness of the Bureau of Indian Affairs has, during the past quarter century, brought with it generous governmental assistance to individual and group enterprise, subsidizing community indus-

As an elected public servant the native Alaskan has reached the furthermost point of civic advancement in his century-long struggle to enter fully and equally into the dominant society. Representing his constituents, he weighs issues affecting their interests and acts on matters concerning the State's welfare. His vote counts the same as the vote of his non-native colleague.

"If it had not been for the founding fathers," declared a recent *Voice of Brotherhood* editorial, "we would still be floundering in the quagmire of ignorance. Signs excluding Indians would still be seen in windows. We would not have equal recognition of native rights as citizens. Many thoughtful Tlingit Indians are thankful to the founding fathers for winning the battle for social freedom. We are free to move around and to live in any area we choose. We are not restricted to certain areas.

tries and providing loans for housing and expensive boats and gear for fishing.

Tremendous legal, legislative and emotional energies have nevertheless been expended over the land payment issue since the Interior Department under Secretary Harold Ickes assumed for the government the obligation of contemporary restitution for aboriginal dispossession. An analogous impasse would have occurred had Queen Elizabeth volunteered to reimburse English Saxons for the Norman conquest.

Morally and practically, the government has no alternative to laying the hundred-year-old ghost to rest. While a recent United States Court of Claims finding that the Tlingit and Haida should be paid $16 million in settlement has been described by the Indians' legal counsel as inadequate, final solution is nearing its terminal stage.

Greater than the monetary value is the psychological break with the vanished past, which clears the way for later generations to meet Alaska's very real present-day problems. Neither the unprecedented wartime building of military installations, nor achievement of statehood, has solved the acute problems of housing, health care, education and the development of a vigorous, stable economic base for industrial growth and year around employment.

With these and the hundreds of other compelling situations demanding answers along the nation's last frontier, native and white Alaskans are concerned alike. "The Tlingit and Haida people are subjected to the same economic forces and desires as their non-Indian neighbors," says the Bureau of Indian Affairs Tribal Enroll-

ment Officer, B. E. Baird. Of a total Alaskan population of slightly over a quarter million inhabitants, the combined native population of interior and coastal Indians, Eskimos, and Aleuts, was counted in the 1960 census at 42,522. Of this number the Bureau of Indian Affairs lists the Tlingit population at 8,482 living in still native communities and in cities where ancestry is mixed. Approximately three hundred and twenty Haida Indians live in the villages of Craig and Hydaburg, on Prince of Wales Island. Baird estimates that considerable numbers live also in Anchorage, Alaska, Seattle, Washington, and Oakland,

California "where chances for employment are greater."

"Locally many of the people are employed in the fishing industry and its related fields. However, this is largely seasonal and does not provide the year-long occupational opportunities present in other types of industry," says Baird. "Increasing numbers of native people work for agencies as well as for private business and in self-employment." The employment effects of the new lumbering activity are apparent in the 1964 Forestry Department figures showing 2,300 Indians, not necessarily all from the southeast district, enrolled in forestry work.

Thus, in the routine matters of the day, employment, education and free movement throughout their state and nation, the Tlingit and Haida of Alaska have all but completed their break with the past. Each is an accepted part of the forty-ninth state. "In Alaska," says former governor, now senator, Gruening, who long worked to banish it, "we have no discrimination." Except for the special native institutions run by the Bureau of Indian Affairs, the schools do not distinguish in their enrollment records between their Indian and non-Indian students. When asked how many natives a department or an industry employs, state officials raise their eyebrows and reply, "We don't keep figures like that."

The erosion of cultural differences is particularly apparent among the teenagers, the generation which has grown up together in the public schools. In Ketchikan, garbed in the extreme, rather startling tight jeans and shifts of contemporary fashion, boys and girls walk together hand in hand. The local coke bar at Wrangell each evening collects a rock and roll audience, which jams itself into booths that surround the indispensible juke box and its stack of pop hits.

"Who else have they got to go with," asks the dour owner of Wrangell's market. In Wrangell, where the Bureau of Indian Affairs gives an estimated Tlingit population of 1,000 for a city of 1,500, the question is well asked. Yet in Juneau, popula-

tion 11,000, where are listed, 1,062 Indians, the proprietor of one of the city's finest shops says with pride edged only faintly by defiance, "My wife is a full-blooded Tlingit."

Klukwan, the last Tlingit stronghold to be penetrated by United States authorities after the purchase, still holds out from absorption into Alaska's mainstream. Isolated even from the twin port cities of Haines-Port Chilkoot at the north of Lynn Canal, the leaders of Klukwan closed the town's doors by unanimous vote of its Village Council, binding the community's two hundred and twelve residents to refrain from showing to strangers any of their seven remaining clan houses in which are stored the last remnants of their valued heirlooms.

Even here, the process of acculturation, assimilation and absorption, goes on. Jennie Warren, last of the weavers of the renowned Chilkat chieftain's robe, who learned the art from her mother, who in turn learned it from hers, says, "One of my sons is a doctor in Seattle."

In a box inside her house were moccasins made of hide and some small, sealskin bags on which *Alaska* was stitched in tiny beads. Mrs. Warren pointed to them. "That's way I raise my children. I make moccasin. Make jelly. My son in Chicago ten year to be doctor."

Mrs. Warren said that she put away an unfinished Chilkat blanket, carefully wrapped and tied, to keep it clean. "No time for making blanket." She shook her head. Then she smiled, "My son's very good doctor now, in Seattle."

Humor, also, is helping to ease the final shock of entry into the white com-

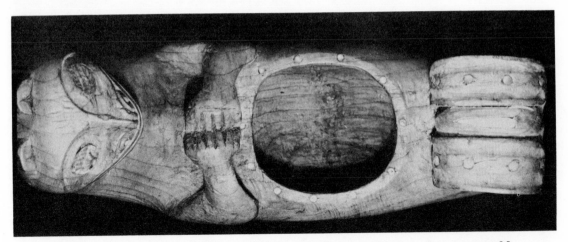

In 1911 the world's sea-otter population had dropped from the uncountable numbers of Bering's day to a scant 500 animals. A half century's careful protection in the Aleutian Islands National Wildlife Refuge nursed them back to some thirty or forty thousand—a renascence that proves men's ability to safeguard nature's world if they so choose.

In October 1965 a joint task force of the Department of Defense, the Department of the Interior, and the Atomic Energy Commission detonated a thermonuclear device far under the bleak, flat surface of Amchitka Island in "Project Long Shot," designed to test United States ability to detect underground atomic blasts. Amchitka is the main island refuge of the sea otter

The need for such tests is not necessarily questioned, but the choice of a site in the public trust, cannot be justified legally or morally. Federal authorities said the animals were driven away several days prior to the blast, and that a post-blast inspection disclosed "no evidence of injury."

Scientists, naturalists, and the man on the street are today fully aware that effects of atomic explosion on habitat cannot be determined, perhaps for years. In this sense the sea otter's fate may forecast man's own—disorderly survival, crowned by ordered death.

munity and to soothe the sting of discrimination which many white Alaskans claim does not exist.

"Look at me," a youthful Tlingit commanded his friends at a bar in Haines. He pulled back the lever of a pin ball machine and sent the ball rolling. "Look what I learned since I got off the reservation."

From potlatch, to politics, to pin ball machines. It might be argued that nonnative America has followed the same course.

Chapter VIII

MODERN ALCHEMY:
ARTIFACTS INTO ART

"Alaska is only a redheaded stepchild," Judge James Wickersham once remarked, "and the other children want the estate."

No description could better sum up the plight of our forty-ninth state in regard to the possession of its own native art. From Maine to California and in museums all over the world, the spectacular arts of the Pacific Northwest Coast Indians may be seen in abundance. Alaska, herself, boasts but a small sampling of the artistic heritage of her native people.

The very first adventurer to set foot on her shores initiated the procedure of removing samples of the carved painted and woven accomplishments of her unusual people. Georg Steller, permitted only ten hours on Kayak Island by an impatient and spent Bering, took from the curious cellar of his visit "arrows and wooden implements for making fire." Captain Cook observed in the hand of a Nootkan chief, "a carved bird of wood, as large as a pigeon, with which he rattled." Today this specimen, or one very like it, rests in the British Museum in London by the side of seventy-five other decoratively fashioned artifacts gathered by Cook and another famed English navigator, George Vancouver.

Other pieces collected by Cook and Royal Navy officers have found their way via gift, purchase, and the auction block, into the museums of Austria, Germany, and Italy. Objects gathered by the expedition's gifted artist, John Webber, whose fine drawing themselves added to the expedition's fame, are treasures of the Historiches Museum in Berne, Switzerland.

Spain was another early visitor to sail off with a sampling of Alaska's Indian art. On his round-the-world scientific voyage, Alejandro Malaspina was ordered to explore the Northwest Coast. In the *Descubierto* and *Atrevida* he made landfalls at Mt. Edgecumbe, site of Sitka, and at Nootka in 1791. Malaspina disappeared into the obscurity of political disfavor, but the trinkets and curiosities that found their way back to Spain are on view in Madrid's Museo de America.

Next to take evidence of Alaska's artistic virtuosity was Russia. Lisiansky arrived at the propitious moment to help retake Sitka and a greatful Baranov gave him masks "very ingeniously cut in wood," a chief's painted copper body armor and other objects which he brought home safely. Housed securely within the Leningrad Museum of Anthropology, they are today, if not lost, at least substantially removed from Western view.

But Russia did not corner the market on artifacts gathered by her early agents in America. Chief Manager Etolin of the

Russian American Company brought back to his native Finland an impressive showing of Kolosh work for the National Museum in Helsinki.

By the 1800's the acquisitive fever burned briskly in the adventurous souls of the fur-seeking Yankees. As a supplement, the Boston men brought back a rich haul of ethnological treasure, much of which still survives, primarily, as might be predicted, in museums of Boston and Salem. Items preserved in the Peabody Museum of Salem date back to 1799 when twenty-two sea captains who had sailed beyond the Cape of Good Hope formed the East India Marine Society of Salem.

From China, Mocha, Zanzibar, the East Indies, South Seas, and North Pacific they brought back beautiful and bizarre mementos of their voyages. Everything from a hairball "from the stomach of a cow in Madagascar," to "the oldest known Chilkat blanket" came into the mariners'

museum, later to become today's Peabody Museum of Salem.

These Yankee sailors brought back some of the earliest slate, or argillite, carvings. Made by the Haida from a carbonaceous shale which is found only on Graham Island in the Queen Charlottes, these intricate sculptures represent their creators' enterprising venture into the tourist trade. Early argillite carvings are patterned after the "scrimshaw" whittlings of the sailors and many reproduce in faithful copy details seen on board ships of the fur traders and later of the whalers who took to wintering in village ports along the Northwest Coast.

To keep up with demand, Haida carvers made unsmokeable pipes, ornamental plates, and beautiful but impractical boxes, all carved as commercial products. Pure sculpture depicting tribal legends and history began to appear and, finally, totem poles carved in exquisite miniature of those made from the tall cedar trees of the Queen Charlotte Islands. Museums today regard Haida argillite carvings as highly as the sailors who collected them.

The nation's first official collector did not even have to set foot on Alaskan soil to acquire examples of its art. As a young republic testing its sails, the United States in 1838 fitted out a major scientific exploratory expedition under command of Charles Wilkes. One of his stops was the Hudson's Bay Company post at Astoria on the Columbia River.

The Company's ship *Columbia* "had just returned from the northern posts," wrote Wilkes in his journal. "The master, Mr. Broughton, was kind enough to give me much information representing the northern coasts, and the Indian tribes. He likewise presented the Expedition with many curiosities of native workmanship, some of which showed much ingenuity, particularly their pipes and masks. The latter are used in their theatrical exhibitions, which are represented by those who have witnessed them as affording them much entertainment, and a pastime in which they very frequently indulge; many of these masks are represented with the spoon-lip. As this ornament belongs to the female sex, they also engage in the diversion. Some of the masks are sufficiently hideous, while others are carved with skill. . . . The wood is variously stained with red, black and yellow marks. . . . The two of them represented in the engraving will give a good idea of those

that are best executed."

The bulk of these pieces are today stored away in drawers of the United States National Museum study collection, tagged simply, "Wilkes Expedition."

An engineering officer, Edward G. Fast, attached to the command of General Jeff C. Davis, was one of the first individual collectors of native art. "The object of this collection is to illustrate as well as possible the history of civilization in our newly-acquired territory, the late Russo-American possessions," he wrote. "The whole collection was acquired during the short period of ten months, (from October 1867 to July 1868) while I was on duty at Sitka."

Fast put his astonishing collection of "Armor, Swords, Fancy Articles, Fishing, Hunting and Domestic Implements, Rare Carvings in Ivory, Stone and Wood, Grotesque Idols, Charms and Ornaments, Masks Carved in Wood, Headdresses, etc.," on exhibit at Clinton Hall Art Galleries in New York from which the Peabody Museum of Harvard University acquired it in 1870.

"My fondness for ethnological researches brought me into the closest connection with the natives," wrote Fast. "I congratulate myself upon having secured the assistance of several intelligent and courageous natives (one of them being a 'medicine man' of old) who at great personal risk scoured the country for hundred of miles, obtaining many of the articles from ancient graves, to touch which is considered such a heinous sacrilege that their lives would have been sacrificed upon the spot had they been detected in the act."

In its third annual report, the Harvard Museum congratulated itself for having come into "possession of so valuable a collection, and . . . in having the advantage of the service of Mr. William H. Dall, whose recent explorations in Alaska rendered him especially cognizant of the value of the different articles."

The smell was in the air. Collecting had turned into something more than a casual accumulation of Indian curios, when such an authority as Dall was called on to evaluate their worth. The next three decades witnessed a massive exodus of native art. Everyone who went to Alaska became a collector, the lowly tourist who quite unabashedly snatched up every object he could buy, the traders, mis-

sionaries, prospectors, school teachers, military personnel, naval officers, and even territorial officials, including the missionary turned governor, John G. Brady. The sudden buying not only disrupted cultural patterns responsible for the creation of the arts, it began to clean out the native inventory as well. Regardless of the jobs which brought them to Alaska, these early visitors moonlighted as collectors on the side.

John J. McLean of the United States Signal Office wrote on December 10, 1881, to Professor Spenser F. Baird, Secretary of the Smithsonian Institution:

"Your 'annual report' pamphlets containing instructions to collectors in zoology, archeology, etc., and accompanying

complimentary letter were received with great pleasure. I feel highly honored to have my name enrolled in the ranks of that noble army of 'Truth seekers,' of which you are the worthy chief, and I promise to do all I can to accomplish the special work you have assigned to me in this portion of Alaska. . . .

"I have availed myself of your offer in your letter of June 3rd to draw on you for the sum of $30.00 for the purpose of making a collection of ancient stone implements, bone carvings, ancient weapons, shields, wood carvings, etc. I have collected 41 pieces labeled and marked and sent them by the U.S.S. *Jamestown* which is about to leave Sitka sometime early in August. You will be drawn on for the sum of $29.75.

"In making the above collection I have learned that the Indians are beginning to discover that the white man desires to make collections of these specimens, hence their value has begun to appreciate considerably. Mr. Paul Schultze President of the NW Trdg. Co. is making a collection for the Berlin Museum through his agent here.

"There is opposition also in another and unexpected direction in my present line of research. The Reverend Mr. Jackson, a missionary, paid a flying visit to Sitka, on his way to Chilcat to establish a mission there, and while in Sitka bought everything, nearly, in the line of specimens, especially of stone, bone, and arms, paying $200 for the same. Mr. Brady of whom he made the purchase informed me that the collection was for the Museum of Princeton College."

Items procured by McLean for $29.75 would turn a modern collector green: "a miniature collection of masks and costumes used by the Indian doctors in their incantations over sick people. . . . Indian pipes ingeniously made of iron pipe and old copper . . . set of gambling pins . . . a ladle made of mountain sheep horn . . . halibut hook, carved . . . halibut club . . . a rattle . . . grease box . . . small war knife . . . carved image of a starving Indian . . . warrior with armor . . . a fish with a man's head protruding from its jaws . . . soup and fish spoon." The same or similar forty-one items would command a price on today's market of well over $5,000 on even a conservative guess. One Tlingit wood circular rattle alone went for sale in 1965 at a Sotheby auction for $1,456.

What McLean may or may not have known when he stowed his "three boxes of Indian implements, ornaments, carvings, etc.," on board the U.S.S. *Jamestown* was that the Navy gunboat's commander, L. A. Beardslee, was another enlistee in Professor Baird's "noble army of truth seekers." A month earlier Beardslee had shipped off his own collection of nineteen "Articles from S. E. Alaska purchased for the Smithsonian Institution." Indeed, as anchor man in the acquisition sweepstakes, Professor Spenser F. Baird back in Washington was laying the foundation for one of the most unwieldy collections of all time.

Only by fortuitous circumstance was the United States Government in the race at all. In 1835 an Englishman, James Smithson, left his estate "to found at

Washington under the name of the Smithsonian Institution, an establishment for the increase and diffusion of knowledge among men." Congress was not eager to accept the gift and debated its suitability for ten years before passing a statute to set up a library and a museum as initial branches of the government institution.

The Smithsonian's first secretary, Joseph Henry, and his successor Professor Baird, dedicated their efforts to fulfilling the spirit of Smithson's will, translating their own ethnological zeal into official Smithsonian policy. In 1863 an instruction pamphlet "for Research relative to the Ethnology and Philology of America" went out to members of the Army, Navy, and United States medical and technical corps, Indian agents, and other individuals stationed in Indian country, soliciting those with scientific training and interest to aid in collecting Indian artifacts.

"It is especially important to make immediate collections," the bulletin emphasized, "as many articles are of perishable nature, and the tribes themselves are passing away or exchanging their own manufactures for those of the white race. It is hardly necessary to specify any of particular interest, as almost everything has its value in giving completeness to a collection . . . In making these collections, care should be taken to specify the tribes from which they are obtained, and where any doubt may exist, the particular use to which each is applied."

The material began coming in. Some speciments, such as the Wilkes collection of Northwest Coast "curiosities of native

workmanship" had already found their way into the Smithsonian. The first really great opportunity for collecting came with the Centennial Exhibition held in Philadelphia in 1876. Both the Indian Bureau of the Department of Interior and the Smithsonian Institution received an actual budget to develop a display of ethnology and archeology of the United States, which at the close of the exhibition was slated for permanent repose in the Smithsonian.

The task of collecting along the Pacific Northwest Coast fell to James G. Swan who was out in Washington Territory as secretary to its first congressional delegate. From Port Townsend at the northern tip of present Washington State, Swan scoured coastal villages of the Nootka, Tsimshian, and Haida Indians. To a nation which thought itself well versed in Indian paraphernalia, Swan's offerings produced astonishment when they went on exhibit in Philadelphia.

"There were fiendish looking little household gods made of bone, inlaid with shell, manufactured by the Alaskan Indians," exclaimed an Exposition historian, James D. McCabe. "A curious feature was a reduced copy of a colossal carving at Fort Simpson, B. C. representing the body and outspread wings of a bird with a head of a dog . . . Here also were two large 'totem posts,' from the Pacific coast" which McCabe explained as "a sort of illustrated pedigree or family tree."

Swan forwarded to the Smithsonian dozens of crates and bales of carefully inventoried carvings, ornaments, implements, and utensils, all noted by date and village of purchase. "My Indian, Johnny Kit Elswa, has proved of great service in purchasing articles at far less prices than I could, as tourists and collectors have advanced prices greatly," he wrote Baird in 1883. "Mr. McKenzie [trader for the Hudson's Bay Company then at Masset] tells me that my purchases are actually lower than he has paid Indians for the same kind of articles."

From Masset came three hundred and sixty-seven objects: an ancient dancing skirt ornamented with puffin beaks and Chinese coins at $1.25, carved and painted rattles representing a man's head, bear, owl, raven, woodpecker, and figures from legends at twenty-five, thirty, and fifty cents each. Ornate dishes representing seals, skates, and beavers carved of wood and of mountain sheep horn were obtained at similar prices. The Masset total, $223.72.

A long list of carved slate columns, the coveted argillite carvings, filled the boxes from Skidgate, priced at six, seven, eight and ten dollars apiece. Altogether the Skidgate collection of two hundred and twenty-six ornaments, weapons and utensils came to $967.09.

To this total of $1,190.81 Swan told Baird, "must be added at least 100 percent to cover expenses of transportation, lodging, etc., incurred on the Expedition. "I have performed all the work of assorting, labelling, packing, inventory and describing this fine collection entirely alone except for the manual labor of an Indian. I think you will be satisfied with the result when the 29 cases I have shipped will have reached you."

Swan's preoccupation with the Queen Charlotte Islands of British Columbia removed him from the competition which

embroiled Alaska. McLean, from his station at the U. S. Signal Office at Sitka, candidly kept Baird up to date in the letters accompanying his shipments.

"Since I wrote last have had the pleasure of seeing one of the most valuable collections of archeological specimens," he wrote Baird in September 1881. "The specimens belong to Captain John M. Vanderbilt Agt. of the N.W. Trdg. Co. . . . The most valuable specimens were presented to him by the chief of the Stikeen Indians near Fort Wrangell, when Capt. Vanderbilt was adopted into the tribe. . . I am doubtful whether the Capt. would part with these specimens, but if he can be persuaded, they would form a very valuable addition to the archeological specimens of your Institution.

"I learned from the Capt. that the Rev. S. H. Young at Fort Wrangell has also a fine collection which I am going down to look at as soon as I can get away from the office."

Compared to his boss, Captain Vanderbilt was a dabbler. "Since writing my last letter of 7th," wrote McLean on the 8th, "I have discovered that the N.W. Trading Co.'s manager has been making a large collection of ancient stone and bone carvings, carved wooden household utensils such as spoons, bowls, dishes, eating trays, a fine collection of war knives with quaintly carved handles and bead embroidered sheaths, and among them a finely carved stone pipe, a stone ax and several pestles and mortars. All of the above fine collection were secured in Hoochenoo among the tribe of that name.

"All of these shew that they have been used for a long time. These specimens are becoming more difficult to get with the arrival of every steamer as they are eagerly sought after and bought up by visitors and others interested in collecting for college Museums etc.,

"I have also heard from good authority that two Germans, scientific gentlemen connected with the Berlin Museum are coming to Alaska, and intend to spend the winter with Indians of the Chilcat tribe to learn their language and to make extensive collections of the archaeological remains. The Chilcats have very valuable collections of carvings in bone, wood and stone and the present would be the best time to secure the best collection of specimens that your Institution has as yet so far secured . . . If you desire the collection to be made without delay, and to be in the field before these German gentlemen, write so that I shall have an answer by the October steamer which leaves San Fran. about the middle of October for Sitka."

While awaiting Professor Baird's reply, McLean bought up one hundred and forty-two objects from Mr. Sphun of the North West Trading Company for a carefully itemized $119.05. In December he sent another shipment from "the villages between Chil-caht and Sitka."

By the time the Krause brothers appeared, the German scientists had been

Port Townsend Washington Territory
December 4th 1883

"Dear Professor Baird:

I sent by mail today a box containing specimens ennumerated on the Invoice I mailed to you November 24th . . . 219 is a stone carving of a mythological legend of the Bear's wife suckling her young. This is specially commended to your notice as a work of sculpture of which the design and pose would have been creditable to a white artist. It has been much admired here by commissioners, and a fabulous price offered me for it. It was not finished when I got it but just roughed out, and my Indian assistant Johnny Kit Elswa finished it on the voyage from Skidgate to Victoria. . . .

Yours truly,
James G. Swan"

out-maneuvered. McLean wrote to Baird in May 1882, "I made a purchase of the largest collection of stone and bone implements and carvings that I have as yet seen at one time. I exceeded the amount you have given authority for, but I think you will be pleased . . . I had just secured the collection when Dr. A. Krause, Member of the Geographical Society of Bremen arrived in Sitka with the special object of securing all the ethnological specimens he could purchase in town.

"The Dr. became my guest and I laughingly told him what I had done, and he seemed to regret very much that he was not in time to secure the collection. Dr. Krause leaves for the East by the May Steamer from Sitka. We shall soon have a valuable report on his labors and researches in Alaskan Ty [Territory]. His younger brothers remains in Chilkat for the summer."

As for Captain Vanderbilt's collection, McLean wrote, "I think he never intended to sell the articles on account of their associations."

During this period a far more formidable collector of Tlingit material had appeared who differed from Professor Baird's captive collectors in that he collected for many museums. Lieutenant George Thornton Emmons of the United States Navy, retired in 1899, spent his life in and around Alaskan coastal waters, serving for six decades as anthropologist without portfolio to the country's forgotten territory. Emmons filled hundreds of lined composition books with valuable ethnological data, some portion of which has been published to form an important part of the anthropological literature. As President Theodore Roosevelt's special agent, he took the stump during the early 1900's on behalf of Alaska's natives, urging Congress to provide them with medical aid and the opportunities of a democracy.

Most of all, Emmons collected hundreds upon hundreds of magnificent examples of Tlingit and Haida art. Few museums are without Emmons pieces, and they are frequently the institution's aesthetic gems. The sheer bulk of his collecting accomplishments gives rise to the suspicion that perhaps Emmons alone emptied Alaska of its native art. The American Museum of Natural History bought twenty-six separate collections from him between 1880 and 1936, each comprising many dozens of carefully documented objects. Other big buyers were Chicago's Field Museum of Natural History which acquired nine lots of masks, rattles, tools, costumes and utensils, and the United States National Museum which through the years bought in gargantuan lots.

Emmons first appeared on the collecting horizon in 1886 when he took Princeton's Professor Libbey and the *New York Times* journalist, Frederick Schwatka, on his gunboat, *Pinta,* to Yakutat for their combination mountain climbing and collecting expedition. Schwatka wrote about the expedition for *Times* readers, while Emmons and Libbey competed with each other for the Yakutat Tlingit's supply of masks, bracelets, combs, hats, and other portable artifacts. Professor Libbey gave his collection to Princeton to supplement the sampling scooped up by Sheldon Jackson on his "flying visit to Sitka." Embarked on the main theme of his life,

Emmons began offering his carefully collected examples of native Alaska's rich creativity to the nation's museums.

"The American Museum of Natural History at New York has recently purchased a very complete collection of ethnological specimens, collected by Lieutenant George T. Emmons," said *The Journal of American Folklore* in 1888. "It is of great value to the student of American folklore as the collector has taken great pains to ascertain the meaning of the various implements, particularly of the carvings and has recorded the traditions referring to them."

The writer was Franz Boas, whose arrival in America coincided with an intensified and broadened interest in the vanishing Indians, an interest which increased in tempo as the Indian culture diminished. An industrial America having completed its pioneer advance across the continent, felt sufficiently secure to study the Indians.

Requisites were ripe for a major scientfic advance: trained and interested men, and the remnants of cultures that in both time and space were accessible to study. Missing only was an instrument to bring them into workable focus.

The catalyst came in 1893, in the form of a great world's fair. Chicago was commemorating the four-hundredth anniversary of America's discovery with an event calculated to put all previous expositions to shame. The World Columbian Exposition enlisted the nation's outstanding minds to prepare exhibits demonstrating scientific and practical progress. It promised in the bargain to establish a Columbus Memorial Museum as a permanent home for the exhibit.

Professor Frederick Ward Putnam was chosen Chief of Ethnology for the Exposition. Putnam was a many-sided man of science who during an energetic life executed numerous government commissions while serving simultaneously and in overlapping capacities as professor at Harvard and Columbia Universities and curator to the Peabody museums of Salem and Harvard and the American Museum of Natural History.

One of the Columbian Exposition's most dramatic offerings in its cross section of the Western hemisphere's cultural fabric was the still living, if no longer flourishing, Indian culture of the Pacific Northwest Coast. From Skidgate in the Queen Charlotte Islands, home of the Haida, a Scotch trader turned ethnologist, James Deans, sent two hundred and eighty-six items including an ancient native house and its totem post.

From the territory of the Kwakiutl came fourteen authentic Indians who lived in native fashion in a large wooden house set up on the premises. Before their return home, Putnam wrote, Boas, who served as one of Putnam's seventy trained investigators for the Exposition, had "secured all their costumes and paraphernalia for the Columbian Museum. He also had moulds made of two or three of them so as to make models which were dressed in their garments."

Emmons sent Tlingit material from Alaska. Swan supplied artifacts from Cape Flattery in Washington Territory. Other Pacific coast exhibits came from the Bella Coola in British Columbia and the Salish of Puget Sound. These rounded out a representation of twenty-five Indian cultures from the United States and Canada which by gift or purchase became the core of the future Chicago museum's ethnological collection.

By providing funds and a forum, the World Columbian Exposition vastly extended the horizon of American anthropology, elevating it in the public consciousness from the realm of curiosity to the region of science and placing its practitioners on a new and higher plateau for twentieth century study.

To Chicagoans, the practical reward came in 1894 with the opening of the Field Columbian Museum, named to honor its primary benefactor, the Chicago merchant, Marshall Field. By virtue of its powerful start the new institution took its place at once as a ranking member of the nation's influential, scientifically-oriented, museum triumvirate. In the next three decades the three big natural science

museums of Chicago, New York and Washington dominated the field of American anthropology.

Chicago's leadership, however, passed to New York where the American Museum of Natural History had hired away the Exposition's directional force, Frederick Ward Putnam. As the American Museum's Curator of Anthropology, Putnam carried forward the impetus of the Exposition. He persuaded his museum president, Morris K. Jesup, to add to the museum's staff promising anthropologists including Franz Boas to gather the necessary arts and artifacts for exhibiting various ethnic groups "dressed in their native costume and engaged in some characteristic work or art illustrative of their life and particular art or industry." The new approach revolutionized the static, typology character (knives with knives, etc.) of museum displays and stimulated desires to collect every detail of cultural accoutrement. Inevitably arose the notion of museum-sponsored expeditions into the field.

Putnam pressed the concept of a major scientific expedition to regions bordering the North Pacific to examine cultural and linguistic relationships of the land arc across which anthropologists theorize early man passed from Siberia over the Bering Straits into the Western Hemisphere. Jesup backed the ambitious undertaking and Boas was put in charge of direction and planning. Between 1897 and 1903, twenty-seven investigating expeditions went to Siberia, Alaska and British Columbia. The Jesup North Pacific Expedition is looked to by American anthropologists as the period in which their scientific discipline came of age.

Siberia and arctic Alaska, Boas parceled out to specialists. "Since the Tlingit had been investigated by Lieutenant G. T. Emmons, U.S.N., who it is hoped may publish the results of his researches," Boas wrote, "the principle work by the Jesup Expedition had to be done in British Columbia and the State of Washington." To these areas Boas assigned numerous investigators, including himself, who brought in data for publication of eleven oversized volumes and carloads of artifacts to swell the museum's fast growing supply.

Choice of the North Pacific rim intensified already keen interest in the Pacific coast and while they did not neglect other Indian cultures, the big-three museums began to vie with each other to build up their Northwest Coast collections. They soon hit on the device of enlisting resident collectors. Two of the most important were Emmons, concentrating on his beloved Alaska, and Charles L. Newcombe, who collected from the Haida, Tsimshian and Kwakiutl of British Columbia. Buried deep in the museums' archives are letters that fill the gap between the densely forested coastal islands and exhibit halls, and dispel any notion that the objects on display appeared by some miracle of immaculate conception. Every museum specimen was a coup, collected by somebody, for somebody, from somebody, in an atmosphere of intrigue and urgency.

Wrote Emmons in 1899 to Secretary John Winser of the American Museum of Natural History, "I have just come across a set of Indian Doctor's implements; it has quite a local reputation and while I have known of the thing for years I have never before been able to see them. There are 20 pieces in all but the value of the things rests wholly in the eight wooden, copper-ornamented masks which stand for the eight spirits personated by the Doctor. . . . No white man has ever yet seen them and I think I have arranged to keep them out of sight for a time until I can hear if Mr. Jesup would wish them. . . . If you wish them let me know at the earliest opportunity as they will be picked up by one who can never appreciate them."

old Alaska pieces without difficulty providing they are catalogued."

Not long after, Emmons sold 1,438 pieces to Dr. George A. Dorsey who, as Curator of Anthropology for the Field Museum of Natural History, was endeavoring to set up his own source of supply. Around 1900 Dorsey approached Newcombe of Victoria, whom he had met earlier on a field trip of his own. Newcombe was interested, but alas, Boas had got to him first. "A sum of $600 to be placed

Emmons's constant worry was the insatiable tourist appetite for creations he felt should be the properly catalogued possessions of museums. In an early letter he chided Boas for turning down a selection of wooden pipes, hair ornaments, masks and utensils from villages of Klukwan, Angoon and Hoonah, and directed Boas to return them for disposal "to tourists who will, as you know, pay anything for such pieces and they will be scattered about where they have no scientific value and this is my regret as I have been at such pains to gather them and each one is a good article ethnologically speaking." Boas took them all in the end, as he knew perfectly well the truth of Emmons's contention, "I find that I can dispose of any

at my disposal," Newcombe wrote Dorsey in May 1901, "provides that out of this sum I obtain one or more totem poles, memorial columns, grave totems, house boards and human skeltons, the more the better, the museum to pay freight from Skidgate . . . travelling, etc., transportation, hire of Indians. In addition, out of this sum I am to collect botanical specimens, birds, etc., to illustrate the stories Swanton is collecting. Also, I am to identify so far as possible exact localities of places, names in the stories. . . . After this my whole services will be entirely at your disposal."

By November he had quitted his obligation to Boas so that Dorsey could write, "Full steam ahead to collect all

Haida material—big, small—simply make the best collection obtainable whether it costs $1,000 or $2,000." In his want list Dorsey said, "Especially am I desirous of having some old carved fronts of doctors' graves and things of that sort, also to get house posts and whatever objects may be secured by a careful search of the houses of Masset itself."

Wrote back Newcombe at one point, "Your capasity for absorbing and accumulating ethnological material fairly astounds me. I had thought that perhaps two or three poles would have been all that you would have cared for—but 10 to 20!! However. . . ." And he did his best to fill Dorsey's requests, gathering materials for fifteen major accessions by 1907.

Symptomatic of changing anthropological interests, the correspondence between Dorsey and his collectors began to cool. Returning from a three-year round-the-world trip, Dorsey wrote Newcombe: "Things are running in the same old way around here, though we have rather shifted the focus of our attention to other continents. We now have a rapid and growing Chinese collection. . . . Likewise our South Pacific collection grows apace. . . . I am inclined to think our Melanesian collections are now the foremost in the world. . . . Little has been done with North America since you left except the acquisition now and then of isolated pieces or small supplementary collections."

To Emmons he had written earlier, "You must be perfectly aware, we are devoting all of our available funds to regions beyond North America."

In a few brief years the big three museums had accomplished their self-assigned mission of acquiring for posterity the cultural castoffs of the nation's aboriginal population. The successes of these frantic two decades had dulled the edge of their domestic appetite and whetted it for the treasures of more distant lands. Instead of gathering up everything in sight, the museums began now to wheel and deal, filling in where they detected a gap, and trading off duplicates.

In 1911 the following set of memos circulated through the upper echelons of the American Museum of Natural History:

March 24th

My dear Doctor Wissler: President Osborn would like to have you examine the Brady Collection, which was sent to the Museum on approval some time ago, and report to him thereon. George H. Sherwood, Assistant Secretary.

April 8th

Dear President Osborn: In compliance with your request I make a report on the collection of Alaskan curios now exhibited in the Museum by Ex-Gov. Brady. So far as I know, there are but two pieces in the collection not easily duplicated in our own and these two are of very little importance. On the whole, the quality of the specimens we now have is superior to that of the Brady Collection. The perishable material is badly moth-eaten, some of the Chilcat blankets, for example, being practically worthless. While it might be a good thing to have such a collection in the Museum for the sake of completeness, I do not see that it would materially add to the effectiveness of what we now have. Dr. Clark Wissler, Curator.

May 11

My dear Doctor Wissler: President Osborn desires you to write him, if you can do so, a letter appreciative of the value of the Brady Collection, calling attention to the fact that, inasmuch as the Museum has the most complete collection in the world which this collection would merely duplicate, we do not desire to acquire it. He desires to send this letter to one of the Trustees, who may be in a position to help Mr. Brady dispose of the collection to some other institution. George H. Sherwood, Assistant Secretary.

In a memo of May 12th, Dr. Wissler obliged, noting, "Such a collection can never be made again as the habits of life of these tribes have changed," and offering Lieutenant Emmons as "fully competent to speak on this collection and will no doubt take pleasure in recommending it to anyone interested."

In December a new set of memos started flowing from Washington, D.C., where Mrs. E. H. Harriman had offered to purchase the collection as a gift to the United States National Museum. Anthropology Curator W. H. Holmes visited New York and found the collection to be much traveled as well as "injured by destructive insects." He placed an evaluation on it of $4,000, found it was mortgaged for $3,000 more and that the American Museum had a lien on it for transportation costs of $300 entailed in its journey from the Alaska-Yukon-Pacific Exposition of 1909. "It appears that this collection has been held for sale since the Exposition at Seattle," he wrote his superior at the Smithsonian.

Mrs. Harriman extricated the wander-

ing collection from its difficulties. On June 20, 1912, a museum memo went out: "Prompt acknowledgement should be made to Mrs. Harriman." On June 21st Secretary R. Rathbunof wrote Mrs. Harriman, "It gives me pleasure to acknowledge the receipt from the American Museum of Natural History of eight boxes containing that portion of the ethnological collection which you purchased from Ex-Governor Brady and have presented to the National Museum."

With his letter to the widow of the United States railroad magnate, Edward H. Harriman, the Secretary of the United States National Museum wrote finis to an era. In a competitive scramble lasting a quarter of a century, the nation's big three scientific museums had cornered the market on the nation's Indian relics. Collections henceforth would bear a more personal stamp and with one notable exception be neither so large nor all-inclusive.

Seattle's Alaska-Yukon-Pacific Exposition of 1909 was one of a series of civic attempts to attract attention to the growing cities of the West. St. Louis celebrated the Louisiana Purchase in 1904, and Portland honored the Lewis and Clark Expedition a year later. Patterned on the U. S. Centennial and Chicago's Columbian, the fairs helped keep alive public interest in dead Indians and stimulated new collecting activities from which smaller museums now benefited.

Emmons's pieces collected for the Alaska-Yukon-Pacific Exposition, unlike Brady's collection, remained in Seattle and for many years were housed in a flammable, vintage structure on the University of Washington campus, until its recent move into contemporary quarters of the Thomas Burke Memorial Museum.

Important survivors of the St. Louis Exposition are thirteen tall Haida totem poles that made the long trip from Alaska to the Midwest and back again to Sitka, where they now stand along the shaded path of Lover's Walk in Sitka National Monument. A. P. Kashevaroff, first curator of the Alaska State Museum in Juneau, then an historical library and museum, credits these early fairs as the Museum's chief means of building its collection. Like an Alaska in microcosm, "The Museum is none too well supplied with specimens of Thlinget antiquities," wrote Kashevaroff, "these being the most easily accessible to tourists, are rapidly leaving the Territory."

Here, "having cleaned Alaska out," as Emmons wrote Newcombe back in 1899, the collector's story might have ended. But in 1912 came announcement of a new acquisitional phase that would persist until the stock market crash of 1929.

"An ethnological collection from the Indian tribes of the Northwest Coast of

America, constituting a part of the George C. Heye collection never before exhibited, has recently been thrown open to the public view," stated Pennsylvania's University Museum Journal. "The visitor is struck at once by the difference between the specimens shown here and those in the other Indian collections; they seem as if they were products of another continent."

George Heye was a phenomenon known in the field as a "box car" collector. He bought at one stroke whole collections and raced across the country in a chauffeur-driven car to buy up the portable environments of entire Indian communities. Using his Standard Oil Company stock inheritance, he followed a lifelong collecting career, carried on personally and through a network of well subsidized agents in both Americas. Called by some the greatest Indian collector of all time, he typifies that emotionally driven breed of accumulators to whom the process of collecting is an end in itself. Only when the massive assortment—from Peru to Alaska—burst the seams of Heye's improvised quarters in New York and a borrowed wing of the University Museum in Philadelphia, did he create and endow the Heye Foundation with its Museum of the American Indian at Broadway and 155th Street in New York.

Meanwhile, the University Museum had become accustomed to its unusual loan collection. It embarked on its own program of securing pieces from the Northwest Coast, enlisting for the purpose the most extraordinary collector of them all—a full blooded Chilkat Indian, Louis Shotridge. Born in Klukwan, an Eagle of the Kaguantan clan, and grandson of the great Kloh-kutz, Louis Shotridge had traveled the acculturation path out of his native village to the urban center of Philadelphia, where he became Assistant Curator in the museum's American section. Through Shotridge the museum built up its highly specialized and incomparable collection of Tlingit clan hats and war helmets.

The museum's future director Dr. George B. Gordon first met Shotridge when he visited Alaska in 1907. By 1913 the handsome, literate man of two worlds was on the museum staff, delighting school children to whom he talked by his stunning presence in full Chilkat ceremonial attire, and aiding such noted anthropologists as Boas, Edward Sapir and others in their research on his people's life and language. His membership in the Alaskan Native Brotherhood and his blood link with the natives of Klukwan gave him access to family and clan treasured heirlooms. One by one, in the name of science, Shotridge collected these priceless pieces and shipped them to Philadelphia.

On the eve of the crash in 1928, Shotridge wrote in the Museum Journal of six clan hats of the ranking Klukwan families: Whale, Raven, Frog, Eagle, Killer-whale and Wolf. "Some of the pieces are unique in character, others grotesque in form, and some of them may appear, to a stranger, as if they had served in a fantastic masquerade. But if one makes a close examination he will readily discover in most of the fine old pieces the aesthetic emotions that played the main part in their creation.

"Like all men who have a desire to accomplish something," wrote Shotridge, "I hope to live to see the day when these old things (each of which has long held the reverence of my people) will help to bring the true character of their makers into the white man's light."

Shotridge did not live to see fulfillment of his hope, although his premature death was less a reason than the superior attitude with which most whites view all cultures different from their own. Shotridge was an employment casualty of the stock market crash, a depression lay-off during the early thirties. His own people, to whom he returned, understood his efforts to interpret them to the white world as little as the white world has learned to understand his people. Versions differ as to his death, but there is little divergent opinion among knowledgeable persons about the still prevailing code of Tlingit justice which demands that wrongs be either righted, or paid for. When Shotridge's body was found near Klukwan, he had already been dead many days.

The death of Louis Shotridge, an uncommon Tlingit, underscores a dramatic reversal in attitude among the Indians of Southeastern Alaska. Since the coming of the first white man, they had bartered their artistic creations freely and watched without too much concern as the white man carried them away. Not until the unreplenishable supply was nearly gone did they clamp down the lid. No one really knows today how much is left, but in every Indian village, Klukwan, Sitka, Saxman, the clan houses—unmarked to the white man but well known to the natives—unobtrusively store the last fragments of their colorful past.

A smattering of masks and rattles,

bowls and boxes have continued to find their way out of Alaska in the decades since the thirties. Emmons continued to collect and sell into the forties. Indians needing money—for actual reasons or for whisky—periodically reduced the native inventory still further. But for all practical collecting purposes, the home source dried up. From the 1930's on, collections coming onto the market had been gathered earlier.

Walter C. Walters, who ran a curio shop in Wrangell during the collecting heyday, gradually came to own more of Chief Shakes regalia than did the last Shakes himself. Today a replica of Shakes' house is watched over by Wrangell's only totem carver, Thomas Ukas, who shows it to tourists. Inside, except for its carved posts, a painted house board once owned by Chief Toyatte, a carved house screen panel, two small totemic carvings and a portrait painted during Russian times of young Chief Shakes, the house is bare.

To see how the Shakes of Mrs. McFarland's day lay majestically in state, surrounded by the carved, painted, and woven evidence of his prestige, one must visit the Thomas Burke Museum in Seattle, which, jointly with the Denver Art Museum, bought up the Walter C. Walters collection of Indian memorabilia from Mrs. Walters in 1953.

A purchase of a different sort was the acquisition of some five thousand masks, baskets, and carvings by the Portland Art Museum, collected over a twenty-year period by Axel Rasmussen, who served as superintendent of schools at Wrangell and Skagway. "He was a quiet, rather lonely man," one of his teachers, Elizabeth Selmer, wrote, "absorbed in three things—a strong interest in the church, a great love for children . . . and a desire to gather and save the art of the Alaskan Indian." Rasmussen died in 1945 at Swedish Hospital in Seattle.

Rumors of the fantastic collection reached the ears of Earl Stendahl, a Los Angeles dealer in pre-Columbian material who at the time was searching out saleable pots and sculpture in Central America. Stendahl wasted no time. He headed north and negotiated the purchase of the entire collection from Rasmussen's heirs. Shortly after, it went on exhibit at the museum, a purchase of the Portland Art Association. Accompanying the exhibit was a handsome picture book in which the museum's former director, Robert Tyler Davis, explained the Cinderella-esque transformation of Northwest Coast ethnological artifacts into objects of art.

Predictably the transformation had occurred under the auspices of a world's fair, the Golden Gate International Exhibition of 1939 in San Francisco, generated in part by the nation's maturing sense of social, economic and ethnic conscience. The presentation of Indian artifacts as art was conceived and organized by Frederick H. Douglas, curator of the Denver Art Museum, and René d'Harnoncourt, General Manager of the Indian Arts and Crafts Board, established by act of Congress in 1935, to promote the economic welfare of Indians through development of their arts and crafts. Full scale art treatment followed at the Museum of Modern Art in 1941 with a similar exhibition that was aesthetically dominated by the arts of the Northwest Coast Indians.

For well over two hundred years these bowls, spoons, masks and helmets, dance leggings and combs, rattles and dance staffs had passed from their original owners via impromptu collectors into the museums of the world. With the Rasmussen transaction, a modern middleman entered the deal, an indispensible member of the modern art world, the dealer. Stendahl's purchase and resale of the vast collection transformed the collecting game into commerce, lifting it once and for all out of the hands of amateurs and turning Alaska's antique art into a commodity.

On Monday, July 12, 1965, the English auction house of Sotheby's announced for public sale "The property of Mrs. L. Ani and Other Owners of Fine African Sculpture, Pre-Columbian, Oceanic, Pacific Northwest Coast and Indian art . . . including Haida Shale Carvings, a Tlingit carved Wood Rattle, a Kwakiutl Female Wood Dance Mask. . . ." Three dozen pieces, all told—similar to the "367 articles of Indian manufacture collected in 1883 by Swan for $223.72—went at auction for $8,794.86.

News of this sort little bothers Alaska's native youth, who through the instant communications and global urgencies of our day, feel more kinship with their contemporaries around the world than with the past. To an inquiry about old carvings, a Stikine teenager at Wrangell shrugged, "I don't bother about that old stuff."

To the young, the once rich fusion of graphic, sculptural, musical and dramatic arts in the daily and ceremonial life of the Indians of Alaska has passed into what the anthropologists describe as "a memory culture." In their stead have come the

work patterns and entertainment forms that—for better or worse—are those of present-day civilization.

Ironically such "old stuff" as still remains in native Alaska is in careful custody of the old timers, many of them, the same earliest Alaskan Native Brotherhood members who urged abandonment of tribal ways. As the last ranking heads of family and clan houses, they are today charged with the responsibility of looking after the reduced inventory of historic heirlooms.

These seasoned, intelligent men are not trying to breathe new life into an extinguished culture. But with the intuitive grasp of human need that led them to press for full acceptance into a modern Alaska, they today urge rich remembrance of things past. This was the theme of the Alaskan Native Brotherhood's fifty-third annual convention in 1965. Resolution No. 36 pledged the Brotherhood to "encourage all camps to assist in recording legends, songs and other data to preserve in written record our heritage."

At the same time, as if recognizing the vacuity of a taped heritage, Past Alaskan Native Brotherhood Grand President Cyrus Peck, editor of the *Voice of Brotherhood*, told the membership that "the heritage of character, the spark or light that passes from father and uncle to son and nephew . . . is the most prized possession we get from our ancestors, the only true possession we ever receive which cannot be taken physically from us. . . .

"Do you hear the whisper of your father—of your uncles? Their example is close to us. It is in the air. It is in the spirit. It is our birthright and heritage. As the men of this organization were vigilant and brave in the battles of the past," he said, "let us be brave in meeting the challenges of today."

ALASKA RE-VISITED

The Living Memory
of a Lost Artistic Heritage

Recognition by the international art community of the significance of the primitive arts is recent enough in time to have many of its early exponents still active in our world of the arts.

For many years the creative works of primitive peoples were viewed and collected as curiosities. Some few observers studied the work from an ethnological or cultural point of view without full recognition of its aesthetic significance. Astute observers among early explorers of the Northwest Coast documented their observations and in some cases collected samplings of the arts to illustrate, on their return home, the curious and unusual customs of its producers.

At the turn of the century and earlier, the rebellion of the European artists against the romanticism, neoclassicism and sentimentality of the official and salon arts brought to the attention of the modern painters, who were searching for new forms and aesthetic experiences, the vital-

ity and sophistication in the work of the Africans, and the stylization and subtlety of design in the work of the Orient. Picasso found inspiration in African artifacts which until then were found primarily in the collections of museums of natural history. Toulouse-Lautrec and Whistler were influenced in their work by Japanese prints and Chinese drawings.

In the United States the recognition of Indians' creations as an art germinated even later in time, beginning with recognition of pre-Columbian accomplishment in the 1920's. An exposition of Indian tribal arts was held in 1931 in New York. The real awakening came with the important exhibition of Indian arts and crafts at the San Francisco Golden Gate Exposition in 1939, followed two years later by an impressive show at the Museum of Modern Art. In each case the outstanding quality of the Northwest coastal art was apparent. Books about these interesting carvings began to appear, and activities sponsored by sensitive men like John Sloan René d'Harnoncourt, Fredrick H. Douglas and others initiated a new approach to evaluating these creations.

Prior to this recognition, the arts of the Tlingit, Haida and their coastal neighbors were collected by explorers, traders missionaries, anthropologists and tourists, much of the material finding its way into museums of natural science and anthropology. At this date in history, the major amount of this work is still in these institutions. Established for scholarship in archeology, anthropology and ethnology, they have become the significant centers where the art student, and the person simply interested in the art of primitive cultures, come to view and study the wealth of these collections. The University Museum, the Heye Foundation Museum of the American Indian, and the American Museum of Natural History are among the institutions today that are performing this dual role.

Very few significant collections are in art museums. The collection assembled by an aesthetically sensitive teacher in Alaska, Alex Rasmussen, was bought by the distinguished dealer in pre-Columbian art, Earl Stendahl, and found its way to the Portland Art Museum, then under the direction of Robert Tyler Davis, a most knowledgeable individual in the field of Indian Northwest Coast art.

By and large the art museums have done little better in recognizing the art value of primitive work within its production period, than they did in the recognition of new expressions in the art of their own culture. The time lapse before the museums' recognition of Courbet, Monet, Cézanne and others was shorter, but the culture that produced these men did not have such differences from our own as does that of primitive societies.

The recent recognition of the aesthetic value of the primitive arts has prompted the creation of a new type of museum, such as the Museum of Primitive Arts in New York, which came into existence to fill the gap between institutions oriented strictly either to science or to art.

Since the work of the Northwest Coast was predominantly produced in perishable materials such as wood, fabric, bark, grasses, it is fortunate that it did have an interest to emerging modern science, for as a result we possess a visual record of the heritage.

The reference to heritage here is in the dictionary sense of a "lost condition or status into which one is born . . . the rights or traditions passed on from generation to generation." In this sense the practicing art of the Alaskan coastal Indian is a lost heritage. The original motivations, cultural conventions, and inspirations that created the environment for this great art are over.

In reporting on a recent study, author Bill Holm refers to his search for valid sources on the interpretation of original data: "Ideally a study of this sort should lean heavily on information from Indian artists trained in the tradition that fostered the art. Unfortunately, I was unable to locate a qualified informant from the area covered, i.e., the coastal region from Bella Coola to Yakutat Bay. That there may be some still living is not questioned, but contemporary work seen from the area reveals a lack of understanding by Indian craftsmen of the principles."

This author's discussions with the Indian carvers Thomas Ukas and George Benson revealed that they have retained the technical skills and applied them to traditional forms, but the motivation and original spirit that produced the vital and creative pieces of past eras are missing.

Current government and private programs in the arts and crafts exist in Alaska, aimed at producing work for exhibit or sale, but none that are part of the heritage. A new product and a new expression related to a new motivation is the driving force. The art has changed from a communal to an individual art.

At all times in history, the element

known as art has been the personal contribution made by the creator to the work, endowing the creation with the power to evoke something of the artist's emotional intent. In the Northwest Coast culture the formal symbolism and its adaptation to utilitarian objects, in both form and limitation, were understood in the minutest detail by the entire clan.

The limitations set by the formal structure and symbolism of the society offered an extra challenge to the creator. Yet, in spite of these limitations the native artist managed to add his personal, creative contribution to the work. Even to the casual viewer, differences in the work of the Tlingit, Haida, Tsimshian and Kwakiutl artists are apparent. Closer scrutiny discloses differences in work within Tlingit territory itself. Given time, an aesthetically sensitive student could begin to single out the work of an individual artist from certain highly personalized techniques and characteristics of his approach.

But in all cases the work was produced within the cultural restrictions of the community, its customs and heritage. Today in the arts and crafts, these restrictions no longer exist. Only the traditional symbols remain for the artist's interpretation.

The coastal Indian saw and appreciated the art of his culture within its proper context. It held little validity for him as a separate and unrelated experience. A totem served a purpose, whether for a potlatch, memorial, or to ridicule a debtor or enemy. After it served its intended use, it was left to nature. Dances, songs and poems were reserved for the appropriate occasion. Today the purpose

and content are gone. Only the forms remain.

The native society that existed prior to the coming of the white man was one of great affluence and abundance, where food from the sea was plentiful, hunting was easy, and berries and roots were adequate. This gave the natives leisure time in which to express, through the arts, the highly formal and stylized nature of their society as it applied to all items used in their daily life.

When white men first came to trade, this culture and balance was not disturbed. The statement of Miguel Covarrubias that, "The coming of the white man was a major disaster to the American aborigines," was not true at the *first* white men's contact with the Indian of the Northwest Coast. The early effects of trading were positive. The Indian of the Northwest Coast was an astute trader who demanded new items of value for his furs. This gave him the metals he desired for tools and added new wealth to his society. The combination of self-sufficiency and added affluence, plus new and better tools, gave rise to a period of approximately eighty to one hundred years of historic art production, which in quality and quantity was unbelievable for so small a group of people.

Unlike the Aleut, who served in serfdom and were decimated by the Russians, the Tlingit, Haida and the others of the coast retained their independence and freedom. For this period of approximately three quarters of a century, all of the requisites were present for the flowering of a great art: affluence, sustenance, creativity and cultural motivation.

Unfortunately it came to a rapid decline soon after the United States' purchase of Alaska.

The decline reflected many factors. The hunting of sea otter had ceased with the animals' near extinction. Fishing, the base of the diet, was being turned over to monopolistic interests. These developments brought the loss of prosperity and even sustenance. Missionaries brought Christianity and education, and with them a change in the social structure. This brought loss of motivation. Louis Shotridge, the Tlingit who was on the staff of the University Museum as assistant curator, said prophetically in a 1919 issue of the Museum Journal:

"It was the method of most of the early missionaries, that if the savage man was to be civilized at all, he must be made to forget, as early as possible, his native ideas as well as his language. This is the mistake that the missionaries of today have to transform, and I think that it might take just as much effort to teach the modernized Indian to be original as it did to make him abandon his originality."

All this plus disease and liquor previously unknown to the Indian and a government that supplied virtually no protection and control, no education and no cultural replacement for the disappearing traditional culture, brought to an end one of the most creative periods in the history of the western continent.

The Indian himself tried to find a way out. He petitioned Congress for schools, government and economic opportunities. A few unusual Alaskans who recognized the full impact of events on the native population raised their voices—men like Lieutenant George T. Emmons, Judge James Wickersham, Governor John Brady, Sheldon Jackson—but their pleas fell like voices in the wilderness. Our government was much too busy with internal affairs and giving away the public's natural resources for private exploitation to concern itself with the natives of Alaska, much less their cultural heritage.

The Alaskan Native Brotherhood had the logical objective of changing the untenable position of being "neither-nor." They interpreted this objective to mean also the discouragement of all native practices from potlatch to shamanism that constituted the cultural and philosophic base for their creative expression in the arts. By the time the Brotherhood was organized, most of the purpose and original motivation for the arts was already gone. The religion was Christian, the potlatch was discouraged, shamanism was outmoded by modern medicine, the family structure was disoriented, and the economy was one of poverty instead of prosperity. Totem poles were rotting in abandoned villages and the ceremonial and clan arts not already picked up by collectors were packed in decorated storage boxes for occasional display to the family.

During this period of cultural decline the anthropologists, Franz Boas, John Swanton, Marius Barbeau and others, were scientifically recording the language, mythology, customs and social organization of the past. Franz Boas established a methodology that made understanding of the cultural expressions possible by analytic evaluation of the symbolism from literal to abstract, and its relationship to the formal structure of the culture.

Earlier scientists such as William Dall and the Krause brothers had recorded their observations. In more recent years Philip Drucker, Viola Garfield, Frederica De Laguna, Erna Gunther and others have devoted themselves to a better understanding of the creative work of the natives and each in his way has added constructively to the understanding of this significant culture.

During Franklin D. Roosevelt's administration the appointment of John Collier as Commissioner of Indian Affairs brought a turning point in governmental attitude toward the nation's native population. It was during this administration that, as a public works program, funds were made available to the Forestry Service under Frank Heintzleman to salvage, recarve and relocate at least a selection of the region's disintegrating totem poles into prescribed Totem Parks. Some $127,000 was made available out of Civilian Conservation Corps funds for employment of Alaskan Indians.

News of the undertaking first reached the public through the Indian Affairs newssheet, *Indians at Work*, which explained that old skilled native carvers were employed to give technical direction and to instruct younger Indians in the art, most of whom had no knowledge of it. Clusters of these poles, "restored with faithful historical accuracy," now stand in public parks at Saxman, Totem Bight, and Klawock.

The intent of the program was primarily economic, but in the process it salvaged many excellent poles, and created some new ones. On occasion it brought unexpected problems. In the attempt to distribute the work where employment was needed, the Baranov pole designed by George Benson of Sitka was assigned for carving to Wrangell. When the pole was returned for installation, the Sitka Indians were horrified—the figure of Baranov topped the pole without clothes. While in Wrangell the bare figure was characteristic, in Sitka it was not, and to this day it is interpreted as a ridicule pole. More than thirty years later, Benson still carries his sketch to show visitors that in his original drawing, Baranov was fully dressed.

Unfortunately the United States Forest Service, which is in charge of the Totem Parks, does not have an adequate maintenance program. In Saxman the poles have been repainted without regard to their original colors. The Johnson pole in Ketchikan, painted by prison labor, has been redone twice because of the lack of understanding of the original intent of the carver.

In Klawock, Alfred Widmark, a past president of the Alaskan Native Brotherhood, said that he had pressed every agency and avenue to have the magnificent poles at Klawock maintained. It was his hope that the Alaska Centennial might open an avenue for funds to salvage the Totem Park put up in the 1930's. The interest of Alfred Widmark in maintaining the poles reflects a new attitude of the Alaskan Native Brotherhood, which has matured fully to recognizing the importance of saving for posterity the remaining evidence of their past heritage. Officially it urges its membership to "preserve their history, lore and art," by taping the words and songs of those who remember, and preserving old photographs as well as clan art.

Yet another trend persists also. A

young business man in Juneau wedded
to a full-blooded Tlingit called to our attention the fact that in native tradition all
creative work, whether song, poem, dance,
or sculpture, is the exclusive property of a
clan or family, passing through the lineage from one generation to the next. Many
lineages have died out, and many are in
process of expiration. Many natives feel
strongly, he said, that their clan arts
should go with them. There have been
three recent fires where clan heirlooms
were destroyed. It may not be coincidence
that these fires occurred upon the death
of a ranking native.

The change of philosophy and direction of the Brotherhood may assist in sal-
vaging, for education, study, and pure display, much of the art and cultural material that is still in the hands of families
and clans. At Klukwan Steven Hotch, former grand Vice President of the Alaskan
Native Brotherhood and Secretary of the
Village Council, strongly denies that the
Tlingit heritage is lost. He has been tape-
recording tribal songs, writing the stories
of the elders and recording the mythology. This community like others has a
treasure of art stored in painted boxes
and chests in the clan houses. The community has voted not to show them to
white men; they say with bitterness that
white men come to them only when they
want something.

Still, in spite of all, the creative heritage is over. The young people go to
Haines or Port Chilkoot for their education and entertainment, and even Steven
Hotch, a heavy equipment operator, lives
in the middle of this century and not in
the past.

The new state has inherited the mu-

seum in Juneau, now the Alaska State Museum. Its collection, considering that it is in the heart of the native area, is relatively small, although much of the material is of aesthetic consequence. The institution is understaffed and unbelievably underfinanced. It has an inadequate operational budget and its accessions budget is less than an Indian would pay for a good Chilkat blanket. Currently the collection is housed in a Scottish Rite hall, although funds for a new building were voted in 1966, indicating some evidence of interest on the part of the electorate. Much of the collection is stored in poorly heated quarters that have no fire protection.

Museum records and documents are sketchy, a condition that echoes general federal failure to make full use of the institution as an educational vehicle, as well as a repository for Alaskana and the work of its native cultures. Individuals currently associated with the museum are aware of the problems, but are aware equally that demands exceed the state's meager resources in all areas.

Nevertheless, the time is now or never to acquire the remaining arts of the natives, before they leave the country or are destroyed. The new attitude of the Alaskan Native Brotherhood, plus a sympathetic government sponsorship, could work wonders toward acquiring native work to perhaps form the nucleus of a new collection along the lines of the Sheldon Jackson Museum, or even the emerging museum maintained by the Forestry Service at Sitka National Monument. The possibility of an Alaskan Native Brotherhood Museum is not even too far-fetched.

The Sheldon Jackson Museum, still the same octagonal structure built by the Presbyterian missionary, recently redesigned inside by Dr. Erna Gunther, has a wonderful collection established early by Jackson which should be continued in Jackson's tradition.

Despite efforts of the Forestry Service to salvage poles for the Totem Parks, many were left on the scattered islands of their origin. Some few remain yet today, quietly succumbing to the elements. These elegant early carvings, such as the Fog Woman on Village Island, are still majestic and deserve more of an enlightened citizenry than to be allowed to sink into final decay. Use of various preservatives, such as applications of plastic, have been discussed, as well as removal to protected quarters. Needed urgently is action, not words, to save the few last eloquent reminders of vanished life in abandoned sites such as Village Island and Old Kasaan.

Looking to the living native artist, the Interior Department through the Indian Arts and Crafts Board maintains a Demonstration Workshop at Sitka National Monument which puts its prime emphasis on revitalizing and upgrading the quality of craft produced by master or potential master craftsmen. Facilities are excellent, although not yet used to their potential. The craft produced is imaginative and of a very high quality; and while it draws predominantly on traditional forms, contemporary expression is also encouraged.

An extension of the Sitka designer-craftsman training program, funded by the Manpower Development and Training Assistance program, has stimulated both contemporary and variations on traditional work among Eskimo artist-craftsmen in a retraining program at the William Beltz State Vocational School in Nome. Responsibility for planning and directing the Indian Arts and Crafts Board program throughout the 500,000 square mile Alas-kan expanse is in the hands of a capable —but solitary, for all the vast area—field representative, George Federoff.

A more spontaneous, grass-roots program, begun nineteen years ago, which

Alaskan Haida village of Old Kasaan astonished early traders and delighted summer tourists who during the 1890's saw this scene as their steamer came in to dock. During Russian rule old Chief Skowl held his people firmly to custom and rebuked Russia's orthodox missionaries by erecting a totem pole to ridicule them. Deserted after the turn of the century, Old Kasaan, with its seventeen great lodges and sixty of the finest totem poles in all Alaska, was set aside as a National Monument by Executive order of President Theodore Roosevelt in 1907 and so proclaimed in 1916 by President Woodrow Wilson. In 1927 Herbert W. Krieger of the Smithsonian Institution's United States National Museum captioned a photograph showing a beach lined with weathered poles: "All that Remains of Old Kasaan. The Forest is Rapidly Encroaching." The last ruins fell apart completely for lack of maintenance. In 1954 the Government abolished the old Haida settlement as a National Monument and gave the site back to the forest.

has recently been helped along by Manpower Development and Training Assistance funds, is that of the Alaska Indian Arts, Inc., which is housed in some of the old Army barracks at Port Chilkoot and is under direction of an able and inspired retired Army major, Carl Heinmiller, who originally turned to Chilkat craft and lore for scouting material. His program encompasses training in wood carving, sculpture, block printing, textile design, lapidary, silversmithing, and adult education. Its intent is to develop art and craft skills that will assist the native to become economically self-sufficient. It is not aimed at developing professional artists. An unusually talented individual in the fine arts, Heinmiller says, would be directed by him to a specialized institution for further study.

Probably the most well-known feature of the Alaska Indian Arts activities are the Chilkat Dancers, who perform contemporary versions of traditional Tlingit and Haida dances. This program offers an opportunity in the performing arts to the native youngster within his present cultural orientation, yet one which stimulates pride in his heritage and background.

These programs and a third, the Alaska Native Arts and Crafts Cooperative, known as ANAC, which is a marketing outlet for eighteen predominantly Eskimo member villages, have validity and value. Their very dissimilarity is valuable, as each stimulates and emphasizes different facets of the creative process. Serving a needed economic function, they are keeping alive the creative impulse of a rich art tradition during the long drawn out limbo of transition.

From all of this, particularly the emphasis on training and retraining of native artist-craftsmen, it is evident that native Alaska is in a final state of transition. The traditional forms and decorative arts no longer have their origins in a living, vital cultural frame. The original purpose and motivation are gone. The heritage is lost as an active art. The creativeness of a strong, alert, vigorous people must be encouraged and given the opportunity to come forth within the framework of their present, not their past.

At the present rate of acculturation of the natives of Alaska, the paintings, sculpture and other work of the forty-ninth state's young artists of native ancestry, will differ little in motivation or direction from those of other young Americans, whose ancestors come from other countries around the world. The April, 1966, issue of *Voice of Brotherhood* reviewed an art exhibit which, in addition to the traditional forms, included oil paintings, pop art, and other international styles. As the Indian has the opportunity to study at the University of Alaska, Chicago, and elsewhere, this cosmopolitan expression will increase and interest in reproducing traditional forms will, for the highly creative, diminish further.

The Alaskan Native Brotherhood's early objective to encourage the native in his advancement from his native state to his place among the cultivated races of the world is almost here. There is hardly a generation from now to the end of personal memory of the early flowering native culture—a culture that is lost as a way of life, but which will remain and increase in recognition as one of the great native art heritages of history.

Bibliographical Acknowledgments

The story of native Alaska poses a fascinating problem in bibliographical anarchy. There is no one set of sources, no one set of people, no single Alaska. Chronologically, Alaska's history is divided between the period of Russian rule, and United States possession after 1867. Classic histories trace white Alaska's long political struggle for self-government and statehood. Anthropologists reconstruct the extinct aboriginal culture. Museums publish picture books on Northwest Coast Indian Art. The adventure narratives tell of first contacts, and the travel writers of curiosities.

But prior to this book, no effort has been directed toward profiling the cultural history of Alaska's native population.

Parts of the transitional history of the Tlingit and Haida are imbedded in numerous, unrelated government documents. Except for Ernest Gruening, who deals with their past and contemporary problems in his definitive work, Alaska's historians introduce the Indian in the state of drunken demoralization described by early government agents, and when these fairly accessible reports cease, abruptly drop him from the historical page.

This account of the coastal Indian's regeneration and triumphant entry into present-day society is drawn, through an extraction process that involved many books, from sources that heretofore have had only a nodding acquaintance. The magnificent collection of current titles and old and rare volumes in the Cleveland Public library, made available by its able and sympathetic staff, helped to supply this broad literary spectrum.

Museums contributed greatly by opening their reserve collections to the authors and by graciously searching out early accessions data. The United States National Museum, American Museum of Natural History, and Field Museum of Natural History opened as well an untapped national treasure in making available accessions files that document the epic salvage and transfer of doomed aboriginal effects to the safekeeping of public-spirited institutions.

Many individuals helped supply information, insights, and illustrative material: Mrs. Ruth Coffin Allman, niece of Judge James Wickersham and keeper of his valuable, as yet unpublished, Alaskana studies; Alex Andrews, early Alaskan Native Brotherhood member, and Father Cyril of Sitka: Dr. Marius Barbeau, anthropologist, National Museum of Canada; Mrs. Will Davis of the Alaska Centennial Commission; George Federoff, field representative of the Indian Arts and Crafts Board; Romaine Hardcastle of the Visitors' Center at Sitka National Monument; Edith S. Harding, secretary of Sheldon Jackson Junior College; Carl W. Heinmiller, director of Alaska Indian Arts, Inc.; Steven Hotch, past ANB Grand

Vice-president, of Klukwan; Mrs. Harold Jenny of Sitka; Ed Kasko of Klukwan; Karl W. Kenyon, biologist with the Fish and Wildlife Service; Cyrus E. Peck, past ANB Grand President and editor of The Voice of Brotherhood; Dr. Helen Shenitz, former director of the Alaska Historical Library; Mrs. Belle Simpson, former owner of The Nugget Shop; Mrs. Louella Smith of The Photo Shop, at Sitka; Emery Tobin, founder and former editor of The Alaskan Sportsman; Thomas Ukas, ANB member and carver, of Wrangell; Jane Wallen, acting director of the Alaska State Museum; Mr. Wanamaker, early ANB member of Sitka; Alfred Widmark, past ANB Grand President, of Klawock.

Invaluable assistance came also from the United States Bureau of Indian Affairs, Indian Arts and Crafts Board, Bureau of American Ethnology, Bureau of Commercial Fisheries, Fish and Wildlife Service, Forestry Service; the offices of Alaska Senator Ernest Gruening and Representative Frances P. Bolton of Ohio; the office of the Governor; the Alaska State Department of Fish and Game and the Alaska Centennial Commission.

The interest and assistance of these many and varied sources have at this overdue date helped to illuminate some portion of the transitional story of the uniquely gifted native residents of southeastern Alaska.

Photographic Acknowledgments

The following individuals and institutions have made available the abundant photographic presentation of art works created by Alaska's Tlingit and Haida Indians and their neighbors along the Pacific Northwest Coast:

Alaska Centennial Commission
Juneau, Alaska

Alaska State Museum
Juneau, Alaska

Alaska Travel Division
State of Alaska
Juneau, Alaska

Ruth E. Allman Collection
House of Wickersham
Juneau, Alaska

American Museum of Natural History
New York, New York

The British Museum
London, England

Canadian Pacific
Vancouver, B.C., Canada

Robert De Armond, photographer
Juneau, Alaska

Denver Art Museum
Denver, Colorado
Tlingit skin drum (page 256)
Courtesy Denver Art Museum

Field Museum of Natural History
Chicago, Illinois

Robert H. Lowie Museum of Anthropology
University of California
Berkeley, California

Marine Historical Association, Inc.
Mystic, Connecticut

Milwaukee Public Museum
Milwaukee, Wisconsin

Museum of the American Indian
Heye Foundation
New York, New York

The Museum of Primitive Art
New York, New York

National Museum of Canada
Ottawa, Ont., Canada

Peabody Museum of Archaeology and Ethnology
Harvard University
Cambridge, Massachusetts

Peabody Museum
Salem, Massachusetts

The Photo Shop
Sitka, Alaska

Portland Art Museum
Portland, Oregon

Provincial Museum of Natural History
and Anthropology
Victoria, B.C., Canada

Rosenkilde and Bagger, publishers
The American Expedition by Sven Waxel, in
which appears the only known portrait of
Vitus Bering
Copenhagen, Denmark

Royal Ontario Museum
University of Toronto
Toronto, Ont., Canada

Saint Joseph Museum
Saint Joseph, Missouri

Sitka National Monument
National Park Service
Sitka, Alaska

Smithsonian Institution
Office of Anthropology
Washington, D.C.

University Museum
University of Pennsylvania
Philadelphia, Pennsylvania

Clark Worswick, photographer
Cambridge, Massachusetts

Photographs taken by the authors of totem poles at Klawock, Wrangell, Saxman, Juneau, Ketchikan, Sitka, Old Kasaan, and Village Island appear in color and at the beginning of each chapter and as vertical margins throughout the text.

Andrews, Clarence LeRoy. *The Story of Alaska.* Caldwell, Idaho, 1938.

———. *Sitka.* Caldwell, Idaho, 1945.

Andrews, Ralph W. *Indian Primitive.* Seattle, 1960.

Baird, Donald. "Tlingit Treasures, How an Important Collection Came to Princeton." *Princeton Alumni Weekly,* February 16, 1965.

Baker, Marcus. *Geographic Dictionary of Alaska.* United States Geological Survey, Bulletin No. 299, 1902.

Balcom, Mary G. *Ghost Towns of Alaska.* Chicago, 1965.

———. *Ketchikan, Alaska's Totem Land.* Chicago, 1961.

Ballou, Maturin Murray. *Alaska, The New Eldorado.* Boston, 1890.

* Bancroft, Hubert Howe. *History of Alaska.* San Francisco, 1886.

———. *History of California.* San Francisco, 1884–1890.

———. *History of the Northwest Coast.* San Francisco, 1884.

———. *Native Races,* Vol. I, *Wild Tribes.* San Francisco, 1875.

Barbeau, Marius. *Haida Carvers in Argillite.* National Museum of Canada, 1957.

———. *Pathfinders in the North Pacific.* Caldwell, Idaho, 1958.

———. *Totem Poles,* Vols. I and II. National Museum of Canada, 1950.

———. *Alaska Beckons.* Caldwell, Idaho, 1947.

* Bartlett, John. "A Narrative of Events in the Life of John Bartlett . . . ," in *The Sea, The Ship, The Sailor.* Introduction by Captain Elliot Snow. Marine Research Society (under present auspices of the Peabody Museum, Salem), 1925.

Beardslee, Captain L. A. *Report on Conditions in Alaska.* 46C: 2s, Senate Exec. Document 105, 1880.

———. *Report to Secretary of Navy.* 47C: 1s, Senate Exec. Document 71, 1881.

———. *Accessions No. 10686.* Smithsonian Institution, United States National Museum, Washington, D.C., 1881.

* Belcher, Sir Edward. *Narrative of a Voyage in HMS Sulphur During the Years 1836–1842.* London, 1843.

Berkh, Vassili. *Chronological History of the Discovery of the Aleutian Islands . . . .* St. Petersburg, 1823. Translated by Dimitri Drenov as WPA. Report 5668, Seattle, 1938.

* Billings, Commodore Joseph. *An Account of a Geographical and Astronomical Expedition to the Northern Parts of Russia and American Coast,* narrated by Martin Sauer. London, 1802.

* Bloodgood, C. D. U.S.N. "Eight Months at Sitka." *Overland Monthly,* February, 1869.

Boas, Franz. "Decorative Art of the Indians of the North Pacific Coast." American Museum of Natural History, *Bulletin* IX. New York, 1897.

* ———. "Gleanings from the Emmons Collection." *Journal of American Folklore.* April-June, 1888.

———. "The Kwakiutl of Vancouver Island." American Museum of Natural History. *Memoirs,* Vol. V. Publication of Jesup North Pacific Expedition. New York, 1905.

* ———. "The Jesup North Pacific Expedition."

* Sources drawn upon for quotations are indicated with an asterisk.

The American Museum Journal. October, 1903.
——. *Primitive Art,* New York, 1951.
* Brady, John G. *The Present Status of the Alaskan Natives.* 29th Annual Lake Mohonk Conference, 1911.
Boit, John. See Howay, *Voyages of the Columbia.*
Campbell, Archibald. *Voyages Around the World from 1806–12.* Edinburgh, 1816.
Chevigny, Hector. *Lord of Alaska.* New York, 1942.
——. *Russian America.* New York, 1965.
Clark, Henry W. *History of Alaska.* New York, 1930.
* Cleveland, Captain Richard. *A Narrative of Voyages and Commercial Enterprises.* Boston, 1850.
Colby, Merle. *A Guide to Alaska.* New York, 1939.
* Collier, John. *Indians of the Americas.* W. W. Norton and Company, New York, 1947.
——. Ed., *Indians at Work,* a news sheet for Indians and the Indian Service. Office of Indian Affairs, 1933–1945.
Collison, William H. *In the Wake of the War Canoe.* London, 1915.
* Colyer, Hon. Vincent. *Report on the Indian Tribes and Their Surroundings in Alaska Territory.* 41C: 2s, Report of Secretary of Interior.
* ——. *Report on Wrangell, Previous to Bombardment.* 41C: 2s, Senate Exec. Document No. 68.
——. "Sketches in Alaska." Article and illustrations in *Harper's Weekly,* February 19, 1870.
* Cook, Captain James. *Voyage to the Pacific Ocean.* London, 1784.
Corser, Rev. H. P. *Totem Lore of the Alaskan Indians.* Ketchikan, 1932.
* *Court of Claims Decision of Tlingit and Haida of Alaska vs. United States:* 147C, C1S., No. 315.
Covarrubias, Miguel. *The Eagle, the Jaguar and The Serpent—Indian Art of the Americas.* New York, 1954.
* Coxe, William. *Account of the Russian Discoveries Between Asia and America.* . . . London, 1780.
Curtis, Edward S. *The North American Indian,* Vols. 9, 10, 11. University Press, Cambridge, 1907–1930.

Dall, William Healy. *Alaska and its Resources.* Boston, 1870.
——. "On Masks, Labrets and Certain Aboriginal Customs." Annual Report, Bureau of Ethnology, 1881–1882.
——. "Tribes of the Extreme Northwest," in *Contributions to North American Ethnology,* Department of Interior, 1877.
Davis, Robert Tyler. *Native Arts of the Pacific Northwest.* Stanford University Press, 1949.
Deans, James. *Tales From the Totems of the Hidery,* O. L. Triggs, ed. Chicago, 1899.
——. *Accessions No. 21.* Field Museum of Natural History (Field Columbian Museum), Chicago, 1893.
De Laguna, Frederica. *The Story of a Tlingit Community,* Bureau of American Ethnology Bulletin 172, 1960.
D'Harnoncourt, René. "Activities of the Indian Arts and Crafts Board Since its Organization in 1936." *Indians at Work,* Office of Indian Affairs. April, 1940.
Denton, V. L. *The Far West Coast.* Toronto, 1924.
* Dixon, Captain George. *A Voyage Around the World.* . . . London, 1789.
Dockstader, Frederick. *Indian Art in America.* New York Graphic Society, 1961.
* Dodge, Ernest S. *The Museum by Navigators.* Peabody Museum of Salem, 1953.
Douglas, Frederick H. Denver Art Museum Leaflets, 1, 32, 34, 72, 79, 80. Denver, 1930–1936.
Douglas, Frederick and René d'Harnoncourt. *Indian Art of the United States.* New York, 1941.
Drucker, Philip. *Cultures of the North Pacific Coast.* San Francisco, 1965.
——. *Indians of the Pacific Northwest Coast.* Bureau of American Ethnology, Anthropological Handbook, No. 10, 1955.
——. *The Native Brotherhoods,* Bureau of American Ethnology Bulletin 168. 1958.
* Duff, Wilson and Michael Kew. *Anthony Island, A Home of the Haidas.* Provincial Museum of Natural History and Anthropology, Victoria, B.C., 1957.
* D'Wolf, Captain John. "Voyage of the Juno." In *Tales of an Old Sea Port,* edited by Wilfred

Harold Munro. Princeton University Press, 1917.

Elliott, Henry W. *Our Arctic Province.* New York, 1887.

Emmons, Lt. George Thornton. "The Art of the Northwest Coast Indians." *Natural History,* May–June, 1930.

——. "Basketry of the Tlingit." American Museum of Natural History, *Memoirs,* July, 1903.

* ——. *Conditions Among the Alaskan Natives.* 29th Annual Lake Mohonk Conference, 1911. *Also* 58C: 3s, Senate Document 106.

——. *Jade in British Columbia and Alaska.* Museum of the American Indian, Heye Foundation, New York, 1923.

* ——. "Native Account of the Meeting Between La Pérouse and the Tlingit." *American Anthropologist,* June, 1911.

——. "Potlatch of the North Pacific Coast." *American Museum Journal,* 1910.

——. *Slate Mirrors of the Tsimshians.* Heye Foundation Monograph, 1921.

——. *The Tahltan Indians.* University of Pennsylvania Anthropological Publications, 1911.

——. "The Use of the Chilkat Blanket." *American Museum Journal,* May, 1908.

——. "Whale House of the Chilkat." American Museum of Natural History, *Anthropological Papers,* Vol. 19, 1916.

* ——. *Accessions, Correspondence, Itemization, Notebooks and Invoices, during Years 1890 thru 1938.* American Museum of Natural History, New York.

* ——. *Accessions Correspondence, Itemizations, Notebooks and Invoices during the Years 1901 through 1930.* Field Museum of Natural History, Chicago.

* ——. *Correspondence, Itemizations, Notebooks and Invoices, Accession Nos. 28072, 37750, 39254, 41512, 42081.* Smithsonian Institution, United States National Museum, Washington.

Ewers, John Canfield. "A Century of American Indian Exhibits at Smithsonian Institution." Annual Report, Smithsonian Institution, 1958.

* Fast, Edward G. *Catalog of Alaskan Antiquities and Curiosities.* Leavitt, Strebeigh and Company, prior 1871.

* Fleurieu, Compte Charles Pierre de Claret. *Voyage Autour du Monde Pendant les Anées 1790, 1791 et 1792 par Etienne Marchand.* London, 1801.

Franchere, Gabriel. *Narrative of a Voyage to the Northwest Coast of America. . . .* Redfield, 1854.

Fuhrmann, von Ernst. *Tlinkit vrs. Haida.* Germany, 1922.

Garfield, Viola. *The Seattle Totem Pole.* University of Washington Extension Series, 1940.

——. *The Tsimshian, their Arts and Music.* American Ethnology Society Publication, New York, 1951.

——. *The Tsimshian Clan and Society.* University of Washington Publications in Anthropology, 1939.

Garfield, Viola and Linn A. Forrest. *The Wolf and the Raven.* Seattle, 1948.

Goddard, Earl Pliny. *Indians of the Northwest Coast.* American Museum of Natural History Handbook Series No. 10, 1924.

* Golder, Frank Alfred, ed. *Bering's Voyages, Vols. I and II.* American Geographical Society, 1922–1925. (Steller's Journal, Vol. II)

——. *Russian Expansion on the Pacific.* Gloucester, 1960.

Golovnin, Vasslie Michailovich. "Voyage Around the World," in *Russian Voyages Around the World,* ed. by N. Nozikov, London.

Greenhow, Robert. *The History of Oregon and California and Other Territories on the Northwest Coast of America.* New York, 1846.

Grinnell, George Bird. *The Natives of the Alaskan Coast Region.* Harriman Alaskan Series, Smithsonian Institution, 1910.

* Gruening, Ernest. *The State of Alaska.* New York, 1954.

Guernsey, Egbert. "The Alaskan Natives at Fort Wrangell." *American Antiquarian,* March, 1891.

Gunther, Erna. "Sitka's Museum." *Museum News,* May, 1964.

——. "Northwest Coast Indian Art." Catalog. Seattle World's Fair, 1962.

Hallock, Charles. *Our New Alaska.* New York, 1886.

* Harriman, Mrs. E. H. *Correspondence, Memos and Itemizations, Accession No. 54171,* Smithsonian Institution, United States National Museum, Washington 1911–1912; *Accession*

No. 38, American Museum of Natural History, New York.

Harner, Michael J. and Albert B. Elsasser. "Art of the Northwest Coast." Catalog, Robert H. Lowie Museum of Anthropology, University of California. Berkeley, 1965.

Haswell, Robert. See Howay, *Voyages of the Columbia.*

Healy, M. A. *Alleged Shelling of Alaskan Villages.* Extract of letter. 47C: 2s, House Exec. Document 9, November, 1882.

* Holm, Bill. *Northwest Coast Indian Art: An Analysis of Form.* University of Washington Press, Seattle, 1965.

Hooper, Captain C. L. *Sea Otter Banks of Alaska.* Treasury Department Document No. 1977, 1897.

Hoskins, John. See Howay. *Voyages of the Columbia.*

Howay, Frederic W. *British Columbia and the United States.* Toronto, 1942.

———. "Indian Attacks upon Maritime Traders of the Northwest Coast." *Canadian Historical Review,* December, 1925.

———. *The Journal of Captain Colnett.* Toronto, 1940.

———. "A List of Trading Vessels in Maritime Fur Trade, 1785–1825," Transactions, Royal Society of Canada, Vols. XXIV to XXVIII, Ottawa, 1930–1934.

* ———. *Voyages of the Columbia.* Massachusetts Historical Society, 1941. (Boit's Log, Haswell's Log, Hoskin's Narrative)

———. "Voyage of the Hope." *Washington Historical Quarterly,* January, 1920.

* ———. "A Yankee Trader on the Northwest Coast." *Pacific Northwest Quarterly.* (formerly *Washington Historical Quarterly*) XXI, (Magee's Log)

Hrdlicka, Ales. "Anthropological Survey in Alaska," 46th Annual Report, Bureau of American Ethnology, 1928–1929.

Hulley, Clarence C. *Alaska.* Portland, 1953.

Huntington, M. R. "The Northwest Coast Collection," *The Museum Journal,* University of Pennsylvania, March, 1912.

Inverarity, Robert Bruce. *Art of the Northwest Coast Indians.* University of California Press, 1950.

* Jackson, Sheldon. *Alaska.* New York, 1880.

* ———. *Destitute Conditions of Natives of Alaska.* 51C: 2s, Senate Exec. Document 14.

Jesup North Pacific Expedition. American Museum of Natural History, *Memoirs,* Vols. I-XI. New York, 1900–1930.

Jewitt, John R. *A Narrative of the Adventures and Sufferings of John R. Jewitt. . . .* Ithaca, 1849.

Jones, Livingston. *A Study of the Thlingets of Alaska.* New York, 1914.

Judson, Katherine Berry. *Subject Index to History of Pacific Northwest and Alaska as Found in Government Documents 1789–1881.* Olympia, 1913.

* Kashevaroff, A. P. "Report of Progress and Condition of the Alaska Historical Library and Museum." Juneau, 1925.

Keithahn, Edward. *Monuments in Cedar.* Ketchikan, 1945; Seattle, 1963.

Kenyon, Karl W. "Recovery of a Fur Bearer." *Natural History.* November, 1963.

———. "The Sea Otter." Annual Report Smithsonian Institution, 1958.

Knapp, Frances and Pheta Louise Childe. *The Thlinkets of South Eastern Alaska.* Chicago, 1896.

Kotzebue, Otto Von. *A Voyage Around the World,* Vol. II. London, 1830.

Krause, Aurel. *The Tlingit Indians,* trans. by Erna Gunther. University of Washington Press, Seattle, 1956.

Krieger, Herbert W. "Indian Villages of Southeast Alaska," Annual Report, Smithsonian Institution, 1927.

———. "Some Aspects of Northwest Coast Indian Art." *Scientific Monthly,* September, 1926.

* Langsdorff, Georg H. von. *Voyages and Travels.* London, 1814.

* La Pérouse, Jean Francois de Galaup. *A Voyage Around the World.* London, 1798.

Laut, Agnes C. *Conquest of Our Western Empire.* New York, 1927.

———. *Vikings of the Pacific.* New York, 1905.

Lindquist, Willes. *Alaska, the Forty-Ninth State.* New York, 1959.

* Lisiansky, Captain Urey. *A Voyage Around the World.* London, 1814.

* McCabe, James D. *History of the Centennial Exposition.* Philadelphia, 1876.

* McLean, John J. *Correspondence, Itemizations and Invoices, Accessions Nos. 12009, 10803, 11616, 12009, 12616,* Smithsonian Institution, United States National Museum, Washington, D.C.

McNeil, William H. *The Rise of the West.* University of Chicago Press, Chicago, 1963.

MacKenzie, Alexander. *Voyages from Montreal Through the Continent of North America. . . .* New York, 1903.

Magee, Bernard. See Howay, *A Yankee Trader on the Northwest Coast.*

Malin, Edward and Norman Feder. "Indian Art of the Northwest Coast." *Denver Art Museum Quarterly,* 1962.

Mason, I. Aldon. "Louis Shotridge," in *Expedition,* Bulletin of University Museum. University of Pennsylvania, Winter, 1960.

Masterson, James R. & Helen Brower. *Bering's Successors.* University of Washington Press, Seattle, 1948.

* Mayberry, Genevieve. *Sheldon Jackson Junior College, An Intimate History.* Sitka Printing Company, Sitka, Alaska.

Meany, Edmund. *Vancouver's Discovery of Puget Sound.* New York, 1907.

* Meares, John. *Voyages Made in 1788 and 1789 from China to the North West Coast of America. . . .* London, 1790.

Morison, Samuel E. *Maritime History of Massachusetts.* Boston and New York, 1921.

* Morris, William Gouverneur. *Report on Customs District, Public Services and Resources of Alaska.* 45C: 3s, Senate Exec. Document 59, 1879.

———. *Shelling of an Indian Village in Alaska, Letter.* 47C: 2s, House Exec. Document 9.

* Mourelle, Don Francisco Antonio. "Journal of a Voyage in 1775," in *Daines Barrington's Miscellanies.* London, 1781.

* Muir, John. *Travels in Alaska.* Houghton Mifflin Company, Boston and New York, 1915.

Muller, Gerhard Friedrick. *Voyages from Asia to America. . . .* London, 1764.

Murdock, Peter George. *Ethnographic Bibliography of North America.* New Haven, Connecticut.

Newcombe, Dr. C. F. *The First Circumnavigation of Vancouver Island.* Victoria, 1914.

* ———. *Accessions Correspondence with Dr. George Dorsay, 1901 through 1913.* Field Museum of Natural History, Chicago.

Niblack, Ensign Albert P. *The Coast Indians of Southern Alaska and North British Columbia.* Washington, 1890.

Nichols, Jeannette. *Alaska.* Cleveland, 1924.

Okun, S. B. *Russian American Company.* Howard University Press, 1951.

Paalen, Wolfgang. "Totem Art." *DYN,* Amerindian Number, Coyoacan, Mexico, 1943.

* Peabody Museum of American Archaeology and Ethnology, Harvard University. Third Annual Report, Boston, 1870.

Petroff, Ivan. *Report of the Population, Industries and Resources of Alaska.* United States Treasury Department Special Agents Division, Washington, 1882.

Porter, Robert R. "Report on the Population Resources of Alaska." 11th Census, 1890.

* Portlock, Captain Nathaniel. *A Voyage Around the World. . . .* London, 1789.

Putnam, Frederick Ward. "History of the Collections Presented to the Museum through the Exposition Dept. of Archaeology and Ethnology," in *An Historical and Descriptive Account of the Field Columbian Museum.* Chicago, 1894.

* ———. "Ethnology, Anthropology, Archaeology," in *The World's Columbian Exposition,* Col. George Davis, ed. Philadelphia, 1893.

* ———. *Correspondence and Memorandums to Morris K. Jesup.* American Museum of Natural History, New York, 1894.

Quimby, George I. "Culture Contact on the North West Coast from 1785–1795." *American Anthropologist,* Vol. 50, 1948.

Ripinsky, Sol. "The Natives of Chilkat." *Alaska Yukon Magazine,* March, 1908.

* Roquefeuil, Camille de. *A Voyage Around the World.* London, 1823.

Sarychef, Govrila Andreevich. *Account of a Voyage of Discovery.* London, 1806.

Schaffer, V. B. "The Sea Otter on the Washington Coast." *Pacific Northwest Quarterly,* Vol. 31, 1940.

Schlesinger, Arthur Meier. *Political and Social*

Growth of the American People. New York, 1933.

* Schwatke, Frederick. *A Summer in Alaska.* St. Louis, 1894.

* Scidmore, Eliza Ruhamah. *Alaska, Its Southern Coast.* Boston, 1885.

———. *Appletons' Guide Book to Alaska.* New York, 1899.

Shapiro, Harry L. *The Peopling of the North Pacific Rim.* Thomas Burke Memorial Lecture Series, 1964.

Shelikov, Gregory. "Materials of the Years 1785 to 1790 on the Activity of the Golikov-Shelikov Company," in *Russian Discoveries in the Pacific,* ed. by Aleksander Andreyev, trans. by Carl Ginsburg. Published for American Council of Learned Societies by J. W. Edwards, Ann Arbor, 1952.

Shenitz, Dr. Helen A. "Father Veniaminov." *American Slavic and East European Review,* February, 1959.

Sherwood, Morgan B. *Explorations in Alaska.* Yale University Press, 1965.

* Shotridge, Florence. "Chilkat Houses." *The Museum Journal,* University of Pennsylvania, September, 1913.

* Shotridge, Louis. "The Emblems of Tlingit Culture." *The Museum Journal,* University of Pennsylvania, December, 1928.

* ———. "Kaguanton Shark Helmet." *The Museum Journal,* University of Pennsylvania, December, 1929.

Shotridge, Louis and Florence. Articles in *The Museum Journal,* University of Pennsylvania, June, 1917; March–June, 1919; September, 1919; December, 1919; March, 1920; September, 1921; March, 1922; September, 1929; June, 1929.

Simpson, Sir George. *Fur Trade and Empire.* Howard Historical Studies, 1931.

* ———. *Narrative of a Journey Around the World. . . .* London, 1847.

Sloane, John and Oliver LaFarge. *Introduction to American Indian Art.* Exposition of American Tribal Arts, Inc., New York, 1931.

Smith, Harlan I. "Canoes of the North Pacific Coast Indians." *American Museum Journal,* December, 1910.

———. "Totem Poles of the North Pacific Coast."

American Museum Journal, February, 1911.

———. "A Visit to the Indian Tribes of the North Pacific Coast." *American Museum Journal,* February, 1910.

Smithsonian Institution. Annual Reports: 1893, 1904, 1905, 1909.

Snow, H. J. *In Forbidden Seas.* London, 1910.

* Sotheby & Co. Catalogue. Monday 12th July, 1965.

Sproat, Gilbert Malcolm. *Scenes and Studies of Savage Life.* London, 1868.

* Steller, Georg Wilhelm. See Golder, in *Bering's Voyages*

* Sturgis, William. *The Northwest Fur Trade.* Old South Leaflets, General Series, Vol. IX, No. 219.

Swan, James Gilchrist. *The Haidah Indians of Queen Charlotte Islands.* Smithsonian Contributions to Knowledge No. 267.

———. *The Northwest Coast.* New York, 1897.

———. "Official Report as Commissioner to Procure Articles for Centennial Exposition." Appendix, *William Gouverneur Morris Report,* 45C: 3s, Senate Exec. Document 59.

* ———. *Correspondence, Itemizations and Invoices, Accessions Nos.:* 13804, 88975, 89232. Smithsonian Institution, United States National Museum, Washington, D.C.

Swanton, John R. *The Indian Tribes of North America.* Bureau of American Ethnology Bulletin 145.

———. "Contributions to the Ethnology of the Haida," *American Museum of Natural History, Memoirs,* Vol. V. Publication of Jesup North Pacific Expedition, New York, 1905.

———. "Social Conditions, Beliefs and Linguistic Relationships of the Tlingit Indians," 29th Annual Report, Bureau of American Ethnology, 1904–1905.

———. *Tlingit Myths and Texts.* Bureau of American Ethnology Bulletin 39, 1909.

* Swineford, Governor Alfred P. *Alaska.* Chicago and New York, 1898.

———. Annual Report, October, 1886.

Sydow, Eckart von. *Die Kunst Der Naturvolker und Der Vorzeit.* Berlin, 1925.

Tompkins, Stuart. *Alaska, Promyshlennik and Sourdough.* University of Oklahoma Press, 1945.

Underhill, Ruth. *Indians of the Pacific Northwest.* Bureau of Indian Affairs, 1945.

* United States Department of the Interior. *Work of the Bureau of Education for the Natives of Alaska, 1916–17.* Bulletin, No. 5, 1918.

Valliant, George C. *Indian Arts in North America.* New York, 1939.

* Vancouver, Captain George. *A Voyage of Discovery.* London, 1801.

* *Voice of Brotherhood.* Publication of Alaskan Native Brotherhood, Juneau, 1954–.

Wagner, Henry R. *Cartography of the North West Coast of America.* Berkeley, 1937.

———. *Spanish Explorations in the Straits of Juan de Fuca.* Santa Ana, 1933.

Wardwell, Alan. "Yakutat South, Indian Art of the Northwest Coast." Catalog, Art Institute of Chicago, 1964.

* Waxel, Sven. *The American Expedition.* trans. by M. A. Michael. William Hodge and Company, Ltd., London, 1952. From Danish translation by John Skalberg. Rosenkilde and Bagger, Copenhagen, Denmark, 1948, first publishers of Waxel's lost manuscript, found in 1938 in a Leningrad bookstore and now in State Library of Leningrad.

Wellcome, Henry S. *The Story of Metlakahtla.* New York, 1887.

White, Leslie A. *The Ethnography and Ethnology of Franz Boas.* Texas Memorial Museum, Bulletin No. 6, 1963.

Whymper, Frederick. *Travel and Adventure in the Territory of Alaska.* New York, 1869.

Wickersham, James. *A Bibliography of Alaskan Literature.* Cordova, 1927.

* ———. "The Oldest and Rarest Lincoln Statue." *Sunset,* February, 1924.

* Wilkes, Charles. *Narrative of the United States Exploring Expedition,* Vol. V. Philadelphia, 1845.

Winter and Pond Company. *The Totems of Alaska.* Juneau, 1909.

Wood, C. E. S. *Among the Thlinkits in Alaska.* New York, 1882.

Woollen, William Watson. *Inside Passage to Alaska,* Cleveland, 1924.

Young, James W. "The Revival and Development of Indian Arts and Crafts." *Indians at Work,* Office of Indian Affairs, April, 1940.

Young, S. Hall. *Adventures in Alaska.* Fleming H. Revell Company, New York, 1919.

* ———. *Alaska Days with John Muir.* Fleming H. Revell Company, New York, 1915.

Index